THE
BILLIONAIRE
SHELL GAME

D O U B L E D A Y

New York   London   Toronto

Sydney   Auckland

THE
BILLIONAIRE
SHELL GAME

HOW CABLE BARON JOHN
MALONE AND ASSORTED
CORPORATE TITANS INVENTED
A FUTURE NOBODY WANTED

L. J. Davis

PUBLISHED BY DOUBLEDAY
a division of Bantam Doubleday Dell Publishing Group, Inc.
1540 Broadway, New York, New York 10036

DOUBLEDAY and the portrayal of an anchor with a dolphin
are trademarks of Doubleday, a division of
Bantam Doubleday Dell Publishing Group, Inc.

BOOK DESIGN BY AMANDA DEWEY

Library of Congress Cataloging-in-Publication Data
Davis, L. J. (Lawrence J.)
The billionaire shell game: how cable baron John Malone and
assorted corporate titans invented a future nobody wanted / by
L. J. Davis. — 1st ed.
p.   cm.
Includes bibliographical references, index.
1. Cable television—United States.   2. Tele-Communications,
Inc.   3. Malone, John, 1941–   .   I. Title.
HE8700.72.U6D38   1998
384.55′5′0973—dc21   98-3294
CIP

This book is for Judy.

Added to all this was the direct stimulus of new inventions; for in the beginning they were still almost toys, and before their potentialities had been transformed into slick routines, they had a power to stir the mind, out of all proportion to their later effects. . . . A good part of all this manipulation and invention came to no good end; let us confess that.

—LEWIS MUMFORD, *The Brown Decades*

CONTENTS

Contents

THE
BILLIONAIRE
SHELL GAME

John Malone in New York

JOHN MALONE HAD HIS FISH ON THE HOOK. NOW THE time had come to set it.

It was as though the gods of corporate irony had conspired in the setting for a situation where the ironies were already multiple. With its Regency furniture, marble fireplace, and crystal chandeliers, the suite in the Waldorf Towers had the air of quiet opulence expected of one of the world's premier hotels, but the Towers suites were subtly different in decor. This particular example—whose sole other occupant was Raymond Smith, chairman of the Bell Atlantic regional telephone company and Malone's chosen mark—closely resembled the one occupied by Barry Diller, living Hollywood legend, when Diller was resident in New York. If Malone was successful tonight—if Ray Smith, as anticipated, made a final supreme effort to pay an imperial ransom for a company that, for its part, closely resembled a phlogiston mine—Malone would also stab Barry Diller in the back. To all appearances, the thought did not disturb him and the prospect did not excite him. Few things did.

He was a strange man, John Malone, strange and hard to read. For a decade, he had been known as the king of cable television, at least in polite company; there were other descriptions of John Malone.

With Bob Magness, the old rancher, roustabout, and oil-seed salesman from the town of Memphis, Texas, he controlled Tele-Communications Inc., TCI for short. By mid-October 1993, when Malone sat down in the Waldorf suite, TCI's coaxial cables—tendrils, some called them—stretched across forty-eight states and had reached the British Isles. The company pumped its television signals into at least 11 million homes and thus controlled access to at least one-fifth of the viewing audience, although the actual number of homes served by TCI's allies, affiliates, and off-the-books subsidiaries was at least triple that number. The best that could be said, without hours of frustrating and often fruitless analysis of TCI's unusually complex financial statements, was that TCI ran its wires into a heck of a lot of homes. The company controlled the Discovery Channel and owned a veto power over the actions of Ted Turner, the brilliant and unstable founder of CNN. It appeared to throw off somewhere in the vicinity of a billion dollars a year, most of it free money not subject to taxation, although this figure, too, was hard to pin down with anything approaching certainty. TCI, like its chief executive officer, was extremely hard to read. This was by design.

There were two things that immediately struck the observer about John Malone—two things that slammed into the observer, actually, if the observer was unprepared. At fifty-two, Malone was a preternaturally handsome man, with the sort of muscular Irish good looks—perhaps accompanied by a touch of the Scandinavian brush—that a thousand 1940s movies had taught a generation of Americans to regard as the standard of masculine beauty. That was the first thing. Like a motion picture actor, John Malone did not resemble a human being; he resembled a photograph of a human being. The second thing was his remarkable self-control.

He could sit, calm and utterly still, for hours, and he often did so, especially when he was negotiating with an adversary or a person who controlled an object of his desire. This often induced a pleasing state of babble in the other occupants of the room, sometimes accompanied by an even more pleasing state of confusion and fear. Malone was an intensely focused man, and his focus was almost invariably directed toward a single objective: money, the getting of it. In the service of this goal, he was also a man with many hidden agendas, and he had a hidden agenda now. In the Waldorf suite, it was his purpose to allow the man sitting opposite him, Ray Smith, to talk himself into paying vastly more for TCI than TCI was worth on the best day the company ever had.

Ray Smith was also pursuing a hidden agenda, although in a way that had grown increasingly strange. He was a round-faced, affable man, a dedicated amateur thespian with a limber tongue and a ready wit that masked, in the despairing opinion of some of his executives, an abiding madness that had now reached its final form.

Like the other six regional telephone companies that had come into independent existence with the breakup of AT&T in 1984, Bell Atlantic had a single great goal in the autumn of 1993. Bell Atlantic and the other six Baby Bells were determined to enter the lucrative long-distance business before the march of science rendered their existing equipment vulnerable, obsolete, or both, but getting there was no simple task. Before Bell Atlantic could offer a long-distance service—even within its own part of the country, using its own lines and switches—sixty years of federal telecommunications law and judicial decisions had to be overthrown, and there was only one certain, reliable, and simple way to do it: persuade Congress to pass bold new legislation that would remake Bell Atlantic's world.

Unfortunately, there was no great public outcry for such a new law. There was, in fact, not a peep from the public, whose indifference on the subject of telecommunications law was as large as the public's very considerable ignorance of it, and it was extremely difficult to explain why Bell Atlantic, a company with annual profits of over a billion dollars, felt a compelling need to overturn more than half a century of lawmaking in order to make even more money. The easy part had already been done; influential congressmen had been provided with large sums of money and more would be forthcoming, but encouraging the legislators to think correct thoughts was only part of the task. It was also essential to provide Congress with a plausible—and, above all, a popular and easily understood—reason for writing the new law. The secret of the trick, Bell Atlantic and the other regional television companies had correctly come to believe, was cable television.

Taken as a whole, cable companies—and particularly Malone's TCI—were roughly as popular as oil companies, law firms, and reporters. Their customer service—particularly the customer service of Malone's TCI—was notoriously poor. Their rates were high and rising. Their motives were suspected, and the fact that most cable companies held regional monopolies was not admired. Former senator and now Vice President Al Gore had long enjoyed a rich political sideline in bashing cable companies in general and John Malone in particular, and by 1993, Gore was not alone; in Congress, bashing cable companies had become the king of indoor sports, because there were votes to be gotten by bashing cable companies. To Bell Atlantic and the other regional telephone companies, opportunity beckoned.

With great fanfare, the telephone companies announced that, if only one small condition was met, they would provide cheap, friendly, and reliable cable television service, using their existing networks. The cable companies would no longer hold the country in the iron grip of monopoly, and the viewing public would soon be happy. All it took was a small change in the existing laws—and, while the legislators were about it, they might as well make a few additional and long-overdue modifications of the statutes in the interest of tidiness and for the benefit of all. To the regional telephone companies,

God—long-distance service—would be found in the modifications. Television was the cover story.

The regional telephone companies had never been interested in television, and most of them weren't interested now. The goal had always been the long-distance business, and the goal never changed. Once the new telecommunications bill was passed and signed, the telephone companies could run a few inexpensive tests in places like Omaha, El Cerrito, and Richardson, Texas. If the tests succeeded, well and good; the telephone companies could make some extra money. If the tests failed, no great harm was done; the telephone companies could claim technical difficulties and public indifference and quietly abandon the undertaking. In the meantime, it was important to feign enthusiasm until the law was changed, and among the captains of the regional telephone industry, no one's enthusiasm was greater or louder than Ray Smith's. By October 1993, it was also clear that he was not pretending. In Smith's imagination, the television business had come to glitter like the towers of Oz and Ilium.

He was an ambitious, romantic man who longed to have adventures, and on the subject of television, his mind was divided by a paradox. On the one hand, he had listened, unwisely and too well, to the promise of new technologies. On the other hand, he knew too little about the cable business. With some justification, he would later claim to have been the father of the 1996 telecommunications bill that gave Bell Atlantic almost everything it wanted, but in October 1993 the commonplace intrigues of his pedestrian colleagues were not uppermost in his mind. Spending an enormous amount of money was.

Smith saw great possibilities in the digital, interactive television that had been invented—in California, more or less as an afterthought, and years in advance of predictions—in 1990, and he believed that his old adversary, John Malone, shared his vision. It was Malone, after all, who had galvanized the cable industry and seized the nation's headlines by predicting a world of 500 television channels, whereupon the urbane and confident voice of Nicholas Negroponte, co-founder of the Media Lab at MIT, made itself heard. Negroponte seemed to be on excellent terms with the future, and he remarked—as though he and the future had just risen from conversation—that the 500-channel world would not be a world dominated by vastly more of the same kind of television. In Ray Smith, practical men of affairs like John Malone and prophets like Nicholas Negroponte found a receptive audience. Great things were at hand.

With interactive television, easy home shopping would at last become a huge reality, offering a vast array of products and services; the few surviving department stores and shopping malls would become the artifacts of a vanished, predigital civilization. With its movies-on-demand, interactive television would replace the VCR and the video store. With its ability to process vast amounts of data, interactive television would consign the home and corporate computers to the dustbin of history, and it would at last make irresistible the Picturephone, a technology beloved by telephone guys like Ray Smith and inexplicably rejected by the American people. But Ray Smith believed he could see even further than that. In 1993, theory held and reason confirmed that a cable television system could be easily adapted to carry telephone traffic; if Smith's telephone lines were combined with Malone's cables, Bell Atlantic would become a colossus of the telephone business instead of a mere giant. And soon, telephones, computers, and television sets would merge into a single household appliance. Bell Atlantic would own that appliance, and it would own the future.

Years would pass before the over-the-air broadcasters—NBC, CBS, ABC, and Fox—could adapt their signals for digital broadcast, but cable television was digital-ready now. No less a figure than John Malone had said so, and the ruthless, intellectually arrogant John Malone was no starry-eyed visionary. Malone had, in fact, matched action to his words, ordering new equipment. Linked by telephone lines, the nationwide network of coaxial cables would become the information and communications highway of the future, a concept much discussed in 1993 but whose precise outlines were obscure to all but a few.

The man who controlled a digital television network held the future in the palm of his hand, and Ray Smith didn't need to stray far from his shaving mirror to see the face of that man. There were billions to be made, perhaps trillions, and he would become a mogul of the information age. For months, trying to buy TCI, Smith had been pursuing John Malone, and Malone loved nothing more than a man whose single-mindedness had gotten the better of his common sense.

In their meetings, Smith and Malone disagreed about many things, but on one topic they were unanimous. Bell Atlantic was the company of the past and TCI was the company of the future. Malone repeatedly said so, and Smith repeatedly agreed. Smith loved to discuss technology. And, following his usual custom, there were a number of things Malone neglected to tell his former adversary.

On many of TCI's cable systems—well, actually, on a whole lot of them—the technology was at least ten years old; Malone had been milking those systems for decades. The technology on the rest of his cable systems wasn't so hot either; Bell Atlantic had more computers in some of its cities than TCI had in its entire company. Moreover, ordering digital equipment—and Malone, hedging his bets, hadn't ordered nearly as much digital equipment as was commonly thought—had also taught Malone a thing or two. For one, a vital component didn't work as advertised; in fact, the vital component didn't work at all. Moreover, it was distinctly possible that some of TCI's systems could never be wired for digital transmission. But Malone was not in a philosophical mood; he did not share his insights with the persistent and determined Ray Smith. As far as Smith was concerned, there was only one important point where their minds did not meet, and it was the rare man who could make John Malone change his mind.

They were not divided by the price that Bell Atlantic would pay for TCI, although it was reported that they were; they had already agreed on the price. No actual money would change hands—they were agreed on that, too—and it was here that their differences arose. Only one issue remained to be resolved: the number of special shares Bell Atlantic would issue to the TCI stockholders, prominent among them Malone and Magness, in exchange for the revenues TCI would guarantee from its cable systems. This was the sticking point. Going in, Smith had known that Malone was a tireless negotiator—always searching for a last concession from his opponent, always eager to secure a special treat, not shared with the other TCI stockholders, for himself and Magness—and so he proved to be; Malone, it soon became clear, was determined to receive a premium for his personal holdings in the company. But by the time of the Waldorf meeting, it was possible for Smith to believe that he possessed an advantage not available to others who had crossed Malone's path. Malone had confessed that he was a weary man, dispirited by the invective that had fallen on his head since he picked his fight with Senator Gore. He seemed ready for retirement, to take the vice chairmanship of Bell Atlantic and assume an advisory role far from the fields of corporate strife. At the Waldorf—one-on-one, with aides and lawyers banished—Smith was determined to press his case and close the deal on his own terms. After all, he and Malone were like-minded men, and a glorious future was theirs for the taking.

James Dickerson, Bell Atlantic's chief financial officer, waited below in the lobby. From time to time, Dickerson placed pseudonymous calls to the suite; sometimes he pretended to be Smith's chauffeur and sometimes his secretary, Phyllis. Repeatedly, Smith had nothing to report to Phyllis. Then, finally, he did. Malone had caved. Bell Atlantic had its terms; it would buy TCI for $33 billion in stock and consummate the largest merger in American history. It was a famous victory.

Afterward, an embarrassed Dickerson encountered an unsurprised Malone in the lobby. "Your boss is ready to go home now," Malone said. Nothing got past John Malone.

ONE

A Wonderful Business

IN AMERICA, CABLE TELEVISION HAD ITS CLASSICAL period, its age of consolidation and renewed vigor, and its time of troubles when new enemies whose motives or strength could not be clearly discerned began to probe the outposts and frontiers of a tired empire. Malone arrived just as the Golden Age of lusty yeomen, swashbuckling piracy, and independent city-states was ending.

The year of its birth can be located exactly; it was 1948. David Sarnoff of RCA had dramatically unveiled practical, consumer-ready electronic television during the New York World's Fair of 1939. The government had established the broadcasting standards in 1941. World War II had intervened. Now, with the return of peace, with Sarnoff's factories going full blast, and with the unlocking of a ravenous consumer demand following fifteen years of depression and global warfare, television was sweeping the country. The public wanted to watch Milton Berle in a woman's dress. Or a test pattern. Or a thermometer, a barograph, and a wind indicator. Or anything. After a decade and a half of nerve-wracking conflict, the public wanted to have some quiet, passive fun. With a kind of cheerful desperate longing, it wanted to believe that the march of progress had resumed and consumer abundance had returned.

Unfortunately, there was a problem; when new technology is involved, there usually is. Unlike radio waves, which bounce off the atmosphere and ricochet off obstacles, television signals travel in a straight line. Any obstacle will blow them straight off the planet. Such as a mountain.

In June 1948, Mahanoy City, Pennsylvania, a hamlet of 10,000 people some eighty-five miles northwest of Philadelphia, did not have television. It was surrounded by the Poconos and lay in a bowl of land. Before the signals reached Mahanoy City from the powerful new stations in Philadelphia, they were deflected to Sirius Major. For one enterprising citizen, this represented an opportunity.

John Walson, Sr., was a lineman for the Pennsylvania Power & Light Company. He also owned an appliance store. Walson was an ingenious fellow, good with his hands—he had once built an automatic door opener for his parents' garage—and after a little thought, the solution to his hometown's dilemma (to say nothing of the key to his future prosperity) seemed obvious. Walson erected a seventy-foot antenna on New Boston Mountain, hooked up some General Electric television sets, and brought prospective customers up the hill to show them the latest marvel of the age. But it soon became apparent that there were a couple of things wrong with his plan. For one, if his prospective customers wanted to watch television in addition to owning a set, they were going to have to build a house on New Boston Mountain. For another, according to a newspaper account, taking prospective lady customers up on the mountain after dark embarrassed him.

Using his lineman's skill, Walson ran a twin-lead wire down the slope, hooked it up to his employer's poles, tactfully provided free television service to a pair of his superiors, and brought the signal into his store. He also wired six additional homes at $100 an installation; the service charge was $2 a month. Walson had discovered a prosperous new business; although he continued to work for PP&L until the mid-1950s, he expanded his television enterprise, introduced coaxial cable, became a pioneer in microwave transmission, wired the city of Wilkes-Barre, and spent his twilight years as a comfortable man.

In that same year, 1948, Ed Parsons of Astoria, Oregon, learned that his wife wanted to watch television. Parsons knew something about the broadcasting business and thought he knew how the trick could be done. The nearest station, KRSC, was in Seattle, 125 miles and three mountain ranges away. Parsons erected an antenna atop a local hotel, tweaked the equipment, and beamed the signal into his penthouse. His neighbors clamored for the service. Parsons, like Walson, was now in the cable business, but Oregon and Pennsylvania were only the beginning, and a modest beginning at that. A few years later, an out-of-work fighter pilot named Bill Daniels brought cable television to Casper, Wyoming, and the world changed again.

Daniels had never seen a television set in his life until he walked into a Denver bar one day in 1952. He was thirty-two years old, a retired naval commander with eleven enemy kills to his credit, and he had been recalled to the colors for the Korean conflict. In his brief adult life, Bill Daniels had known almost nothing but war. Now he was heading north to Wyoming from his father's home in New Mexico, intent on making a little civilian money by practicing the only other trade he knew: selling insurance in the oil patch. He was familiar with radar but had no idea how television worked, and he never learned. But he came to think that this thing, television, might be one hell of a business.

There was oil near Casper, Wyoming, but there was no great call for insurance. On the other hand, the town didn't have television, and Daniels sensed an opportunity. Wearing his cowboy boots, he took a plane east to Pennsylvania, then the hotbed of the cable business, and hooked up with John Malone's subsequent corporate abode, Jerrold. Run by Milton Shapp, a future governor and presidential hopeful, Jerrold was one of the few companies that manufactured cable equipment, and it owned a few small systems. For $500 a day in 1953 money, it would teach someone like Daniels how to set up and run a cable company. Daniels paid the fee, took the course, and went home.

Following Jerrold's teachings, he went to the city fathers and obtained a permit to use the streets and alleys. The nearest television station was in Denver, 275 miles away, a distance that had never been bridged in cable's short history; when the Jerrold people showed up to sell their pupil his equipment, they thought Daniels was out of his mind. Still, they were perfectly willing to pick his pockets; it was either buy from Jerrold or purchase the hardware off the shelf and adapt it, and Daniels knew nothing about electrical engineering. In the unlikely event that he ever got the business off the ground, he would also pay Jerrold twenty-five cents a month for every one of his customers. One way or the other, Bill Daniels was a goose for the plucking.

As the Pennsylvanians chuckled all the way back to their Pottstown headquarters, Daniels set about constructing his impossible system. He erected an antenna on a mountain near Laramie, paid $125,000 in cash for a performance bond, rented a microwave relay from the Bell System at around $8,000 a month, and pumped the Denver signal over the remaining 200 miles to Casper. He was able to import one channel.

"We were charging 150 bucks per connection because we had a monopoly," Daniels recalled many years later in his oral history. "With every 150 bucks we got, we built a couple more blocks of plant down the alley to get more customers, and we charged $7.50 a month. . . . Every ninety days we would send our then-customers a poll, and they'd pick what programs they wanted to watch. . . . The majority ruled. If more people wanted to watch *I Love Lucy* than Sid

Caesar, then that's what we showed . . . and that was the true democracy in those days."

He wired Rawlings, Wyoming, and picked up the Denver signal again, more easily this time; he wired Farmington, New Mexico, and picked up Albuquerque. Then something occurred to him, and he moved to Denver. Like the shopkeepers and lawyers during the California Gold Rush, Daniels decided to make some real money. He would find cable opportunities for eager entrepreneurs, give them a crash course in the business, arrange the financing, and introduce them to Jerrold. If it worked, he would find himself shooting fish in a rain barrel. Doing cable was easy, but almost nobody knew it. If Bill Daniels could do cable, anybody could do cable. On the other hand, everybody who examined the business immediately realized that people in towns like Casper and Rawlings would actually pay to watch television; if you built or bought a system in a place like Casper or Rawlings, you owned a license to coin money. Daniels would be the essential middleman and take his cut in fees.

Still, in the mid-1950s, it seemed impossible that cable would ever get big; it was only a matter of time before the broadcasters built powerful transmitters in every city and town, and there would no longer be any need for the cable companies to import a signal. A niche business would probably persist in remote corners of the country and in places like Manhattan and parts of Los Angeles, where spectrum clutter and atmospheric conditions gave cable, with its static-free signal, a clear edge when it came to the quality of the transmission. In the immediate short run, however, everything went cable's way. Over-the-air transmitters were expensive, the geography of the country was temporarily in cable's favor, and so, as it happened, was the government; the government froze the construction of new broadcasting stations between 1948 and 1952, first to sort the situation out and then because of the wartime emergency caused by Korea, and cable was the only way a televisionless town or city could get itself some television. Even in cities with one or even two television channels, cable could usually offer a superior picture, and as the technology improved, cable could offer more and more channels—soon, many more than were available locally—and fill at least some of them with signals imported by microwave; in cities where only NBC and CBS were available, it could bring in ABC and DuMont, and it could tap the local programming of the nearby big cities. Another opportunity arose when David Sarnoff of RCA finally rolled out color television in 1954 after a lengthy battle with CBS. Early color television was not user-friendly.

"If you have a color television set," said GE chairman Ralph Cordiner, "you've almost got to have an engineer living in the house." There wasn't a lot of color broadcasting in 1954 (or 1955, or 1956), but it was far easier to view on cable and the quality of the color was (and remained for a long time) considerably better. When color was combined with cable, superior television resulted. For the sort of people who always rush into a new consumer technology and delight in starting up their gizmos and making them go, cable was the conduit of choice.

Moreover, early cable had almost no enemies. Municipalities welcomed it eagerly; for a brief and giddy time, cable pioneers like Daniels were heroes. Utility and telephone companies usually didn't mind if cable companies strung wire on their poles and usually didn't charge; a cable guy could drive out in his pickup, throw a roll of coaxial over his shoulder, and start climbing. The major broadcasting companies didn't object when their signals were snatched out of the air and sold for a fee the broadcasters did not share; cable increased the broadcasters' viewership, made people eager for over-the-air broadcasting when it finally arrived in their communities (or so the reasoning went), and pleased advertisers who now reached even more prospective customers. The Internal Revenue Service occasionally glanced at cable, trying to figure out what kind of business it was, what kind of taxes it was supposed to pay, and whether it was legal, but the occasional IRS scrutiny usually came to nothing. The Federal Communications Commission was indifferent, although at least some cable operators wished the situation were otherwise; in the

America of the 1950s and 1960s, a respectable communications business was a regulated communications business, a sign that it was a serious undertaking. But in 1952, there were just seventy cable systems with 14,000 customers, and the mighty government regarded the tiny upstart with the sort of smiling indulgence usually reserved by a basking lion for a very small kitten.

Even so, cable could be a modestly wonderful business for a small investor and a long-dreamed-of chance for a penniless drifter in search of a break. A classic early system was expensive to build, but it was not prohibitively expensive for someone who could raise a little cash—or someone with nothing to lose who was willing to take a tremendous chance. A certain amount of the original outlay would be recovered almost immediately as customers paid their installation charges. From then on, revenue from the subscribers was recession-proof; people would have their telephones disconnected before they gave up cable television. The cable operator had to pay interest on his loans if he had any, but the mantra chanted by a Texas cable guy named Bob Magness was correct as far as it went. Interest really was cheaper than taxes, and if the operator and his investors were using personal loans (as Daniels and his investors had done in Casper), the interest was tax-deductible.

Moreover, a shrewd cable operator could arrange things so that his company paid no taxes at all. A cable operator could write off his investment over a period of five or eight years, preventing the company from making a profit—and in the absence of profits, there were no taxes. Because the system was fairly new and rugged, maintenance wasn't usually a major item. Neither were operations and overhead, because a classic cable system picked up somebody else's signal for free. The owner of a classic cable system, in short, had placed himself on the receiving end of a reliable stream of cheap money without—as Bill Daniels had discovered to his immense enrichment when he imparted the secret to others for a fee—the bothersome necessity of acquiring complicated broadcasting or station management skills. Some of the money could be spent on expansion, a source of further write-offs and more cheap cash, and the remainder could go into the owner's pocket. Yes, classic cable was a wonderful little business. A small system might not make a huge amount of money but it would make money steadily while—in a masterpiece of legal humor—it was legally making no money at all.

Nor did the wonders cease when the tax breaks expired. At the end of the depreciation period, the owner could cash in by selling his system at a handsome price, build another one, and start the process all over again, while the new owner avoided taxes by writing off the cost of his investment. As time wore on and the rules of the game were perfected, cable became only incidentally a business that delivered television to the masses. Increasingly, it was a business of flipping and trading systems. And with Bill Daniels standing by, ready to match any willing seller with his many willing buyers, it was as close to a foolproof enterprise as had ever been devised by the mind of man.

"I WAS KIND OF TRAPPED OUT HERE," RECALLED GLENN Jones as he relaxed in the conference room of his corporate headquarters in Englewood, Colorado, the Denver suburb of the cable barons. Thirty years ago, he had been a dyslexic young lawyer with no prospects whatever, a man who scratched together his living, such as it was, from the kindness of strangers and the sympathy of his friends. At the end of 1996, Jones Intercable was one of the ten largest cable companies in the country.

"I'd just graduated from law school," Jones continued, warming to his subject—it was an old story and a favorite one—"and I didn't have enough money to go back to Pennsylvania. So I decided to start my own firm. I worked out of a coffee and bakery shop on Florida Avenue. When I had a client, we'd eat doughnuts and drink coffee and conduct business. After a few months, it was pretty obvious that it was hard to operate like that, so a friend of mine talked me into representing some cable companies that he had—keeping them clean, keeping them qualified to operate in various states—in exchange for office space. Then I got excited about politics, and I ran for Congress in 1964 with Barry Goldwater. I lost.

"I was broke again. I lived up in the mountains in my car, trying to find a cable system that I could buy. My cable clients would track me down. I'd take off my Sears and Roebuck boots and Levi's and put on my blue suit and go to Los Angeles to monitor the franchise hearings at $350 an hour. That was the money I used in my search. I closed a lot of deals and I handed a lot of checks to people in bibbed overalls. They weren't financial wizards. They were ordinary people, nice people. They were farmers, basically, and they owned a cable franchise and they built it and they sold out. Fifty thousand dollars. A hundred thousand dollars."

Jones, living in his car up in the mountains, intensified his search for a system of his own. When he finally found one, the hour was very late.

CABLE WAS CHANGING. FOR EX-FIGHTER PILOTS LIKE BILL Daniels and failed lawyers living in their cars like Glenn Jones, the window of opportunity had begun to close. Most of the country was still wired with the small classical systems of the Golden Age, where Pop in his coveralls and Mom in her apron would see their investment pay for itself in an astonishing three years, but big money had finally seen the same thing. So had the government. So had the telephone company.

In 1964, Jack Kent Cooke, a wealthy semiretired Canadian publisher, was looking for a place to double his money with a minimum of risk. He discovered cable, invested $22 million, and never looked back. GE and Westinghouse were interested. Daniels, always ready with a deal, was able to attract the attention of Cox Communications and Storer. He also sold Irving Kahn his first system, in Silver City, New Mexico. It had 750 subscribers.

Just after World War II, Kahn was a vice president of 20th Century Fox when the FCC came calling to offer a deal that, with the wisdom of hindsight, had not been equaled since a bunch of Indians made the acquaintance of certain Dutchmen on a place called Manhattan Island. For a song, Fox could have bought permits to establish television stations in the nation's major cities. Kahn, with the justifiable exaggeration of a very frustrated man, recalled that they were as cheap as marriage licenses. Later, they were worth billions. Kahn's superiors weren't interested.

Now Kahn was head of a company called TelePrompTer, whose patented device enabled politicians to give the impression they were speaking with marvelous extemporaneous fluency. TelePrompTer also brought exclusive broadcasts of championship boxing matches to local movie theaters. Daniels, who had the born salesman's knack of improving a prospective customer's thought processes by adding a customized spin to his proposed deals, suggested that lucrative possibilities might materialize if TelePrompTer's sports business were combined with cable. TelePrompTer didn't have a lot of spare change, but it had enough to take a small flier in the market and buy the Silver City operation. Kahn immediately made the usual discovery.

Daniels had been right. Cable television was the closest anyone (except a tobacco company) had ever come to an ideal consumer product: something that cost pennies, sold for a dollar, and was addictive.

The tiny Silver City system, with its handful of customers, was a miniature gold mine. And Kahn also saw something else. Silver City could be the foundation of an empire. Cable still wasn't a huge business, but it was no longer small; by 1968, the industry had 3.5 million subscribers, 6.4 percent of the population, and revenues of $240 million. Kahn, ever mindful of his instructive experience at Fox, found the necessary funds to expand. By the end of 1969, TelePrompTer was the third-largest cable company in the land, with 140,000 customers. By 1980, just before it sold the business to Westinghouse, it was the largest, with more than a million, although by then the hand of Irving Kahn was no longer on the corporate tiller. Kahn had gone to jail in

1971 for bribing, among others, the mayor of Johnstown, Pennsylvania, in exchange for a cable franchise.

But Kahn's temporary departure from the scene—his sentence served, he was soon back in the game, selling New Jersey cable systems to the *New York Times*—was little more than a regrettable incident, despite the colorful copy in the press and the importance of the event to its protagonist. As the cable industry began to change after the mid-1960s, it found itself impaled on the horns of a dilemma that took the form of two questions. Now that cable was an established business, just what was it supposed to do for a living? And, equally to the point, what would the telephone company, the broadcast networks, and the government allow it to do? The answers were not as easy as they might seem.

SHORTLY AFTER HE INVENTED—OR, DEPENDING ON OTHER interpretations, did not invent—the telephone in 1876, Alexander Graham Bell tried to sell it. At the time, the nation's first and only telecommunications company was the telegraph giant, Western Union. Bell offered the telephone to Western Union for $100,000. Forgetting that the inventor of the telegraph, Samuel F. B. Morse, had also tried to sell his technology (an effort, had Morse succeeded, that would have deprived Western Union of a bonanza if not its very existence), Western Union decided the telephone was a temporary fad. It passed on the offer. Years later, Western Union was a wraith of its once mighty self, and AT&T ruled the telecommunications roost.

AT&T was determined not to duplicate Western Union's fatal mistake. Moreover, the telephone company had noticed something else, something that was extremely hard to miss. The Bell System no longer owned the only communications wire entering the house. It was hard to tell just what, exactly, this meant, but coaxial cable—increasingly, the cable companies' wire of choice—was, at least theoretically, a two-way conduit. At least in theory, cable television could become interactive, importing data (and who knew what else) into the home at the customer's request. At least in theory, a coaxial-based, interactive cable system could also become a telephone system. AT&T was not amused. At least in theory, the Bell monopoly seemed to be in jeopardy. Steps were taken.

"I was trying to build a little cable system up in Idaho Springs," said Glenn Jones. "I intended to be on telephone poles up there, and I applied for a contract. Mountain Bell decided they didn't want to lease poles; they wanted to pick on some little guy like me. They'd give me five channels or ten channels, and they'd use the rest of the capacity for themselves. And I would have no control over service or anything. I didn't want to do that. I ordered a bunch of twenty-five-foot creosoted telephone poles with absolutely no money to pay for them and had them delivered to Idaho Springs. I had to set them fast enough that by the time the bill came, I'd have customers up and running. So up in Idaho Springs, there are still poles on both sides of the street."

Although few cable operators were driven by the impoverished Jones's desperate ingenuity, many of them were confronted with the same problem. AT&T was forbidden to get into the television business, but it definitely owned its poles and wires, and in the matter of poles and wires, AT&T was no longer inclined to be indulgent, although the precise manner of dealing with the problem and the threat of cable was left to its regional subsidiaries.

In the simplest of the preferred methods, the local telephone company charged the cable operator rent for the use of its right-of-way, which produced revenue and put a dent in the cable operator's all-important tax-free revenue but otherwise did little to address the threat: that the cable companies would get into the voice and data businesses. In the more complicated but preferred method, the telephone company forbade the cable operator to string his own coaxials, built and maintained the system itself, leased it to the cable guy with written stipulations governing what the cable guy could and could not run over the wires, and reserved the excess capacity for its own use in the event anybody figured out what—aside from television—it could be used for. The ball seemed to be in AT&T's court; not only did it own the poles, but it didn't have to apply to local government for permission before it began building a cable infrastructure. The cable companies were weak and powerless, and the telephone company was rich and politically sophisticated, with an army of state and national lobbyists—but not quite as sophisticated as it imagined. When it came to television, the telephone companies usually weren't.

For one thing, remarkably few politicians ever lost a vote by attacking the telephone monopoly. For another, politicians just loved—and would do almost anything—to see their faces on television. Just as the telephone guys seemed to have the loudly caterwauling cable guys over a barrel, Congress limited the fees the Bell System charged for pole access, and the FCC forbade the operating companies from owning cable systems in their home regions.

In the early history of cable, it was a famous—but rare—victory; the cable operators had developed some other enemies. The broadcasters no longer regarded cable as a hayseed operation that modestly expanded their advertising base while preparing the populace for some real television. The Hollywood studios, the independent television producers, and the New York networks no longer regarded the purloining of their movies and programs as a harmless prank—not with more than 6 percent of the country wired up and no money coming in as a result.

In vain—and more than a trifle disingenuously—the cable operators protested that broadcast signals floated invisibly in the air for anyone to take, cable systems were just another form of aerial, and if the broadcasters, networks, film studios, and producers felt ticked off about the situation, they ought to charge the homeowners who picked up their programs with rabbit ears and rooftop antennas. It had been child's play to take on the telephone company, but when the interests of the networks, their broadcasters, and the studios were involved, the tables were turned. The broadcasters, carrying both network fare and the programs generated by the studios, reached 90 percent of the country—and politicians, as noted, loved to see their faces on television. For the first time in almost three-quarters of a century, the nation's copyright laws were rewritten. Henceforward, if the cable operators wanted to sell a program or a movie that belonged to somebody else, they would have to pay royalties for the privilege. Cable was still a wonderful business—it was still largely tax-free—but it was no longer the wonderful business it had been. And it had developed another problem, perhaps the most serious problem of all. Cable technology had outrun the cable operators' ability to make use of it.

Cable's capacity had expanded from one channel to three channels, then five channels, and—when Jerrold finally got some competition in the hardware business—twelve channels, creating a dilemma that would persist for years. Outside the Chicago area and the Coasts, there simply weren't enough signals that could be snatched out of the air and used to fill cable's growing capacity. In most of cable's service areas in the late 1960s and early 1970s, there were plenty of channels—for the time, an unimaginable abundance of channels—but there wasn't a heck of a lot to watch.

The modernized cable systems carried the broadcasts of the major networks, which took care of three channels out of twelve. It was left to the cable operator to fill the remaining nine channels with whatever he could rustle up. Some operators serving large populations set up small programming arms like Home Box Office, but going national with programs created specifically for cable was prohibitively expensive—which was why there were so few cable programmers in the late 1960s and early 1970s. Cable systems were widely scattered. Most of them were rural, semirural, or confined to smaller cities and their suburbs; to the studios that made original programs, cable was not an enticing market. To provide the relatively few viewers on any given cable system with regularly scheduled, non-network sports and entertainment, the operators had to turn to wholesalers and rent films and old programs that usually weren't very good, run the promotional films of local industries or special-interest groups like Ducks Unlimited, send a camera crew to the county stadium, or buy regional news and sports footage from someone with his own camera crew. Before the passage of the new copyright law and the proliferation of empty channels, cable had been a form of almost effortless, risk-free piracy that required no broadcasting skills whatever; the networks provided them. After the passage of the copyright law and the proliferation of channels, most cable operators still had no broadcasting skills.

As a stopgap until someone thought of something—as the cable business outgrew its primitive roots, it continually seemed to be waiting for someone to think of something—some system operators turned their unused channels into an early equivalent to video-on-demand. At one upstate New York cable system, the first person who called and requested a film was the person who controlled the channel for as long as the film ran; if the caller wanted to watch a movie about trout fishing, everybody watched a movie about trout fishing. Then the cable operator moved on to the request of the next caller, and everybody tuning into the channel watched that. In the immediate short run, there seemed to be only one reasonably good, moneymaking answer to the problem of channel proliferation: move cable into the big cities, where plenty of broadcast signals could be picked up. It wasn't nearly as good an idea as it seemed.

IN THE MID-1960S, A SMALL COMPANY CALLED STERLING Manhattan Cable, 20 percent of which had been acquired by Time Inc. in what resembled a fit of absentmindedness, began wiring the lower half of Manhattan while Kahn's TelePrompTer wired the upper half. Much water would pass beneath a number of bridges before either company saw its money again. The reasons were various. In the now dying days of classic cable, a system operator received a permit from a city council whose constituents were mad for television, any kind of television, especially if it was clear and static-free. In Manhattan, the citizens could receive seven broadcast channels, and remarkably few of them proved willing to pay money to watch an improved signal. Most big-city people, it turned out, were willing to watch a bad picture if the sound was clear. There was no great groundswell for cable television in Manhattan and no way to blackmail the city council with threats of a voter backlash. Sensing its own opportunity, New York City demanded and received a franchise fee, teaching a lesson to other city councils that cable operators soon wished they had never learned. Then the hard part began.

In a classic system, the operator strung his cables on telephone poles. There were no telephone poles in Manhattan. Instead, the cable had to be snaked through underground conduits owned by the Empire City Subway Company, a subsidiary of New York Telephone. The streets had to be opened, the telephone lines had to be pushed gently aside, and sometimes the conduit had to be enlarged, all of which cost money. In a classic system, the operator and his salespeople would fan out to the houses along the route, persuading the homeowners to purchase the new service. Manhattan was an island of apartment buildings and multiple dwellings; building superintendents and landlords demanded a piece of the action before they would allow a cable operator to set foot inside the door. Thus admitted at a price, the cable operator then tried to sell a new kind of television to a populace that was largely indifferent to the latest wonder of the electronic age. Until somebody thought of something, big-city cable was not going to be a wonderful business. Ted Turner thought of something.

THOUGHTS OF HIS FATHER'S SUICIDE WERE NEVER FAR from the mind of Robert E. (Ted) Turner. In his high-rise Atlanta office, there was a sliding glass door overlooking an unbarred, fourteen-story drop to the pavement below. "In case," he explained, "I need to get out."

He was twenty-four in 1963 when he bought the bankrupt billboard company his father had once owned and made it the foundation of his empire. In 1969, he bought Channel 17 in Atlanta, an almost worthless UHF television station with an uncertain signal, and gave it the call letters WTCG for Turner Communications Group or, alternatively, Watch This Channel Grow. The unimposing studio building on West Peachtree Street had to be dusted for fleas every week. Turner was brash and eager, a bright young lad, with David O. Selznick in him for good or bad. His love of the movie *Gone With the Wind* bordered on obsession. He sported a Clark Gable mustache, and he named one of his sons Rhett. Years later, when he could afford a skyscraper with a special door and a fourteen-story drop to certain death, the movie played on the video monitors of the Turner Broadcasting Corporation all day long.

Within his personal sphere of influence, he did nothing by half measures. He was a devoted and talented sailor with an eye for beautiful long-legged blond women who were not his wife, and he was extremely fond of his glass. But when it came to television broadcasting he was, at first, a distinctly small potato. He was dyslexic.

Although he claimed, repeatedly and forever afterward, that he was a keen fan of quality television and family values, and further claimed that WTCG viewers were much smarter than the average audience, because it took a homeowner of genius to find his station's weak and elusive signal, his success was based on the least well-kept of television's many dirty secrets: a huge hunk of the audience wasn't remotely interested in information, uplift, or culture. Turner flooded his airwaves with professional wrestling, cheap old movies and cheap old sitcoms, the games of the Atlanta Braves baseball team (always ready to seize a main chance, he later bought the team with the team's own money), and stunts—his news anchorman sometimes wore a bag over his head when he reported the dismal scores of the local sports franchises.

Turner was lucky: the second independent Atlanta television station withered and died. He was smart: in broadcasting parlance, he was a talented counterprogrammer who put on *Star Trek* reruns when his rivals were doing their evening newscasts, picked up NBC network shows when the local affiliate refused to clear airtime and bragged about it on his billboards, and came out of nowhere to scoop up the broadcasting rights to the Braves. When he bought a second, even worse station in Charleston, South Carolina, against the explicit wishes of his own board of directors, in a sheriff's sale on the courthouse steps, and with nothing more than his signature on a document, he organized a "beg-a-thon" during which viewers were asked to donate the price of two movie tickets to keep him on the air. He collected $30,000, and kept right on going. Ted Turner was never a man to hide his light under a bushel.

In a few short years, he became a regional television power who stubbornly, noisily confronted the national networks on their own ground and either prevailed or held his own, but national prominence eluded him. For one thing, he couldn't afford to build the microwave towers that would allow him to expand beyond his Atlanta base. In many ways, he resembled a twelve-channel cable operator scrambling for programs; Turner was trying to fill an entire broadcasting schedule. But there was a difference between Ted Turner and most cable operators. Turner knew how to do it, and, like Bill Daniels, he sensed an opportunity that had eluded others. The Turner formula worked splendidly in Atlanta. It would undoubtedly play just as well in the rest of the South or, for that matter, the entire nation, where hundreds of cable systems were clamoring for just the sort of programming he knew how to do so well. WTCG could become a superstation with an audience in the tens of millions. In the broadcasting industry, a superstation was a station whose unusually powerful signal made it audible over a vast geographical area. In the cable industry as Turner envisioned it, a superstation was a station whose programming was sold to cable operators. But no sooner had Turner conceived his latest new idea—a little ahead of its time, it was true—than the FCC made it impossible. The FCC was another entity that had once paid remarkably little attention to cable, but everything was different now. For the time being, Ted Turner, who made no secret of his consuming thirst for greatness, was instructed to stay home and tend his garden.

In 1968, the FCC imposed its so-called blackout rule: if a cable system imported a distant signal from, say, Atlanta, a period of days must elapse before it could show programming that was also available from the local broadcasting outlet. Cable operators and would-be broadcasting suppliers like Turner were set a difficult and sometimes impossible task. Because Turner was a broadcaster, his station's daily schedule was announced in advance and set in stone. It was economically and technically unfeasible to cherry-pick a broadcast television schedule; under the blackout rule, the programming fare of Turner's proposed superstation would have huge gaping holes—"like Swiss cheese," in the words of one commentator. It was just as well that Turner couldn't afford to build one. Under the blackout rule, building a cable-ready superstation made no sense.

The commission also imposed a four-year freeze on the further expansion of cable into the country's top 100 markets—the major cities—starting in 1968. TelePrompTer and Sterling could continue to wire Manhattan, but they couldn't wire Pittsburgh. The FCC, the commissioners said, wanted to rethink the whole question of cable television.

FOUR YEARS LATER, THE BLACKOUT RULE HAD BEEN overturned in the courts. Turner could build his superstation after all, and he was soon in a position to do so. The freeze on the cities had expired the year before, in 1972. The cable companies could move into the big time again, provided Turner (or the usual unknown somebody) supplied them with the sort of unique programming that would give them a competitive edge over the established broadcasters.

The usual unknown somebody, as it turned out, was an obscure Time lawyer named Gerald Levin. Levin's equally obscure Time cable subsidiary was preparing to broadcast its signal from an RCA communications satellite. Any cable operator with an earth station could pick up Time's programming and sell it to its customers. Everyone had known satellite transmission was possible, but it was Levin who did it, inventing an entirely new form of cable television. Meanwhile, over at Warner Communications, the charismatic chairman Steve Ross repeatedly alarmed his executives and bored his stockholders by obsessively talking, not very clearly, about something called a "frame grabber." Boiled down to its unclear essentials, the frame grabber seemed to be a form of interactive television. It was not only the telephone companies that had noticed that coaxial cable was, potentially, a two-way street, and Ross was not alone in loudly trumpeting its possibilities. In the early 1970s, all the major cable operators were talking about interactive television. They talked about it so much, in fact, that in 1972 the FCC passed a rule requiring cable television to become interactive. The entire industry seemed to be entering an unprecedented period of expansion and creativity. Certainly it was about to change in ways that could not be foreseen. There was money to be made, perhaps a huge amount of money. It was a wonderful business.

This, then, was the situation prevailing in the industry when John Charles Custer Malone, a young executive with a formidable intellect, a dangerously unhappy wife, and a peculiar personality, shook the dust of his native East from his feet and came West to seek his fame and fortune in the High Plains of Colorado.

A surprise was waiting for him in Denver. Tele-Communications Inc., the company to whose wagon Malone had hitched his star, was broke.

TWO

A Mirror in the Sky

ALL HIS LIFE, UNTIL HE WENT TO COLORADO, JOHN Malone had been one of Fortune's favorite children. In Colorado, he became a young man with a world of trouble on his hands.

Born in 1941, he was raised in an eighteenth-century house in the comfortable precincts of Milford, Connecticut. His father was a General Electric vice president and, by some accounts, both an inventor and a hard-driving man who came home on Saturday, drove to work on Sunday, and spent the rest of the week away from home. His mother, by Malone's own account, was distant. Also by his own account, he early exhibited the youthful genius expected of an American entrepreneur, buying surplus GE radios for a buck, repairing them, and selling them for seven times his purchase price.

He took his engineering degree from Yale in 1963, married young, joined Bell Labs, and continued his higher education at AT&T's expense. "Part of their development program was furthering your education in electrical engineering," he said. While at Bell Labs, he took his master's at NYU and his doctorate at Johns Hopkins. He tried his hand at teaching on the side and found it wasn't something he wanted to do. For Ma Bell, in a portent of things to come, he wrote a 300-page paper on the problems of running a regulated company. He thought he was interested in computers and discovered that he wasn't.

"To tell you the truth," he said, "I never liked computers. I mean, I found them to be exasperating, requiring an immense amount of detail. And I, really, like somebody said one time, I'm a mathematician, not an accountant. I may be accurate, but I'm not precise, and precision is very important in the computer business. Sure, I could have gone into the computer business. I could have gone into any technologically based business. But my real ambition was always to get involved in the business side."

He didn't like teaching. Computers disappointed him. At Bell Labs, he could see exactly what he would become: a diligent soldier of science, perhaps a lavishly decorated one (Bell Labs had produced four Nobel laureates and a dazzling succession of breakthroughs), but he would not be a towering figure in the eyes of the world. Only a handful of people had ever heard of Claude Shannon, the Bell Lab mathematician and co-author of the information theory that was central to the computer revolution. A few more had heard of William Shockley, the principal inventor of the transistor, but only much later, when Shockley developed a harebrained plan to breed an artificially inseminated superrace of mental titans, most of them white. Neither of them had become rich. (Shockley had merely been wealthy; Shannon was otherwise remembered for having ridden his unicycle through the halls at Bell Labs while he was thinking.) John Malone was an ambitious man. He wanted to be rich, he wanted to be powerful, and he believed his profession showed the way.

"Electrical engineers," he remarked in an interview a few years ago, "used to end up running insurance companies, because they had one of the few rigorous educations in statistics and math." A complicated company in a complicated industry would suit him just fine, where he could make the best use of his skills, make his mark, and make his fortune.

He left Bell Labs and joined McKinsey & Company, a celebrated consulting firm with a notorious sideline: on more than one occasion, the undeniably talented McKinsey consultants were called into troubled companies, picked the brains of middle managers who, unlike their superiors, actually knew what was wrong, and often replaced the middle managers with themselves. Outside the executive suites of the client companies, McKinsey consultants were not ecstatically welcomed. Louis Gerstner, latterly the chairman of IBM, had been a McKinsey consultant until he saw his chance and took it.

Malone stayed at McKinsey for two years, although he was clearly marked for higher things. His wife was not happy; the hours were long and a McKinsey consultant was frequently on the road. Leslie Malone wanted her husband to come home for dinner. Her husband went looking for another job.

In 1970, not yet thirty years old, he was named group vice president of the General Instrument Corporation and president of its Jerrold subsidiary. Jerrold was at the same old stand, manufacturing equipment for the cable systems that were then called community antenna television. Because many cable operators had almost no cash to speak of (but a bonanza down the road, if only they could get there), Jerrold also extended credit, which meant that Malone knew as much or more about some of his customers than their own bankers did—provided, of course, his customers were lucky enough to have a banker; many didn't. He made the acquaintance of Bob Magness, an outwardly unimpressive small-potatoes cable operator with a sharply defined notion of how to do business. The two of them hit it off, and Magness offered him a job. So did Steve Ross, the chairman of Warner Communications, whose cable system was either the second or third largest in the country depending on the monthly to-and-fro of the dealmaking that characterized the business. Malone found Ross hypnotic—most people did—but he refused.

"Some of the senior management were very good friends of mine that I admired very much," he explained—unpersuasively, in view of his subsequent and richly deserved reputation for dealing ruthlessly with anyone who got in his way, "but their continued involvement would probably have been inconsistent with me coming in, if you know what I mean. They were going to continue to run it, or I was going to run it. I just didn't want to be the vehicle for that."

Perhaps more to the point, his wife still wanted her husband to come home at night; Malone had traded the long road trips of McKinsey for the long road trips of Jerrold, and Leslie Malone's mood was growing dangerous. In Colorado, he could live close to the office, and running a cable company—which more or less ran itself—would not be a consuming occupation. Moreover, he would find the political atmosphere more congenial. Malone's politics were libertarian bordering on the antediluvian; he had begun to see the specter of socialism everywhere in his native East, and the cowboy culture of the High Plains would be to his taste and liking. On the subject of his private life, Malone was normally a tomb of silence, but one thing was suspected about him to the point of certainty. John Malone was deeply in love with his wife. For both of them, things would be very different in Colorado. Leslie could keep horses.

"I was really looking to get my family out of the New York metropolitan area," he said. "I was always a country kid, growing up in distant suburban Connecticut. And I wanted to have a career. You know, you strive to pursue those two goals well, you can't spend a lot of time on a train or in a limo stuck in traffic."

The year was 1973. He was thirty-two years old.

MAGNESS WAS A FERRET-FACED, GAP-TOOTHED, JUG-EARED Texan who looked exactly like the man he had very recently been: a roustabout with no visible prospects. He was also considerably smarter than he looked.

In 1956, Magness had sold his cattle, mortgaged his home, and started to build a cable television system in a flyspeck of a Texas town called Memphis. Many people like Magness were building cable systems then. He climbed the poles and strung the wire; his wife, Betsey, kept the books on the kitchen table. They had 700 customers. In 1958, they moved their operations north to Bozeman, Montana. By 1970, they were in Denver, sitting at the feet of Bill Daniels, ready to cut some deals. The number of their customers had grown to nearly 37,000.

Magness's company, Tele-Communications Inc., seemed to be about the right size for an unprepossessing operation run by such an unprepossessing entrepreneur, but there was one unusual thing about Bob Magness. The typical small-time cable proprietor usually sold his systems after five or seven years. Selling the systems, not delivering television, was where the money was. Magness was different.

"Bob never sold anything," recalled Glenn Jones. "Bob just bought."

Magness liked to keep things simple. He always said that it was cheaper to pay interest than to pay taxes; it was the guiding principle of his business life. Everyone in cable knew that, of course, all the ranchers in bibbed overalls, ex–fighter pilots, and failed lawyers who traded cable systems out of Denver as though they were portfolios of penny stocks; remarkably few of them paid any taxes to speak of. But Magness took it one step further. If he kept borrowing and buying, he would eventually reach a point where he was rolling in dough and he would still never have to pay a penny of tax. The trick was to keep expanding.

By 1973, Magness had it all worked out, including the last element that would make the plan work. He needed a skilled partner, someone very different from himself, who would be the public face of the enterprise, and whose appreciation of the central, simple idea was identical with his own. His choice was John Malone.

To all outward appearances, they were an oddly mismatched pair. Neither then nor later, when he owned a stable of three hundred Arabian horses and a fortune in the vicinity of a billion dollars, was Bob Magness overly fond of contemplating his likeness in the newspapers. John Malone was not opposed to it, provided the text accurately reflected his thoughts as he chose to reveal them, the publication was prestigious—the *New York Times, The Wall Street Journal, Barron's*—and the story suited his purposes. To the end of his life, Magness had terrible taste in clothes and he never got his teeth fixed. Malone was as handsome as a movie star, with the long muscular body and physical grace of a collegiate oarsman. He was an Easterner by birth and upbringing and a product of its schools. He had a Ph.D. He had worked at Bell Labs and written scholarly papers. No one had ever confused Bob Magness with destiny's darling, but great things had always been expected of John Malone. Now he had turned his back on all that. He had upped stakes, moved to the middle of nowhere, and joined a jerkwater outfit owned by a guy who looked like a refugee from central casting.

At Jerrold, his annual pay had been $150,000. At Tele-Communications Inc. it was $60,000. But TCI was not without its redeeming features.

At Jerrold, Malone had been president, but he was still an employee in charge of a subsidiary. At TCI he was a partner in the firm with a free hand to run things under the guidance of a man he regarded—or so he often said—as a father figure and a mentor. Moreover, TCI was a company after his own heart. Magness had given it a freewheeling style, and it had thrown off the dead hand of government taxation. Properly managed, the company could grow very large indeed. Irving Kahn had done it at TelePrompTer, and Kahn had known nothing about the cable business. Malone and Magness would reap wealth beyond the dreams of avarice.

Unfortunately, the wealth part had to be postponed. TCI, buying new systems and hardly ever selling them, had become overextended, and the disgrace of Irving Kahn, the industry's role model, had just slammed shut the door of the bank. To all intents and purposes, TCI had no money to speak of and no clear way of raising more.

"For three or four years," Malone recalled, "it was impossible for an entrepreneurial cable company to borrow money." TCI was a company that lived on borrowed money; borrowed money was central to its corporate strategy. Then, in 1974, the stock market crashed. Wall Street wasn't going to save TCI either. It was impossible to float an issue of stock. "We were lower than whaleshit," Malone said. There was no way he could charm his way out of his dilemma. Malone had no charm. Years of battle lay before him, and Leslie Malone saw her husband at the dinner table even less often than before. It was not what they had planned.

THERE IS A STORY PREVALENT ON WALL STREET—AND never confirmed by Malone—that he once physically fought an equipment supplier, beat the man to a pulp, and improved his opponent's thinking. It was said that when his creditors came to call, he would slam the keys on the desk, inform them that they now owned a cable company, and ask them how they proposed to run it. Once, not long ago, Malone had been a respectable young executive in an industry that had its origins in piracy. Now, as the new prince of the pirates, he was about to show his colleagues a trick or two about running a leaky ship.

Malone insisted that cable television was a creature of the governments—city, state, and national—that granted the franchises, made the rules, and wielded the whip hand. But although he never talked about it, Malone had made an interesting discovery: with the public addicted to television and dependent on the cable company for its fix, a city could become a creature of its cable company, especially if the cable company—unlike Warner and Time—didn't care what anyone thought of it.

Early in Malone's tenure, Vail, Colorado, demanded that a battered and reeling TCI improve the quality of its programming without raising its prices. Malone, the man who had expressed such tender feelings for his friends at Warner, immediately retaliated. During one memorable weekend, the viewers in Vail found nothing on their television sets but the names of the mayor and the city manager, together with their telephone numbers. Vail capitulated.

For a time, it seemed like an isolated episode, the desperate act of a desperate company. "That story has whiskers on it," Malone said dismissively. He neglected to mention—Malone was a man who neglected to mention many things—that variants of the Vail gambit became a standard way of doing business at TCI. If a TCI city rebelled, it would feel the weight of Malone's wrath.

Meanwhile, the rest of the industry seemed to be galloping away from him at top speed. While Malone was preoccupied with TCI's problems and the feeble protests of ski resorts and jerkwater towns, Jerry Levin put the cable signal on the bird and created a mirror in the sky.

THERE ARE AMERICAN ORIGINALS AND AMERICAN TYPES. Malone was a durable type, the brilliant and driven loner. Levin was an original, a man of no visible qualities and only a single achievement to his name, who rose to the top of a giant entertainment conglomerate because no one knew what else to do with him. Levin outlived or outlasted his colleagues, and he assumed command in the end because he was the last man standing.

He resembled Malone in one important respect. As a youth, great things had been expected of him, and he had expected great things of himself. He also differed from Malone in one important respect. After his youth had passed, no one expected much from him at all.

All accounts agree that Levin, born in 1939, had been the perfect child and the perfect student. He was raised in suburban Philadelphia. His father was in the food business, his mother was a piano teacher. There was some thought that he might become a rabbi, and he knew enough Hebrew to conduct services in his synagogue before

he was ten. At Haverford College, a small, traditionally Quaker institution, he majored in biblical studies and wrote his senior thesis on
the convergence of Jewish and Christian traditions. On graduating
first in his class in 1960, he burned his college papers as an act of
humility, as he believed the poet Virgil had done. He took a law
degree from the University of Pennsylvania, was invited into the
white-shoe New York firm of Simpson Thacher & Bartlett, and
worked for the firm's high-profile partner, Whitney North Seymour.
He was launched, but he was not a happy man. It was his clients who
did the big things. As their lawyer, Levin stood anonymously by and
lent a hand in the execution of other people's plans. Levin did not
believe he had been placed on earth to become a bag carrier.

After four years, he left the law and joined the development firm
of David Lilienthal, former head of the Tennessee Valley Authority
and first chairman of the Atomic Energy Commission. Starting in
1971, Levin worked on a massive project, involving three hundred
engineers, to make the deserts of southern Iran bloom as lush and
verdant farmland. He was finally a part of the big picture. For the first
time, he was in his element, where he believed he had learned many
valuable lessons that would serve him well in his future work.
"There's not a lot of difference [between] distributing electronics and
distributing water," he once said. But the deserts did not bloom. It
was not long before Levin was also out of a job.

In 1972, a friend led him to Time Inc., a company that was trying
to figure out what to do for a second act after the darkly glorious,
darkly mischievous years under its late founder, Henry Luce.

There were those who believed, and believe to this day, that Luce
was almost single-handedly responsible for the McCarthy witch
hunts, the Formosa crisis that brought the country to the brink of war
with China in the 1950s, and the long tragedy of Vietnam, and there
was some justice in this view. There was, however, little danger that
anyone would entertain similar views about Luce's successors. *Time*,
the company's namesake and flagship publication, was a fading imitation of its former self, and while the company had successfully rolled

out *People* and *Money*, they were ventures that resembled blots on its escutcheon rather than jewels in its crown. Time Inc. assembled task forces that examined almost every magazine concept known to man, only to decide for a variety of excellent reasons (primarily, a fear of failure) that most of the good ideas were already taken and the others wouldn't work. And, more or less by accident, it had turned itself into a cable television company.

In 1970, trying to figure out what to do with the proceeds from the sale of its five television stations—stations whose product Henry Luce had profoundly mistrusted—Time finally bought the rest of Sterling Manhattan Cable. With Sterling Manhattan came a pay-TV service called Home Box Office, which had been established to sell the games in Madison Square Garden to Sterling's subscribers. Later, HBO tried to expand its offerings by adding movies, which turned out to be—put charitably—an idea well in advance of its time.

Film distributors quite naturally wanted to know how large an audience their products would reach through the medium of cable television. The discouraging answer was: not a heck of a lot. Six percent of the nation looked like a threat to the telephone company and the broadcasting networks, but to a film distributor, 6 percent was a joke. Yes, it was important to ensure that the studios got paid for the use of their products when cable managed to get hold of a film, but that was a problem for the studio lawyers. For the large distributors of popular films, cable could come back to the store when it grew up, had a real audience, and could pay some serious bucks.

There were only two ways to expand the audience, neither of them appealing. A film or a primitive videotape could be physically delivered to a client cable system—a practice called "bicycling"—whereupon HBO would come to resemble a messenger service rather than the programming arm of a mighty corporate empire. Anyway, the distributors could do it themselves if they wanted to. As an alternative, HBO could either buy or rent microwave systems, as Bill Daniels had done. Microwave transmission is a line-of-sight technology; depending on the terrain, the towers have to be spaced roughly twenty or thirty miles apart. Building microwave towers to deliver HBO movies to a relative handful of viewers was prohibitively expensive. Renting them was merely expensive. An exasperated Time tried to shut the entire programming service down, only to be stopped in its tracks by an adamant New York City Council. To preserve its cable franchise in the nation's largest metropolis, Time Inc. had to continue to show the games at the Garden. To fill up the rest of the schedule, it needed some movies. And it was at Time Inc.'s despised and unwanted corporate orphan, Home Box Office, where Jerry Levin became chairman in 1973, that he found the home of his heart and the inspiration for his single stroke of genius.

AROUND TIME INC. HE BECAME KNOWN FOR HIS PRODI-gious memory, his ability to win the trust and friendship of the magazine people, his poor taste in clothes, and his tendency to carry on endlessly during staff meetings about the difficulty of sending microwave television programming to Wilkes-Barre, Pennsylvania, the city John Walson had wired and a subject of utterly no interest to anyone else in the room. Levin's fellow executives were astounded to discover that, when the company met with stock analysts to explain its plans and goals, the analysts had begun to regard Jerry Levin as one of the most interesting people in the room.

His ability to master every fact that came to his attention and remember every event that occurred in his immediate vicinity was regarded as slightly humorous, slightly dweebish, and more than a little annoying. Although he bore his erudition lightly, it had a way of keeping everybody in his vicinity just a little bit off balance. In an interoffice power struggle, such a mastery of detail could become a potent weapon, but Jerry Levin was safely tucked away in an odd corner of a company that regarded itself primarily as a publisher and purveyor of news. When most Time executives gave thought to the future, cable television did not figure prominently in their ruminations. Most Time executives, like most people outside Pennsylvania and Denver, didn't even know much—or anything—about it. Power struggles occurred when corporate titans clashed by night, and Levin was not a corporate titan. When he wasn't working on his microwave transmissions or irritating his fellow workers with his encyclopedic knowledge of just about everything, he devoted his time to ingratiating himself.

Because he spoke in prose and knew his way around the English language, Levin was regarded by the custodians of Luce's journalistic legacy as a more sympathetic executive than the other suits who ran the company; Levin seemed to understand what writers and editors did all day long. (J. Richard Munro, the otherwise well-regarded chairman of the company, was heard to boast that he had never spent a day behind a typewriter. Levin had once wanted to be a writer.) He also had a way of standing out in the executive crowd, although he was a small and unassuming man to whom the adjective "gentle" was often attached. In a sea of Brooks Brothers pinstripe and blue, he wore double knit—just a step above polyester—and he seemed to have chosen his ties while thinking of something else. To the writers and line editors of Time Inc., the friendly, talkative, sartorially challenged Levin seemed touchingly human. The editors and writers didn't know it, but Jerry Levin was the worst enemy they ever had. He was obsessed with television.

Levin seemed to know the plot of every video episode and movie ever made. He had great hopes for HBO, even if these hopes were not forcefully expressed. When he was told that Time Inc. was not overly fond of his movies and wrestling matches, he plaintively replied, "But you're not going to stop me, are you?" And in 1975, he somehow—no one seems to remember exactly how—persuaded the company to give him $7.5 million to undertake an experiment.

Everybody knew you could send people to the moon. The trick

was to persuade somebody to pay an immense amount of money for it. Everybody knew you could bounce a television broadcast off one of the new communications satellites—somebody already had, in a 1973 broadcast of a speech by Speaker of the House Carl Albert, and Levin had seen it. The trick was to persuade somebody—in Levin's case, his corporate masters—to spend a very considerable amount of money to do it all the time, and the subject matter had better not consist of Carl Albert. Not for the last time in his life, Levin had all the theoretical answers, and some of them were even correct.

In theory, the rewards would be great. HBO would no longer have to bicycle or microwave its signal to small, uneconomical audiences. Its signal would blanket the country; any cable operator with an earth station could pick it up and pump it out to the customers over its wires. Nobody knew if enough cable operators would buy earth stations.

In theory, the audience could be huge, almost network scale, especially if cable systems kept expanding at their current healthy pace. Nobody could say for certain that the audience would be huge.

In theory, programmers would flock to the new technology, creating a whole new type of cable-based television. No one knew if that would happen either.

Getting onto a satellite would be expensive—Levin proposed to hitch a ride on RCA's new $150 million bird—but it would be almost maintenance-free. Satellite broadcasting involved almost no moving parts, and it operated in a vacuum. This was all well and good, just the sort of project for a cable-programming operation with deep pockets and a name that was known across the width and the breadth of the land. There wasn't one. HBO, the unwanted urchin in Time's cellar, had never made any money, and almost no one outside of New York City, Allentown, and Wilkes-Barre had ever heard of it. Still, Levin was persuasive, the occupants of the Time executive suite had a strange way of lurching into new television ventures, and in 1975 the company gave him the money.

Under Levin's leadership, HBO had already broken significant new ground in the desired direction. A milestone of sorts had been passed in March 1973, when HBO sent its customers the first live event ever to appear on pay-TV: the Pennsylvania Polka Festival at the Allentown fairgrounds, using old-fashioned microwave transmissions. (In pay-TV, the viewers coughed up a small sum of money—in addition to their cable subscriptions—to watch a specific show.) In June of that same year, it had experimented with putting its signal on a bird, using a Canadian Anik II satellite to deliver the Ernie Shavers–Jimmy Ellis heavyweight boxing match to the National Cable Television Association convention at the Disneyland Hotel. Unfortunately, many of the conventioneers missed the demonstration because Shavers knocked out Ellis in the first round. Moreover, there was nothing particularly earth-shattering about the event. Everyone who paid attention to the technology already knew you could bounce video off a communications satellite; Levin had not been the only person who had gazed at the visage of Carl Albert, and every fledgling technology—including a great many fledgling technologies that never made a penny for their investors—knew how to pull off a stunt. A demonstration would qualify as earth-shattering only if Levin could show the industry how to make some money from it, lots and lots of money. Which, for his next act, Levin proceeded to do.

On September 30, 1975—a date that would always dwell fondly in Jerry Levin's memory—HBO used a satellite to deliver the Muhammad Ali–Joe Frazier fight, the Thrilla in Manila where Ali decked Frazier after fourteen rounds, to paying customers in Jackson, Mississippi, and Vero Beach and Fort Pierce, Florida. History was made. An actual home audience had watched a satellite-borne event taking place thousands of miles away and the home audience had forked over money for the privilege. This was no stunt. Levin had discovered a bonanza, solved the cable industry's most persistent and intractable problem—and, in the process, had transformed the nature of the business. It was his greatest moment.

The market for earth stations boomed—at first, to pick up HBO, which came roaring out of the chute and soon provided nearly half of Time Inc.'s revenue where it had once produced no revenue at all—and so did cable-specific programming services. Pat Robertson put his Christian Broadcasting Network on cable in 1977; it evolved into the Family Channel. CBN was followed by, among many others, the Cable-Satellite Public Affairs Network, C-SPAN, and the Entertainment and Sports Programming Network, ESPN. For the first time since John Walson grabbed the Philadelphia signal out of the air and brought the irresistible novelty of television to Mahanoy City, the cable business had something entirely new to offer. Inevitably, some of the ideas were slightly strange.

"I got the feeling that things had gotten out of hand," said Bud Rukeyser, a former vice president of NBC, "when someone brought us a channel for old people, showing old people doing things with other old people. Call it the Geezer Channel. Old people don't want to watch old people. Old people want to watch young people. We passed."

In Atlanta, Ted Turner was quick to sense the implications of Levin's breakthrough, suited action to his (many) words on the subject, transformed WTCG into the WTBS superstation, and watched as his Atlanta Braves became America's team. Turner, who had always hankered after greatness, sensed that his goal was at last within reach. WGN in Chicago followed suit; its regular programming—including advertisements for companies that existed only in Chicago—became visible all day long in unlikely places like Boise, Idaho.

Everything seemed to be happening at once; it was like an algae bloom, the Reagan administration, or the invention of the home computer. The telephone company had been vanquished. The FCC had opened up the cities. Levin had given the industry access to a whole shelfful of programming that would not have existed without his breakthrough and was not available on network television—and at first, much of the new programming was free, just as the network signals had once been free. The good times had returned. Cable was once again a wonderful business, but in an entirely new way. Or so it seemed.

IN DENVER, JOHN MALONE CONTINUED TO STRUGGLE with TCI. When other cable barons looked at Levin's HBO, they saw the possibility—the certainty—of untold riches. When John Malone looked at HBO, he saw a possible way out of his dilemma—provided he played his cards both cleverly and well. The untold riches would come later.

THREE

The Bystander, the Land Rush, and the Wired Nation

AROUND THE OFFICE, HE WAS CALLED "YOUNG DR. Malone," after a popular radio soap opera. It was one of the few known jokes that were ever made at John Malone's expense. (Years later, there was another. You are in a room with Saddam Hussein, Abu Nidal, and John Malone. You have a gun and two bullets. Q: Who do you shoot? A: John Malone—twice, to make sure he's dead. John Malone and the people around him did not like this joke.) In truth, TCI was rather proud to have a genuine Ph.D. as its chief executive officer. In good times and bad—and at first, the times were very bad indeed—it added a touch of class to a company that never looked back, took no prisoners, and never counted its dead. The Doctor was always operating. In the early years, he had his work cut out for him.

For Malone and TCI, the turnaround came in 1976, thanks to Jerry Levin. In exchange for access to Malone's 660,000 cable subscribers—TCI, despite its struggles, had become one of the ten-largest cable companies in the country, fifty times its size only six years before—Time Inc. lent TCI several million dollars on highly preferential terms to buy the earth stations to grab the HBO signal off the satellite. It was a meeting of minds in a flawless deal; all gained, none lost. HBO received a large number of valuable viewers for its national cable programming service, Malone finally laid hands on some real, almost free money after a long drought, and several million dollars bought a lot of earth stations. With the instrument maker Scientific-Atlanta offering a special bargain rate, an earth station cost $65,000. Almost immediately, things began to come together for TCI.

The company's cash flow improved. Malone was earning a reputation as an impressive young executive. Large and solvent companies blessed the bright future of the cable business by entering it, or, like Time and Warner, expanding vigorously. Not least—the sins of Irving Kahn had been forgotten. In 1977, a year after the Time-HBO deal, TCI was finally able to cast off dull care and borrow $70.5 million from a consortium of insurance companies and pension funds. At the time, it was the largest loan in the history of cable. Next, Malone agreed to give the new, non-HBO cable programmers access to TCI in exchange for advance royalties. TCI could fill up its empty channels, the new programmers found an audience, and Malone obtained yet more tens of millions of dollars in what amounted to interest-free loans.

"The green lights were starting to come on for us," Malone said. Renewed prosperity did not, however, improve the company's disposition when it came to its customers.

IN 1981, WELL AFTER TCI WAS OVER ITS ROUGH PATCH, Jefferson City, Missouri, decided to throw the company out of town.

TCI's service was poor and had not improved, its franchise was up for renewal, and Jefferson City put the contract out for bid. Jefferson City discovered that Vail, Colorado, the city that felt the kiss of TCI's lash, had gotten off lightly.

"We know where you live, where your office is, and who you owe money to," a TCI employee wrote to a television consultant hired by the city. "We are having your house watched, and we are going to use this information to destroy you. You made a big mistake messing with TCI. We are the largest cable company around. We are going to see that you are ruined professionally."

Malone later explained that the man had "psychological problems," but he failed to add that the man with psychological problems worked for a company with a very bad attitude. TCI withheld a $60,000 payment, threatened to go dark until its franchise was renewed, informed the city that it would allow its wires to rot rather than hand them over to a competitor, and vowed to sell satellite dishes at a substantial discount unless it was given its way. At the end of the ensuing lawsuit, TCI was ordered to pay $44 million—for, among other things, practicing "commercial blackmail." Jefferson City renewed TCI's franchise anyway. Commercial blackmail, it seemed, was a little expensive but otherwise worked just fine.

Boulder, Colorado, became the next municipality to experience the negotiating tactics of its cable television provider. After a decade-long wait for TCI to provide satisfactory service, all patience exhausted, the Boulder city fathers also tried to get rid of the company. TCI strung cables, city workers tore them down, and the legal battle finally reached the Supreme Court. "They have an unfortunate company philosophy," a city official observed. In 1982, Boulder lost its case.

Vail was not an exception and Jefferson City and Boulder were not isolated victims of a company with pathological employees and poor internal controls. By the early 1980s TCI was no longer a dying company. It was back on its feet and ready to join the big time in a big way, and in one important respect it bore a distinct resemblance to the Irish Republican Army. Once a municipality signed on, it could be fired (Vail was eventually fired) but it could not quit. As they said in Belfast, once in, never out.

"That's the dark side, if you will, of TCI," said Richard J. Mac-Donald, a New York-based media analyst, who pointed out that such methods were not uncommon in the cable industry when municipalities were its prime regulators. But as the 1980s proceeded and the cable business grew from large to huge, with institutional investors who were deeply concerned about the corporate image (if, for no other reason, because a company with a bad image problem often developed a bad problem with the price of its stock) and management eager to be perceived as captains of industry, cable increasingly tried to portray itself as a friendly uncle with a basketful of nifty programs for all the family. TCI did not. Nor, although TCI was one of the few television companies with a trained engineer in the topmost ranks of management, was TCI conspicuously interested in technology. It didn't even seem to be very interested in television, if television was defined by the quality of its delivery system, the quality of its programs, or its cultural impact. Most other television executives had at least three sets in their offices, tuned to different channels and playing constantly, but Malone's office contained not a single set. One wag remarked that if Malone thought he could make a fortune and pay no taxes by owning taco stands and funeral homes, he would have bought taco stands and funeral homes. The prime objective—too often, it seemed, the sole objective—was to make a very large amount of money while spending as little of the stuff as possible.

By Malone's own admission, TCI's employees worked longer hours at half the wages of its competitors—and, he claimed, were delighted to do so in exchange for the stock options that would make them rich. (By the end of the decade, some of the secretaries at the Denver headquarters were millionaires, at least on paper and at least for a while.) It did not seem to occur to him that doling out peppercorn salaries for sweatshop hours would fail to attract a top-flight workforce eager to serve a public that paid the bills. In fact, the public was regarded as the enemy. An interesting corporate syllogism was at work.

The public always seemed to want something, and almost invariably, the things it wanted happened to cost money. If TCI spent money, its cash flow would diminish. If the cash flow diminished, the stock options that represented the workforce's ultimate reward would diminish in value; the size of TCI's cash flow—not its profits (which did not exist) or its dazzling technology and happy customers (ditto)—determined the price of its stock. The trick, then, was never to give the public what it wanted. Even in the user-unfriendly cable industry, TCI was known for the poor quality of its service and the unresponsiveness of its employees. At a time when other cable companies were pressing thirty or more channels on their customers, many of TCI's old-fashioned and poorly maintained systems offered only twelve, and Malone was not eager to install more. He claimed that he was only listening to the marketplace. Unlike his blue-sky rivals, he said, he would not tart up his systems with a lot of needless and costly bells and whistles until he was certain the marketplace would accept them. In practice, when his marketplace demanded better television, he continued to bludgeon it into silence. It worked. As long as TCI's lawyers continued to win their cases against municipalities like Boulder, the marketplace had nowhere else to go. And the marketplace was addicted to television.

Malone claimed that he was not a monopolist because his company had plenty of competition and his customers had a rich abundance of entertainment choices—movies, radio, or the inferior signals of the regional broadcasters. As someone remarked at the time, this was a little bit like saying that the telephone company was not a monopoly because people could always write letters. Until Levin broke through with satellite transmission in 1975, however, the cable monopoly—no matter how good it was to its practitioners, how badly it occasionally treated its customers, and how much it worried the telephone company—was a distinctly local phenomenon that did not loom large in the concerns of the nation.

As a cable guy, Malone—like just about every other cable guy—was a monopolist for a simple reason. In most cases, it made remarkably little (or no) sense to allow more than one cable system to compete for the same customers in a single geographical area. Cable systems bore a certain resemblance to telephone systems: they were expensive to build and maintain, and the revenues, though large in the aggregate, were small from each individual household. If cable companies were forced into direct competition, they would either beat each other's brains out, make no money, or both, which was hardly the point of the exercise. Almost all cable systems, therefore, were regional monopolies; no one would enter the business if they weren't. But the regional monopolies were scattered all over the countryside; even the regional monopolies of a single company like TCI were often separated by wide swaths of landscape and the regional monopolies of other companies. Taken together or viewed separately, they did not constitute a television juggernaut, and they still appeared to be part of a self-limiting, temporary phenomenon. The regional audiences were small. Cable still delivered a superior signal, but its advantage was rapidly being canceled by the march of technology. With a few, not very promising exceptions like HBO, cable was able to offer nothing that wasn't already available from local broadcasters and the national networks. Cable would no doubt persist in places where the signal stubbornly remained poor or nonexistent—and technology would doubtless take care of that problem, too—but by the early 1970s, cable seemed to have peaked. All the remaining slopes led downward. Jerry Levin had changed all that.

Thanks to HBO and the other proliferating and cable-specific programming services like ESPN, cable could offer its customers something that the networks didn't have, and the number of new choices could only grow. The FCC had lifted the freeze on new franchises in the major cities, where an immense new audience was waiting. For the first time, it made economic sense for the cable companies to compete with the broadcasters for the popular movies that drew in even more viewers, and cable could make movies on its own that the broadcasters could not have; at ABC, a talented young executive named Barry Diller had shown how the trick was done with the network's popular in-house movies of the week. And cable had a hole card. With the urban audience ripe for the picking, it could finally live up to its potential and introduce the wonder of the age that Steve Ross and others had long predicted, the telephone company had long feared, and the FCC had ringingly endorsed by ordering the cable companies to make it so: interactive television.

Equipped with its irresistible new products—and with one outstanding exception—the cable companies raced into the cities. The exception was TCI.

FOR ALL OF ITS BRIEF LIFE—IN THE EARLY 1970S, THE industry was barely out of its teens—cable television had lived in a seller's market. In the large cities, the situation was dramatically different.

Previously, it had made a certain amount of sense—small, as it turned out—to wire New York, at least the Manhattan part of it, and certain sectors of Los Angeles, where local conditions (such as Manhattan's signal-distorting buildings) meant that cable's signal was not merely superior, but vastly superior. Otherwise, cable in the large cities had no advantage in particular; large-city audiences could receive plenty of broadcast channels, and the broadcast channels were free. Levin had changed all that in 1975, and viewers in the tens of millions were waiting, an audience (and its money) that would fall into cable's lap like ripe fruit. Or so it seemed.

Blinded by greed and a kind of childlike eagerness, the cable operators were willing to do anything, anything at all—provided it was either legal or impossible to detect—to cut the legs from under their competitors and seize control of a previously forbidden hunk of urban real estate. In the untidy process, brandishing their irresistible new product, many cable operators failed to realize, others forgot, and still others ignored a couple of singular facts: cable had changed but the cities had not, and most cable guys didn't know a heck of a lot about large cities. The cable operators, with Malone conspicuously absent, hadn't quite thought the matter through.

It was the time of the great franchise wars, accompanied by many comical interludes. In the classical age of rural, suburban, and small-city cable television, it had been a relatively simple matter—the telephone company notwithstanding—to obtain permission to use the rights-of-way, often at no cost. In the larger cities, the old easygoing rules did not apply, and in the largest cities of all, where a quid pro quo was automatically expected in return for municipal favors, the cable operators might have been dealing with the legislators of a foreign, not overly friendly country. New York had already shown the way a decade before, when it sold access to its notoriously fractious citizens in exchange for the city's favorite substance, money. That was then, when there had been only a tiny handful of cable operators—TelePrompTer, Sterling—with the inclination and resources to try their luck in the big time. This was now, with a multitude of cable operators clamoring to be the first to lay a hand, a foot, or even a head on the chopping block in exchange for access to the promised land. Money was still nice to have, and large quantities were extracted. But it was also possible to obtain many other pleasing things.

Choosing a cable company was probably the largest decision a city council would ever make, the water and gas lines having long been laid and the telephone and power grids completed. This interesting fact was not lost on the city councils in question—where it was usually not seen as an opportunity for the exercise of civic virtue—along with a second, equally interesting fact: the cable operators seemed to have lost their minds. As the council members pondered the cable operators who jammed their chambers waving fistfuls of cash, a bubble formed over their collective heads. It contained a single word. Prey.

Although the many and persistent rumors of under-the-table payoffs remained just that, rumors, there were plenty of ways to make a buck off the cable guys. Gifts to local charities were thought to help the cable companies in their quest. The cable companies gave generously. They identified the most influential members of the local plutocracy, scanned the electoral records for the largest political contributors, and offered these worthies cut-rate stock. The practice was called rent-a-citizen. Cities were supposed to charge the lucky winner 5 percent of his revenues. Many cities charged much more.

But such crude monetary transactions often took a back seat to the noble goals of urban improvement, beautification, and demonstrations of public spirit. The winning cable company in Sacramento not only agreed to charge the citizens a trifling sum for their new television service but to plant tens of thousands of trees. Newton, Massachusetts, received a new library. A town in Illinois got a million-dollar interest-free loan for a water system. Larger cities demanded and were promised dozens of channels, ignoring—sometimes because the city fathers didn't know it and the winning cable operator chose not to enlighten them—the fact that many dozens of channels were still technologically impossible. Other channels were set aside for public-access television, open to anyone who wanted to put on any kind of a show that conformed to community standards of decency, a highly flexible concept in places like New York, San Francisco, and Los Angeles. In New York on a Christmas Eve, one amateur producer repeatedly showed a videotape of himself killing his dog.

Even after a franchise was won, the follies of the cable operators sometimes did not stop. Warner Amex spent a bundle of money wiring downtown Dallas before it discovered that almost nobody in downtown Dallas wanted cable television. At the time, it seemed a small matter. The chairman of Warner Communications, Steven J. Ross, was a man who lived and thought on a large scale. To carry the day in the franchise wars, Ross realized, you needed highly motivated troops. Few troops were more highly motivated than the troops of Ross. To seize control of desirable urban landscapes, you needed an edge. It couldn't be money. Everybody spent money, bags of it. You needed something else, and Ross didn't have to search far to find it. It was his old dream, interactive television. Nothing, absolutely nothing, won the hearts and minds of the targeted cities like interactive television.

JERRY LEVIN HAD INVENTED A NEW KIND OF CABLE television, but it was not a new kind of television. Satellite transmission enabled the cable industry to show popular films and develop its own programming—and make money beyond the dreams of avarice—but the broadcasters had been doing the same thing for decades. But well before Ross actually did it, Levin's colleagues in the business had seen further than that.

Coaxial cable, their fat pipe into the home, endowed the cable operators with powers and abilities far beyond those of mere broadcast television, or so they confidently believed. The television signal used only a portion of a coaxial cable's carrying capacity. Once the industry figured out what to do with the rest of the coaxial cable, cable television would become a competitive weapon of awesome force. Addressing an industry convention in the 1960s, Ralph Nader warned darkly of the consequences if cable fell into the wrong hands.

There were, of course, a couple of highly pertinent questions. Just how, exactly, would the cable industry make use of its vast but untapped powers? And just what shape would the new form of television assume? These were mere details; the cable barons were not technologists. No doubt someone would think of something. But one thing was certain: cable would inevitably perform the same miracle promised by every new technology from gunpowder to the staple gun. It would transform society and make its owners rich beyond the dreams of avarice.

The cable barons would create the Wired City, then the Wired Nation, and finally the Wired World. Cable, done properly, was obviously destined to uplift the national taste with cultural fare unavailable on the airways. Cable would abolish poverty by flooding the slums with educational programs and vocational seminars that would lift the yoke of ignorance from the shoulders of the poor. Cable would transform the practice of medicine, as illustrious doctors made diagnoses and supervised operations from locations miles away. Cable would allow people to work at home, shop, vote, enter into a national debate with their elected representatives, give the President a piece of their mind, abolish the government, and bring world peace. None of these ideas were very new. In fact, almost all of them were very old.

The broadcasters had once entertained similar hopes for the transformative powers of television until they discovered what people really wanted to watch. So had, to a lesser extent, Edison when he invented the phonograph and Marconi when he invented the radio, but the cable guys believed that, this time, they had gotten it right. Cable, said TelePrompTer president Hubert Schlafly, was "a genie in a bottle . . . a modern version of Aladdin and his lamp." Over-the-air broadcasting could deliver *Bonanza*, *I Spy*, and Walter Cronkite, but once cable had wired the entire country, there seemed no limit to what it could do. Cable, clearly, was destined to replace the networks. It was only a matter of time, and the time itself often seemed to be next Thursday in the morning.

In 1963, Ball Brothers Research Laboratories of Boulder, Colorado—an offshoot of the Muncie, Indiana, manufacturer of glass canning jars—announced that digital television and digital compression were just around the corner; as soon as a few glitches were worked out of the system, Ball Brothers would roll out a prototype and vastly improve the quality and economics of broadcasting. Perhaps, but the cable guys were convinced that the game, the set, and the match were already theirs.

Once Ball Brothers perfected its system in, say, 1964 or 1965, it would be coaxial cable and not broadcasting towers that would be the transmission vehicle of choice. The cable companies owned the fat pipe, the second wire into the home, and they would inevitably introduce the miracle of digital television while the broadcasting lads were still twiddling their dials and fiddling with their vacuum tubes. In the meantime, cable's own technologists had finally come across—as expected—with an ever expanding multiplicity of new channels. These were the channels that would resemble weed-choked empty lots until Levin put the signal on the bird, but the cable guys regarded them as a marvelous opportunity until they swiftly learned otherwise. The new channels would not necessarily be devoted to television.

Instead, with a tremendous fanfare now forgotten, it was announced that the Wired Nation was imminent. Cable television would become interactive. There would be videotext services and video telephones, home banking and home shopping, burglar alarms, brokerage services, games, and much more. Cable television would deliver the morning newspaper. This last marvel would be accomplished by a roll of newsprint atop the family set and, one gathers, some kind of home Linotype machine.

Some of it actually happened, sort of. In 1972, a primitive form of pay-per-view allowed the customer to view movies or special programming by inserting a punch card or a plastic ticket in a slot in a set-top box. The experiment went nowhere. In 1976, with Levin's satellite revolution well underway, TelePrompTer unveiled a radical new delivery system, splicing the reliable old coaxial cable to the recently perfected fiber-optic filaments called light paths. Other cable companies rushed to duplicate Kahn's achievement; shortly thereafter, filled with rage, loathing, and visions of dollar signs equipped with wings, they ripped it out, because it didn't work.

There were other possibilities. Levin, having discovered his technological prowess, opened Time's checkbook and tried them all.

Dubbed Time's "resident genius" by corporate chairman Andrew Heiskell, he experimented with subscription television. It was to be Levin's next great idea: with subscription television, a properly equipped viewer would pay HBO a monthly fee, and HBO, eliminating the middleman in the form of the independent cable operator, would send the signal to the home. "I don't think we understand it fully," Levin said, "but there's something very profound about the subscription system." Apparently they didn't understand it at all. HBO lost an estimated $100 million on subscription television.

Next, Levin became enamored of videotext. Videotext enabled a home viewer to call up data—a bank statement, a news story—on his living-room screen and scroll through it as though the television were a computer. The *Times* of New York and the *Times* of Los Angeles were all for it, in part because many of their executives watched television only for the news and sports, did not know how a computer worked, did not know how a television set worked, and were unaware of the all-important difference between fourteen inches and fourteen feet.

As a rough rule of thumb, the user of a mainframe computer terminal—and later of a home PC—sat fourteen inches from his video monitor. The picture on the screen was progressively scanned, one line of the picture followed by the next line of the picture, which made for a tight and readable picture; the picture resembled a projected frame of photographic film. The average television viewer sat approximately fourteen feet from his set. The picture on the television screen was interlaced. A television picture bears approximately the same relation to a filmed picture—or a picture on a computer screen—that a helicopter does to an airplane. They do much the same thing, but they don't do it the same way at all.

A frame of film is a chemical artifact delivered to the movie screen by a mechanical device, the projector. The film is made of chemicals, the image is painted on it with more chemicals, and the projector does the rest. A television picture is an electronic artifact projected on glass that has been treated with phosphors, also produced by the chemist's art. A frame of film is projected on a screen in much the way a painting inhabits a wall: the entire picture is there. A television picture is written on its tube as though it were a letter, but not in strict linear sequence; although the eye cannot perceive it, the entire picture is never there. The set writes a line, skips a line, writes another line, skips, and continues until it reaches the bottom of the tube, whereupon it returns to the top and fills in the blanks. It does this thirty times a second. Fixed-wing pilots often say that God did not intend for a helicopter to fly. God also did not intend for a television screen to be a medium for masses of the printed word. On a television screen, smallish text is hard to make out. Because of interlacing, if the viewer moves closer, the experience can become painful, the smallish text is even harder to read, and people do not want to do it. Computer makers, dealing largely with text and diagrams, had solved the problem with a quick progressive scan where one line followed the other in logical sequence and the images on the screen—which usually did not move rapidly—were continually refreshed. Television, whose images were expected to move rapidly down a narrow broadcasting band, was wedded to an interlaced picture.

Jerry Levin knew that people didn't want to read their television sets; unlike many newspaper executives, he watched a lot of television. "In order to breathe new meaning into the word 'cable,'" he said, not very clearly, "we have to weave all of the current offerings together within this new teletext service to create something that is not just more television, as we have known television to be for a generation or two—into something that is really a connection, a plug-in to all the accessories and peripherals and the electronic programs that are necessary to make that television set into a display unit. Now I can't articulate it for you because I don't know quite what it is." He never did quite figure out what it was. Time's television operation lost an estimated $30 million on videotext. Newspaper publishers lost millions more.

Amid all this costly and unproductive ferment—the Wired Nation, the land rush in the cities, and one crash-and-burn experiment after another—Steve Ross introduced his interactive television.

Within its limitations, it worked just fine. For a time, it swept everything before it—except the audience.

LIKE JOHN MALONE, STEVE ROSS OF WARNER COMmunications was an American type. He was W. C. Fields in the body of Cary Grant.

Ross loved many things: beautiful wives, of which he had three; the good life, which he lived in abundance; the thrill of the chase, which he indulged by buying any company that took his fancy; the glitter of Hollywood, a substantial portion of which he owned; and celebrities, movie stars, who loved him in return.

Given his capacious appetites, it seemed odd that Ross became so wildly enthusiastic about a plain-vanilla, wires-in-the-ground business like cable television, but the technology enthralled him. So did the huge amount of money that could be made. Ross was extremely fond of money, not least—indeed, primarily—because he could then proceed to shower it on his friends, his colleagues, and himself.

He had gotten into cable at a seemingly auspicious moment in 1972, buying a small operator for the then huge sum of $50 million and offering the job of running it to Malone. It was true that Ross was a romantic, but he was usually a romantic with something very specific and very unromantic in mind. Cable, he foresaw, was an ideal vehicle for distributing films. Ross, who controlled Warner Brothers, was the only cable operator who owned a movie studio, and if the resulting income from cable was small, it had two compelling advantages. It was an income that he hadn't had before, and it cost him nothing. He would release the movies in the normal fashion and make money from the ticket sales; he would sell them to the television networks, again in the normal fashion, and make more money; he could put them on his cable systems and his subscribers would pay him to watch; and at a time when cable had very few advertisers of its own, he would attract advertisers and make even more money. The new money might not be much—in 1972, his cable operations were not large—but it would be reliable. With his huge film library, he could put his films on cable again and again. And when it came to cable, Ross did not intend to remain small for very long. His secret weapon, never very well concealed, was the frame grabber.

Although he talked about it incessantly to the despair of his executives, Ross had never been very clear about what a frame grabber did, exactly, aside from grabbing frames. Sometimes it seemed to be a way of banking and shopping at home, and at other times it seemed to be a way of stopping the television signal and rewinding it like a VCR. Nobody even knew what a frame grabber looked like—although it sounded like something the rest of the cable industry had discussed for years. Ross was a newcomer to cable, but he was a newcomer with deep pockets. In 1977, in Columbus, Ohio, he rolled out an entirely new kind of television called Qube.

THE WORD QUBE STOOD FOR NOTHING BUT ITSELF. IN ITS launch city of Columbus, Ohio, it first reached 26,000 and later 31,000 homes at a basic price of $10.95 a month. Depending on who made the estimate, it had cost Warner $12 million, $15 million, or $20 million, and it cost another $1 million a month to run. Steve Ross was a man who made no little plans.

In Columbus, a computer scanned the system every six seconds, recording the channels to which each set was tuned, nine of which were reserved for movies. A Qube subscriber could survey the available films and, thanks to the computer, choose one, pay for it, and not pay for anything else. This, in itself, was a revolutionary breakthrough. In 1977, a viewer who signed up for HBO or another of the cable-specific channels bought the whole package whether he watched it or not. Modern pay-per-view television was born in Columbus, Ohio. So was a crafty marketing strategy.

Qube was the only cable system allowed to show Disney movies, always a reliable draw with the audience. Qube also offered something called a drive-in movie channel that featured, in the *Economist*'s dry description, "crashing cars and beatings-up with blood and vomit." And there was a soft-core pornography channel. Warner soon developed great hopes for its pornography channel.

It was known—suspected, really—that a good many people would fork over cash to watch pornography on their home screens. Unfortunately, unlike Presbyterians or Republicans, it was impossible to tell just how many of these people there were; in an age before talk radio, most people who wanted to watch pornography on television did not declaim their proclivities from the rooftops. The Qube computer could count the sets tuned to the porn channel, but it could only count the number in Columbus, Ohio, which might very well be either a pillar of sexual virtue or a sink of iniquity; it would be folly to project a national market for Qube based on the pornography hunger (or drought) in Columbus. By a happy chance, Japan and New York City soon showed a solution to the problem, as they so often did.

First, the Japanese introduced the first mass-marketed videocassette recorders, Matsushita's VHS system vanquished Sony's superior Beta, and the usual question arose: just what, exactly, would persuade millions of Americans to buy videocassettes? It would not be mainstream movies. The movie studios had fought television tooth and claw before submitting to the inevitable and making billions of dollars, but the film industry had learned only half its lesson. It would no longer resist new video technologies, but it would not commit itself until a proven market existed. Here, New York City led the way.

In 1979, the first Video Shack opened on Broadway at Forty-ninth Street, next to an X-rated movie theater. Video Shack sold the theater's movies for home consumption. For a time, it was the only retail videocassette outlet in the nation, but it did not enjoy the honor for long; there was simply too much money to be made. By 1981, between a quarter and a half—nobody knew for sure—of all prerecorded videocassettes in America were pornographic, and the foundation of a major industry had been laid. The necessary VCRs had been bought, the audience had been trained in their use, and the audience could be measured. Hollywood wholeheartedly committed itself, and more billions were made. The Warner Brothers studio was part of Hollywood, but the Warner cable operation had its own take on the situation. Warner's video people weren't just selling films. Like the Japanese, they were selling a whole new video technology. The videocassette experience had proved that a national marketplace existed for the sort of home-viewed smut that would cause the consumers to clamor for Qube just as they clamored for VCRs. The Qube audience would then experiment with Qube's revolutionary interactive features, new interactive programmers would rush forward to satisfy the need—just as new cable programmers had proliferated after Levin found his mirror in the sky—and Qube, true interactive television, would take the country by storm. Moreover, the figures from Columbus seemed to prove it.

In Columbus, Qube's nine movie channels generated $128,000 in revenues during February 1980. Half the sum came from the sex channel. Pornography would be the killer application that would make the nation clamor for interactive television. And Warner had a huge head start.

There was a flaw in this reasoning.

When a person rented or bought a pornographic tape at a video store, only the clerk knew what the customer had taken home. On Qube, the central computer knew what was playing on every television set in the system. Moreover, it printed the information on the monthly bill, sparking many a lively conversation at the family dinner table.

Pornography was not destined to be the killer application of interactive television. Doggedly, Warner soldiered on.

Qube subscribers could tune in a town meeting, register their responses to the City Planning Commission's latest proposals, and press another button to urge their public servants to stop nattering and stick to the point. They could press a button and make reservations at a local restaurant or obtain holiday information from a local travel office. College courses were offered and credit was given. Students could query the professor—although not at length or in detail—by pushing more buttons. Viewers were invited to sit in on the hour-long adventures of a fictional young woman named Lulu Smith, help determine the direction of the plot, and vote to name the drama something other than "Lulu Smith." Voting, as the system evolved, was an activity that happened a lot on Qube, sometimes in strange ways.

Qube enabled 1,200 people to cast ballots on the question of whether a woman should have been allowed to commit suicide. Nearly half the respondents said she should have, 32 percent were against it, 20 percent weren't sure; 55 percent of the respondents indicated that they had contemplated suicide themselves.

Qube offered a local talent show where the viewers voted on the performers after the first forty seconds of the act, allowing them to continue or giving them the hook. "In the privacy of their homes," the *Economist* remarked, "viewers can be heartless. A mongoloid-looking youth playing his clarinet barely survives the minimum time. A little black girl with spectacles and braces on her teeth has to stop in the middle of her song."

Mr. Qubesumer, an investigative shopper, asked viewers to name the topic of his next show. When the viewers asked Mr. Qubesumer to look into automobile tune-ups, Mr. Qubesumer discovered that there were a lot of different prices for automobile tune-ups. Viewers were invited to second-guess the judges at the Sugar Ray Leonard–Roberto Durán and Sugar Ray Leonard–Thomas Hearns fights. The viewers and the judges, it turned out, pretty much agreed. Viewers were also invited to call the plays—by majority vote—at a semipro football game. A little bit of this sort of thing, Warner discovered, went a very long way. Many viewers were bored by the interactive features of Qube, and many others didn't use them at all. Without professional and inventive programming, Qube was pay-per-view television attached to a toy whose charms faded with time.

When President Carter delivered his "crisis of confidence" speech in 1979, Qube viewers were invited to evaluate his message, and the results were flashed across the nation as a revelation of the citizenry's mood. But, as many commentators pointed out, Qube had no idea who had punched the buttons—or why. It never did, and without the information, Qube couldn't take the pulse of the nation, the town, the neighborhood, or a single home. The poll was worthless.

A New York psychiatrist, Dr. Lawrence J. Hatterer, almost beside himself with excitement after his appearance on Qube, reported that 49 percent of his viewers admitted they were addicted to something, or that a member of their family was. Dr. Hatterer was eager to continue his researches on Qube, ignoring the fact that a number of his respondents might be—almost certainly were—four years old, mischievous teens, drunks, or a family cat batting the Qube touchpad around the floor.

Qube experimented with home banking. Many thoughtful people believed that home banking was a certain winner, perhaps not as wonderful as pornography, but the sort of thing that would draw the consumer to interactive television and the home computer in droves. They continued to think so until Qube and a handful of big-city banks actually tried it.

Qube displayed the daily contents of the local newspaper, the *Columbus Dispatch*; if a viewer took an hour to read it, his morning newspaper cost $5. Qube could turn a subscriber's television set into a state-of-the-art fire and burglar alarm. In practice, the alarms functioned only if the cable system was functioning, and cable systems had a way of going off the air at unexpected moments. Qube featured games and interactive quiz shows where viewers could win prizes and money; winning money on games and quiz shows was the most popular thing Qube allowed its customers to do, but not many of them did it for very long. Soon, it was promised, Qube would offer its subscribers home energy management, allowing them to curl up for a long evening of watching and adjusting their refrigerators.

Still, there was no denying that, as far as interactive television was concerned, the world of tomorrow had become the world of today in Columbus, Ohio. Whether Warner would ever see its money again was another matter; Qube lost an estimated $50,000 a month. In the short term, however, whether Qube made any money in Columbus was entirely beside the point. Other cable operators, bidding for urban franchises, could offer trees, waterworks, and libraries. Only Warner had Qube and the millions of dollars of free publicity it had received in the national press. A city without Qube was a city that had turned its back on the television of the future. Perhaps, as Qube expanded its installed base, the sheer number of people with access to the system would finally attract the national programmers and the killer app would be born at last. Or perhaps Warner could simply shut it down; other cable operators, confronted with catastrophic losses and unkept promises, had gone back on their word. Steve Ross was a man who knew how to weigh the odds and cut his losses. In the interval, Qube suited his purposes perfectly.

With Qube as bait, Warner Amex won the contract to wire Cincinnati and its suburbs. It snatched the coveted Pittsburgh contract from under the nose of a stunned Time Inc. It moved into Dallas despite stiff competition. It scooped up Houston and the St. Louis suburbs; by the end of 1981, Warner Amex Cable had won the bidding for 1.1 million of the 1.6 new households that entered the cable market. Qube was now available on six systems, and it was finally possible to draw some real-world conclusions about the nation's first up-and-running interactive television.

Most people—aside from city councils, professional futurists, and the sort of citizen who can't wait to get his hands on the next great thing—will not buy a new technology unless it enables them to do things they have always done, although in a significantly better way, or if it continually entertains them. Qube's pay-per-view feature fit the bill. The rest of Qube did not. Home banking had failed. Home burglar alarms were a dud. Remarkably few people wanted to pay $5 to read their morning newspaper on the television set. The home shopping market contained some nasty surprises for almost everyone who tried to exploit it, but Qube never seriously went in for home shopping; the national retailers—rightly, it turned out—weren't interested. It was said, both then and afterward, that Qube had never been given a real chance, that if it had ever reached critical mass in the form of a large potential audience, inventive and irresistible programming would have magically appeared and Qube would have taken the country by storm. But almost twenty years later, when futurologists and cable executives once again contemplated interactive television, they spoke with unrestrained enthusiasm about home banking, video newspapers, and video games as though Qube hadn't tried all of them, Jerry Levin hadn't tried one of them, and all hadn't been found wanting. On Qube, video games were another dud.

"Out-of-town writers talk about this as if it were the second coming of Christ," Jeff Border, a media reporter for the *Columbus Dispatch*, told the *New York Times*. "They are much more impressed with Qube's operations than the people around here."

In the early 1980s, the average cable system was able to sign up 40 percent of the houses passed by its wire. Qube signed up 41 percent, a slight and statistically meaningless difference. On the six systems where Qube was available, only one-third of the viewers— 350,000 households—opted to pay for the interactive features, the PANS, or pretty amazing new stuff, that Ross so enthusiastically offered. The rest preferred to watch POT—plain old television. Even when viewers took the service, only 2 percent of them watched Qube's most popular offerings, the interactive game shows. During the course of a month, only a quarter of the subscribers watched anything, anything at all, that was interactive, and there wasn't much of that. In the last year of its existence, 1984, Qube offered interactive programming only ninety minutes a day. Ross never found the killer app. No one even knew what it was, or if it existed at all.

FOUR

The Troll and the Wizard

WHETHER THE WORD CAME BY LETTER OR TELEGRAM WAS a matter of some dispute, but in the television industry, Malone's terse and pointed message soon achieved the mythic stature previously reserved for Alexander Graham Bell's summons to Mr. Watson. How one felt about it, of course, depended on one's perspective.

Fred Pierce, the chief of ABC television, was attending the 1984 Olympics when he heard from an obscure Colorado cable operator named John Malone. ABC had recently purchased ESPN, the popular sports channel. Until then, ESPN, like most cable-specific programming, had made its money from its advertisers and had been provided to cable systems for free. ABC, after decades of eating the CBS and NBC dust, was now the leading broadcasting network in the country. ESPN was far and away one of the most popular channels on cable, and the time had come for the programming service to begin making some real money for its powerful new owner. ESPN had just imposed a fifty-cent-per-viewer charge on the cable operators who carried it. Malone's abrupt reply was terse and to the point.

Unless Pierce agreed to sit down and talk, either immediately or before the end of the day, TCI would remove ESPN from its systems at midnight, period and end of discussion. John Malone had arrived on the national scene. Unfortunately, almost nobody outside the cable industry seemed to have any idea just who John Malone was.

Several things, however, were immediately clear. The broadcasting networks were still extraordinarily powerful—and their executives still luxuriated in the aura of that power—but cable had begun to seriously erode their 90 percent share of the national audience. Cable's unruly rush into the large cities, no matter how badly handled or ill-advised, had seen to that. (By the mid-1990s, after years of steady decline, the network share of the national audience was less than 65 percent. By 1997, a very bad year for the broadcasters, it had slipped to less than 50 percent.)

John Malone had not joined his colleagues in their mad dash; his systems remained largely rural or in small cities. Still, there was no denying that TCI, with more than a million subscribers, was the third-largest cable company in the country. It couldn't be ignored; the loss of more than a million viewers would blow a huge hole in ESPN's revenues. Attention must be paid, but for a cable guy to personally take on the president of the nation's premier network . . . this was an unheard-of and flabbergasting event; recalling it years later, Pierce was nearly speechless. Malone was either very foolhardy, very sure of himself, or both. In any case, ABC would have to deal with him. It was not an easy task. Malone immediately proved himself to be a resourceful and determined negotiator. Like the far-better-known Steve Ross, he made no little plans.

To drive home his point and improve ABC's thinking, he immediately entered into talks with Anheuser-Busch, with the objective of establishing a rival sports network. This was an extremely serious development. Even with its million and more subscribers, TCI probably lacked the resources to buy the sort of sporting events that would enable Malone to launch a credible threat to ESPN, but the maker of Budweiser beer had very deep pockets. Moreover, Anheuser-Busch was a heavy sponsor of sports programming. If it owned a piece of a cable sports channel, the channel would almost automatically receive the advertising revenue it needed to become a viable undertaking. And with Malone threatening to pull the plug on ESPN, ESPN's new competitor would be born with a silver spoon in its mouth in the form of a large guaranteed audience. As Malone anticipated, the thinking at ABC improved remarkably, and a satisfactory compromise was reached. Malone may have made no little plans, but unlike many of his cable colleagues, he was not a man whose reach exceeded his grasp.

ESPN, it was announced, would still charge a fee for its services, but the fee would not be nearly as large as the one that had attracted Malone's attention and ESPN would devote the new revenue to improving its programming. The TCI-Anheuser alliance was heard of no more, and Malone announced a mighty victory on behalf of his subscribers—concerning whom he didn't otherwise seem to care not a tinker's darn as long as they kept quiet and paid their bills. Henceforward, it was said with only slight exaggeration, nothing got on cable (or stayed on cable) unless TCI wanted it there. Wall Street and the entertainment industry suddenly became very interested in John Malone. And John Malone, the reporters from the financial and trade publications soon discovered, was a very peculiar fellow.

"Ask him if he has any friends," one of his business associates suggested to the *Barron's* reporter Maggie Mahar. "We'd all be real curious to know." Another Malone colleague told Mahar, "I'd love to be his friend. We all would. But he's distant."

Malone came to be known as many things, some of them printable: he was the king of cable, its Bill Gates, its Sam Walton, its 800-pound gorilla, its Genghis Khan, and its godfather—a term that could be taken in one of several ways, although Senator Albert Gore of Tennessee perceived only one. John Malone, said Gore, was the ringleader of the cable Cosa Nostra.

In person, he was a polite, self-contained, and sometimes startlingly profane man. He could also be artless; "I am an intellectual," he once told a visitor. If a visitor to TCI's Englewood offices raised a question about new technologies, Malone, who sometimes claimed that he had forgotten everything he once knew about engineering, reminded the visitor that he was an engineer. He also reminded the visitor that the visitor was not. He was pleasant and he was visibly—almost eerily—serene, a man without gestures, almost a man without movement. As an engineer and a businessman, he would stress, he was not greatly interested in new technology.

"All these visionaries, these pioneers, they go around hyping all these way-out high-tech ideas," he told Daniel Burstein and David Kline, the authors of *Road Warriors: Dreams and Nightmares Along the Information Highway.* "Well, pioneers often end up with arrows in their back because, you see, technology isn't necessarily a business."

He had no small talk, did not attend social functions, and regulated his time according to a personal clock. On most days, he drove eight miles home to have lunch with his wife, Leslie, and to walk his dogs. When things were quiet in his professional life, he worked only five and a half hours a day, just as she had always wanted.

He lived beyond the reach of his own coaxial cable, received his television on a homemade dish, and his office was decorated with sailing memorabilia rather than pictures of its occupant in the company of the famous and the mighty. The phone there never rang unless his wife was calling on her personal line. Every winter and summer, he and his wife traveled to Boothbay Harbor, Maine—usually by recreational vehicle, because Leslie didn't like to fly. In Maine, he owned a restored 1904 Stanford White house and a sixty-three-acre estate, pottered about in his apple orchard, ran a small marina, sailed his boat—first a 59-foot Hinckley Sou'wester, later a 64-footer named *Ragtime,* a 1929 motorized commuter craft that had been built to carry passengers from Long Island to Manhattan—and lived what his wife regarded as a normal life. When he was in Maine, he tried to keep his work time down to an hour a day. By the end of the decade, his collection of antique cars included Gary Cooper's old Mercedes. Aside from the fact that he had two grown children, a son and a daughter, remarkably little was known about his personal life.

When people spoke of John Malone, they mentioned first his utter ruthlessness and then his formidable intellect; his longtime associate Peter Barton was put in mind of a Rubik's Cube. Barton did not say, although he could have, that Malone resembled the puzzle rather than the skillful man who could solve it.

"John Malone's opinion and attitude is surmised at, guessed at, speculated at in every sports-rights negotiation, in every conversation investment bankers might have about the formation of a new cable service," said the former president of one of the four broadcasting networks. "Although John is a likable man, when you're negotiating with him, he will let you see his fangs. His power is real. And some of his rhetoric about the people he competes with, his rhetoric about the networks, certainly suggests that he considers himself intellectually superior to all of us. With some reason, I think, by the way. John Malone is the troll that sits under the bridge."

Malone took no pleasure in the suffering of his victims.

"I learned a long time ago in business, you have to be distant," he told *Barron's* Maggie Mahar. "Otherwise, you get manipulated and then you get conflicted."

In his politics, he was antediluvian, and he came to them by inheritance; his engineer father, whom he deeply loved, loathed Franklin Roosevelt. To Malone, the heroes of the age were Dwight Eisenhower and Ronald Reagan.

When he spoke to trade groups, he spoke without notes. When he came to close a deal, he arrived with Peter Barton and a handful of aides, and he conducted the negotiations himself. In a decade characterized by the art of the deal, other executives came to the negotiating table accompanied by a small army of investment bankers and paid them tens of millions of dollars for their advice and counsel.

Malone saw no point in paying an outsider tens of millions of dollars for anything he could do himself. He knew more about the financial structure of the cable industry than any investment banker who had ever lived, and he quietly let everyone know it. His mere physical presence was eloquent with understatement; he was alone with a handful of trusted aides, he was motionless and utterly calm, he had all the necessary figures in his head—or so he pretended; usually, it was Barton who had the distasteful job of dealing with the details— and he was ready to eat someone's lunch. His headquarters staff was lean, 250 people, with no public relations department and a telephone answered by a machine. It became popular to liken TCI to a submarine, sleek, silent, and deadly. The larger world had discovered—and perhaps considerably exaggerated; Malone's very strangeness made good copy in the press—its leader's talents, his company had plenty of money, and in 1984 and a few years afterward, the cable industry seemed to be made for a man like John Malone. The same could not be said of Steven J. Ross.

IT WAS ATARI THAT HAD DONE IT. BOUGHT BY WARNER IN 1975 for $25 million—not a serious price by Warner's standards— Atari was a low-end example of the pretty amazing new stuff that was beginning to come out of Silicon Valley, Seattle, and similar venues. It was not a serious company; Atari manufactured electronic arcade games like Space Invaders, and Pong, an early home video game where the players bounced a tennis ball back and forth on the television screen. Atari seemed bombproof. It controlled 80 percent of a rapidly growing market, it threw off vast amounts of Ross's favorite substance, money, and it was fun. Ross liked things that were fun. He (and a gratifying number of other people) became addicted to Atari's products; Ross would play them far into the night.

In 1981, Atari's profits were an astonishing $300 million. The following year Atari accounted for more than half of Warner's $4 billion in revenues, and the prospects for the future seemed limitless.

The company gave $23 million to Ross's great friend Steven Spielberg—all of Ross's friends were great friends, and Ross loved to give them money—to create a computer game from his hit movie *E.T.*, whereupon Spielberg demonstrated that he had no idea how to create a computer game. Charging hard into the new home computer business, Atari introduced Mindlink, an electrified headband that could be used, at least in theory, to control the activity on a computer screen. The secret of its use was a creatively furrowed brow. Mindlink gave its users headaches and the device kept falling around their necks. Warner offered an Atari computer, free, to any Columbus Qube user who wanted one. With the computer, the customer could call up Compuserve, the Ohio-based on-line information service that almost nobody wanted to watch on their television sets. There was vague talk of something called Ataritel, a telephone service that would link Atari's computers with Qube's televisions in some way that was never very clear. There was nothing unusual in any of this. The early 1980s were the dawn of the home computer age, the air was thick with ideas and plans, some of them actually worked, and Atari could afford it, or so it seemed. The movie business, the home of Ross's heart, was also in the business of losing huge amounts of cash in pursuit of the hit film that redeemed everything. Somewhere out there, Atari would no doubt stumble onto something.

In other ways, however, Atari was precisely the sort of business that did not interest Ross at all. Its main products were pleasingly frivolous, but at its core Atari was a straightforward manufacturing operation, with plants, blue-collar workers and engineers, a fleet of trucks, and a bunch of socially challenged computer nerds who were no fun at all. Ross had done that sort of thing back in the 1960s, when he made his first fortune with parking lots and window-washing companies, and he had put that part of his life behind him. Moreover, there was the question of Atari's immense profits. The Atari profits began to bother Ross; they looked too good to be true. Ross was extravagant, but he was not dumb, and he possessed an uncommon ability to do corporate math in his head. If someone in Atari was cooking the books and the company was in trouble, the person who would emerge from the experience with a whole skin would be Steve Ross.

The early 1980s were not the best years of his life. He suffered a major heart attack. His second wife, Bill Paley's stepdaughter Amanda Burden, left him. He lost two important executives—one of them his closest adviser and best friend in the company—during a widely publicized kickback and mob-related scandal surrounding a Warner-owned dinner theater in Westchester County, and Ross had narrowly escaped prosecution himself. The movie studio was in one of its periodic funks. Now word began to reach Warner's New York headquarters that shipments of Atari's games were being diverted—stolen—by its distributors and perhaps some of its executives. Thanks to the introduction of another popular new game, Pac-Man, the first half of 1982 had broken new records for profitability, but Atari's inventory had risen to dangerous heights, which meant that Atari was manufacturing far too many products that could not possibly be sold. By the end of 1982, a year that began with such bright promise, the Atari division had all but collapsed, taking Warner's profits with it. To save the company, drastic surgery was required.

Atari's bloated inventory was trucked into the desert near Alamogordo, New Mexico, buried in a hole, and sealed with concrete. Hard-won cable franchises were put up for sale, including Dallas, one of the most hard-won franchises of all. Qube was shut down and never revived. It was a remarkable thing for the head of a publicly traded American company to survive such an experience intact, but nobody laid a glove on Steve Ross. And John Malone, as began to often happen when trouble brewed in the cable industry, stood by to help.

"Drew Lewis was brought in by the Warner Amex people to rationalize their cable systems," Malone recalled, "and I went up to meet with Drew. I said, 'Here are your seven problem systems.' And he came right back at me. He says, 'No, you got the order reversed. Pittsburgh, they're telling me, is the most difficult one to fix.' And, boy, when I heard that, I said, 'Drew, I'll tell you what. How much money have you got in Pittsburgh?' See, we had all the suburban systems. And he told me, I don't know, a hundred and thirty-five million bucks, something like that. And I said, 'I'll tell you what. I'll buy it from you for what you got in it.' And we shook hands. That was it."

In the end, Malone paid $93 million for Pittsburgh. He immediately ripped out the Qube technology, moved operations into a former tire warehouse, decimated the staff, and reduced the number of channels from 60 to 49. Four years later, Pittsburgh was generating a lovely $14 million in cash flow, and no one in America was interested in interactive television any longer.

NO ONE, THAT IS, EXCEPT FOR AN ARCHITECT AT THE Massachusetts Institute of Technology named Nicholas Negroponte. Malone had buried Qube in Pittsburgh in 1984. In 1985, Negroponte founded the MIT Media Lab. Under his leadership, the Lab announced that interactivity was the destiny of television, and the destiny of television was the destiny of the world. Or at least it was the destiny of television (and the world) for as long as Nicholas Negroponte said so. He had a way of changing his mind.

Although Negroponte, like Malone, was reticent where his personal life was concerned—probably an understandable precaution on the part of a member of a Greek mercantile family that had watched in horror as Aristotle Onassis and Stavros Niarchos had lived their lives at the top of their lungs—he had once let slip that he was not unfamiliar with the quarterdeck of a yacht and a glass of fine Montrachet. Born on New York's Upper East Side in 1943, he had been educated in the private schools of Switzerland and America. His parents lived in Klosters. He summered on the Greek island of Patmos. It did not seem to occur to him that, as a man accustomed to wealth and comfort, he might know remarkably little about the daily experiences of 90 percent of the human race.

Moreover, he was dyslexic. By his own admission, the longest document he willingly read was the front page of *The Wall Street Journal*, where he claimed, somewhat oddly, that he kept track of his investments. Either he was not familiar with the front page of *The Wall Street Journal* or he sacrificed accuracy for the sake of a memorable phrase. His enemies said that he sacrificed accuracy a lot, especially when he was talking about himself, and Nicholas Negroponte was a man with many enemies. Much of the work at the Media Lab seemed devoted to creating a world where its founder would never have to read anything ever again.

According to a brief biographical sketch he supplied to *Scientific American*, the youthful Negroponte scored a perfect 800 in the math section of his SATs, completed a five-year MIT architectural course in four (B.A., 1965; M.A., 1966), worked briefly for IBM in the fledgling field of computer-aided design, returned to MIT, and stayed there. The IBM experience, he wrote, persuaded him that he was "too naive architecturally" to thrive in the private sector.

At MIT, he continued his work with computers, his second but greatest professional love. When it came to computers, architecture, and people, there was something seriously strange about Nicholas Negroponte.

Le Corbusier, the seminal and often misguided French architect, had often called the human home "a machine for living." To the Frenchman, the machine function, such as it was, occurred when the inhabitants of a building reacted to the elegance, sensitivity, and efficiency of its design. To Negroponte, the machine function would occur because the home of the future would actually be a machine. Among many other things, Negroponte's idealized digital house would, so to speak, sit down with its owners, together they would plan alterations and additions, and the house would perform the work while the owners took a much needed vacation. It did not seem to occur to Negroponte that the house's first task would be to bribe the city building inspector. Le Corbusier's followers took his vision and produced the modern high-rise public housing project, for which the world has yet to thank them. Negroponte's followers took his vision and produced a lot of talk.

In the evolving vision of Negroponte and the associates he gathered around him in something called the Architecture Machine Group, the house of the future would inevitably be the house-as-pal, the house-as-illusionist, and the house-as-Jeeves. If Joe and Jane Beercan, the owners, wanted to wake up in a virtual Switzerland, a country with which the Beercans were intimately familiar, the house would oblige: the aroma of an Alpine meadow would waft through the doors and visible through the windows would be the Jungfrau. The house would recognize its owner, know its owner's exact location, and understand what the owner was doing; if the owner approached the house from the outside, laden with grocery bags, the house would automatically open the door. It did not seemed to occur to Negroponte that in places like Brooklyn, this might not be such a hot idea. The house would sense its owner's mood and respond accordingly, especially when it answered the telephone, an instrument that Negroponte seemed to regard with loathing and fury. Sensing the owner's mood, the house would screen his calls. It did not seem to occur to Negroponte that this was an excellent way of getting the owner fired if the owner was mad at his boss, the boss called to apologize for the unfortunate misunderstanding, and the house told the boss to take a hike.

Like many other specialists in the future, including Karl Marx, Negroponte had an uncanny knack for identifying a real problem, proposing an idealized solution, and behaving as if the idealized solution was, in fact, the actual solution. This was to ignore certain rules of thumb that were repeatedly discovered, and repeatedly forgotten, by countless philosophers, farmers, politicians, industrialists, and just about everybody else as mankind continually blazed its trail into the world of tomorrow. For one thing, the future almost never turns out as predicted, because most dazzling new inventions either don't work the way they're supposed to, don't work at all, or work exactly as designed but in ways that annoy the hell out of their owners. The world of the future always takes a lot of fixing up. It was clear that Nicholas Negroponte had never heard the cautionary tale of the Waltzing Tycoon.

At the end of the 1980s, Bruce Wasserstein was the reigning boy wonder of Wall Street. At the First Boston Corporation, he had gone from strength to strength, merging gigantic corporations to form even more gigantic corporations. Then, with his longtime partner, Joe Perella, he had cut loose from the old firm and set up shop in midtown Manhattan. Empty pizza boxes littered the desktops; cables snaked across the floor. In his new private office, the master of the game spoke to a reporter about his bold and far-reaching plans for American capitalism.

Suddenly, the room dimmed. Without interrupting his speech, Wasserstein slowly raised his hand, as though asking permission to visit the washroom. The reporter said nothing. Still talking, Wasserstein then raised his arms and began to waggle them up and down.

"Mr. Wasserstein," asked the reporter, "is everything all right?"

"Perfectly," said the magnate. He continued to talk, now with an air of annoyance. Abruptly, he left his seat. Neither a small nor an agile man, he began to move swiftly around the room, waving his arms and sometimes joining his hands high above his head, as though doing jumping jacks. He also climbed onto a piece of furniture.

"Mr. Wasserstein," said the reporter, "should I get Mr. Perella?"

"I'm trying to turn on the lights!" the tycoon explained.

Actually, Bruce Wasserstein really was trying to turn on the lights. His office, like the office of many another financier, had been equipped with a lighting system attached to a motion detector. The idea was to save energy. There was no wall switch. When you came to your office, the office turned on the lights, because the office knew you were there. The lights remained on for as long as you were in residence, because the office sensed your presence. Or so the theory went. All over Manhattan, men in Savile Row suits and women in

Chanel dresses were pirouetting madly about in their workspaces, trying to turn on their lights.

Negroponte would say, correctly, that the problem could have been solved with an improved motion detector. The trick was to develop an improved motion detector that didn't do something else wrong—and then persuade the maddened customers that it really, really didn't do anything else wrong. An even better trick was to install a wall switch. In the meantime, the broad, sunny highway to the future had taken a small educational detour, prominent members of the financial community had been given a salutary lesson in new technologies that were just smart enough to be extremely stupid, and the human race stumbled on. Generally speaking, the company or the individual who makes a bundle out of the future is the company or individual that makes the least bad guess about something and then makes it work, often in unforeseen ways. For example, James Watt, the supposed inventor of the steam engine, did not invent the steam engine. He repaired a pump. This was not, however, the way Nicholas Negroponte viewed the future. To Negroponte, the future would conform itself to his vision, arrive at daybreak in the morning next Thursday, and work perfectly.

There was no denying that Nicholas Negroponte possessed a vivid and fertile imagination—too much of one, his critics said. There was something to this. During his early years in the visionary business, even when he produced a real accomplishment, he had a curious tendency to claim that it was something it was not, and his claim was usually designed to bring greater glory to Nicholas Negroponte. For example, he and his early MIT associates created a virtual-reality video version of Aspen, Colorado.

On-screen, you could drive through the streets. You could stop, enter a building, and talk to the inhabitants. You could see the buildings as they had been years before. You could view them in all weathers. It was an altogether stunning achievement, one that the military found extremely useful. Building on the work of Negroponte's team (and others, unmentioned by Negroponte), military planners could present a field commander with a visual representation of his objective's terrain and allow him to examine it from a variety of angles in a variety of weathers. Gilding the lily, Negroponte claimed that the Aspen video was a pioneering effort in multimedia. It wasn't. It was monomedium. Then there was something called Talking Heads, and here Negroponte moved from the boastful into the weird.

If the Soviet missiles had ever come over the Pole, they would almost certainly have plastered two specific targets. One was Strategic Air Command headquarters in Omaha. The other was Mount Weather in Virginia. There, carved from the living rock, was the national underground command post. As half the world vanished in nuclear fire, the President, Vice President, Secretary of State, and Speaker of the House were to burrow into the Strangelovian chamber and do their level best to destroy the other half. The plan contained only one flaw: the Soviets knew where Mount Weather was. It would be better, the Pentagon reasoned, if the nation's leadership were dispersed—one in an airplane, one in a submarine, one in Sonoma—and equipped with a means of communication that would enable them to complete the destruction of the planet.

Negroponte's solution was to create three mannikin heads and mount them on gimbals. The Speaker of the House, say, would take up his position in the wardroom of the *Los Angeles*. With him would be the three heads. On the surface of the heads were the televised visages of the absent dignitaries—the President, certainly, and perhaps the Vice President and the Chairman of the Joint Chiefs. If the Speaker had the floor, the heads would swivel in his direction. If the President spoke, the heads would swivel back. The heads could also nod. It was, Negroponte admits today, a somewhat bizarre idea. It also demonstrated that, given enough resources, he would come up with a high-tech solution even if nobody in his right mind would ever use it. Third and last, the Negroponte team produced Dataland.

Dataland was a wall-sized video display broken into picture-window-sized segments and manipulated by an instrument-equipped Eames chair. From the chair, a user could visit a video clip of Peter Falk in *Columbo*, not exactly a groundbreaking achievement. But the user could also direct his attention to a Rolodex, look up a number, and make a call. Or he could open a file on a desktop and rearrange its contents. Once again, Negroponte, thinking like an architect rather than a computer scientist, was actually on to something.

In those days, the march of computer science was only a few steps ahead of the march of the computer industry. The personal computer was in the process of being invented at Xerox PARC, the Palo Alto research center that proved to be a source of wonderfully lucrative ideas for just about everybody except its corporate patron, but the whole idea of personal computers repeatedly came a cropper when confronted with a single, immovable fact: you could fit one of the things onto a desktop, but there was almost no way for an ordinary citizen who wasn't some kind of scientific and mathematical whiz to use it. In order to start up a computer and make it go, a person had to know computer language, and to an ordinary citizen, computer language was impenetrable gibberish. Which, in turn, led to a second and related question that was not nearly as simple as it seemed: how did you solve the problem in a way that would make the average citizen want to buy one of the things?

As a nonscientist—and a dyslexic nonscientist at that—Negroponte was far closer to the thinking processes of the normal citizen. Moreover, his life of privilege had led him to expect certain things from his surroundings, such as a silent servant who brought him his sundowner without Negroponte having to bother himself with any intervening business involving glasses, ice cubes, and bottles. When it came to computers, Negroponte wanted a silent electronic servant who would do exactly what he wanted, instantly. He wanted to fire up the computer, give it a simple instruction, and be obeyed. The solution, he correctly felt, was icon-based computing, the sort of computing where the user pointed an arrow at a picture of something rather than typing in a command that was sometimes long and often hard to remember, and Dataland was his demonstration. In Dataland, when the Rolodex was activated, the Rolodex was ready to use. But Negroponte went further. He claimed that he and his team had invented icon-based computing. A whole lot of other people, with varying degrees of vehemence, said that was flatly wrong; someone else invented icon-based computing, and Negroponte should have either known it or looked it up. When it came to curbing his tongue and moderating his ego, Nicholas Negroponte had a problem. Negroponte, though a man of considerable charm, was not a popular figure outside his immediate circle. But in Jerome Wiesner, he made a powerful friend.

WHILE OTHERS CAME TO BELIEVE, WITH MORE THAN A little evidence, that Negroponte had a highly flexible notion of the truth in toxic combination with an opinion of himself they did not share, none of his detractors enjoyed the stature and power of Jerome Wiesner, whose confidence and patronage Negroponte had won.

Wiesner was the president of MIT, a former national security adviser to Presidents Kennedy and Johnson, a respected expert on international arms control, and the man Negroponte credits with talking him out of some of his wilder ideas, such as a computer program that communicated with dead artists. By 1979, the two of them had conceived the Media Lab, an MIT facility where scientists, musicians, painters, sociologists, architects, writers, and industrialists (together with the latter's money) would gather under a single roof to ponder and create the digital future. To raise the necessary funds, they set out on the global travels that, in Negroponte's case, would never end. Six years and $50 million later, they had their faculty, their student body, their corporate sponsors, and their new building. It was designed by I. M. Pei—the irreverent students called it "the Pei toilet"—and it was named for Wiesner.

"Our charter," the Lab's literature said, was ". . . to drive technological inventions and break engineering deadlocks with new perspectives and demanding applications." It would be Bell Labs, Xerox PARC, and the Bauhaus rolled into one. The idea was to examine the world of the binary code, identify trends and possible new uses that were five years or ten years out—Negroponte expressed boredom at any idea that promised to arrive in a year or two—and identify something that might become an actual commercial product. The Media Lab, as it seldom ceased to remind the world, was inventing the future.

As far as the executive suites of certain corporations were concerned, it was high time somebody did. Clearly, there was gold to be mined in the digital revolution. The question was where to dig. Corporate suites tend to be heavily occupied by lawyers and accountants who are not exactly well versed, if they are versed at all, in binary technology.

Moreover, the attention span at many a corporation was roughly as long as a mayfly's life span. Since the 1980s, companies had increasingly concentrated on delivering "value to the shareholder" in the form of a lofty stock price, which meant that the things a company did in the immediate present were far more important than the things a company planned to do in five years. Worshipping the bottom line, many companies had cut back on basic research. At many companies, there was no longer an in-house scientist who could describe all the splendidly profitable things an electron could probably be made to do if only the scientist was given several million bucks and an unlimited amount of time. This was where Nicholas Negroponte entered the picture.

Like many descendants of the seafaring Greeks who settled in Britain and America, Negroponte spoke a fluent English that was graceful, entertaining, and clear. He was witty and clever, but never too witty or too clever. He had a way of explaining complicated concepts that was instantly understandable. He was poised, urbane, freshly barbered and shaved, and tastefully dressed. When he walked into a corporate suite, he was at one with his hosts, a man you could safely sink money into. He had not yet grown arrogant, hectoring, or impatient with visions less comprehensive than his own; that came later. For the moment, he brought the captains of industry the digital future almost as a gift; access to the Media Lab could be purchased for less than the price of a full-page ad in the *New York Times*. In exchange, the Lab's scientists would display their wares and invite the industrialists to rethink their production and manufacturing processes. The industrialists would bring their problems to the Lab, and the scientists would be invited to make suggestions. In many important ways, the Lab more closely resembled a cheap substitute for a corporate research and development facility than it did a home of pure and disinterested research, but its broadest endeavors were guided by Nicholas Negroponte's intuition. In 1985, his intuition told him that interactive television was the television of tomorrow, and Negroponte had a very precise idea of the form it would inevitably assume.

He wanted the family television set, like the servant with the sundowner and the unbuilt intelligent house, to know its owner's tastes and habits and to be its owner's helpful friend. In his ideal world, once you walked into your home through doors that swung open (and caught up with your telephone calls by barking a command to the hatrack or the floor lamp, another of his persistent visions), your television set would be instantly aware of your interested presence, and would say:

"Hello [your name here]. While you were out, I recorded the Met's live production of *Coppélia*, von Karajan conducting but, if I may be permitted to say so, a step off his usual game. From C-SPAN, I have selected and stored today's congressional hearings on the bills to abolish the Supreme Court and the Federal Communications Commission, together with Speaker Gingrich's statesmanlike comments. For your amusement, I have also stored Congressman Gephardt's comically bumbling attempts at a rebuttal. The city council continued to discuss the tax breaks and zoning relief for your new headquarters structure. I regret to say that nothing of importance was decided, but the material is available for review. I have also recorded a selection of advertisements for the products in which you have recently expressed a certain interest. Turnbull and Asser, if I may be permitted to say so, is offering a wizard discount on their latest shirtings."

Nicholas Negroponte, like John Malone and a large, perhaps dominant, number of computer people, was of the libertarian persuasion. He also continued to be a man to whom a great many things did not occur. It did not occur to him, for example, that the television was perhaps equally likely to say:

"Hello [your name here]. While you were out, I stored eight prosthesis advertisements and downloaded the day's programming from the New Jersey Bondage Network. What would you like to see first, hotshot?" The television, presumably, would have the good sense to make certain you were alone before it made this announcement.

The Negroponte television would have at its beck and call the full menu of broadcast network, cable channel, and local station programming, but with a significant difference. The viewer could watch the existing programming whenever the viewer pleased, forever liberated from the tyranny of the daily television schedule—an event that Negroponte seemed to rank with the storming of the Bastille and the thought processes of James Madison as a landmark on the road to human liberty. Perhaps better yet, the viewer could alter the content of the programming as though it were a computer game. In the process, although Negroponte did not say so and probably did not know it, the newly liberated interactive viewer would bankrupt every movie studio, television studio, and independent production company across the width and breadth of the land.

In order to alter the content of a movie or a television show, filmed alternatives for every scene had to be available. Anytime a scene in a movie or show was changed, Heisenberg's Uncertainty Principle kicked into operation. The entire remaining content of the film or show had to be altered. It did not seem to occur to Negroponte that this would cost an enormous amount of money.

The average movie script consists of 120 pages. As a rule of thumb, let's say that it costs around $250,000 to shoot a page, about average for a mid-range studio film whose budget and/or star has failed to go out of control. Under extreme but not unheard of conditions, such as a director gone out of control, each page might have to be shot as many as thirty times. Because a number of modern thespians have failed to learn the rudiments of their craft, the voices in the final version of the shot might have to be rerecorded another thirty times. In the end, the director will have produced a single, usable camera shot based on a single page of script.

To render the filmed page interactive, a large number of alternative versions will have to be shot and redubbed thirty times. Assume that the number of alternative versions is twenty-three—in computer terms, not a large number. The cost of filming the first page of a script has risen to $5,750,000. The situation worsens on page two. There are now twenty-three variants of the plot, but the movie remains interactive; there are also twenty-three variants of all twenty-three variants. Shooting the second page of the script now costs $132,250,000. There are 118 pages to go. There is not enough money in the world to pay the production costs of a single interactive movie studio with a full schedule of releases. Moreover, there was one final thing that hadn't occurred to Nicholas Negroponte.

Stripped to its essentials, the core technology of Negroponte's interactive television bore a singular resemblance to Qube, the interactive television that John Malone had just ripped out in Pittsburgh because no market for it existed.

FIVE

In the Hall of the Mountain King

O N NEW YEAR'S EVE 1989, MALONE'S RIGHT-HAND MAN, Peter Barton, stopped by his office to pick up some papers. On his desk was a telegram from ESPN, the company Malone had blindsided five years before. The message was short, to the point, mischievously derivative in its prose, and accompanied by a faint dry chuckle of vengeful glee. As of 12:01 A.M., New Year's Day, the telegram said, TCI was to cease carrying ESPN everywhere in the country—unless TCI agreed immediately to a huge increase in ESPN's fees. TCI had no wiggle room and no choice; a situation familiar to the owners of ESPN, where memories were long and revenge was a dish that was best eaten cold.

For Malone and TCI, it had been a great ride while it lasted, but in the annals of American capitalism, it had been remarkably short—

as perhaps befitted the nation's television-shortened attention span. The humbling of AT&T had taken more than a hundred years. General Motors bestrode the automotive world like a colossus for half a century. John Malone had been put in his place just five years after he sent his ultimatum to the president of ABC and sat down to dictate terms. But it had been, at least as far as Malone and TCI were concerned, a great five years. In 1989, the year nemesis finally began to knock on TCI's door, the company's cash flow exceeded the revenues of all three major broadcasting networks combined.

MAGNESS HAD FOUNDED TCI WITH SMALL, RURAL systems. Malone built more rural systems and invaded the suburbs—"little bites," he said, "rather than great big swallows." As far as it went—and once TCI had some money again—Magness's original plan worked just fine. In the early 1980s, its million subscribers placed it in cable's big leagues and allowed it to make an object lesson of ESPN without violating the two prime directives of Bob Magness. "Keep it simple," Magness had said. And: "It's cheaper to pay interest than taxes."

"The scheme of the company," Malone explained, "is contrary to what they teach in business school, which is to earn money, pay taxes, issue dividends, and then have your stockholders pay 70 percent taxes on those. We think that's stupid. TCI is a company of the future."

To become a company of the future while violating the teachings of every business school in the land, however, it was essential for TCI to meet a couple of conditions. It had to grow much larger while avoiding the sort of constraints that were usually placed on companies controlled by many stockholders—among them, sophisticated investors like pension and mutual funds—with bad nerves and strongly held opinions about the latitude granted to chief executive officers. To grow along the anticipated lines, TCI would have to retain the management structure of a much smaller company with no powerful or nervous stockholders at all. Simplicity was sacrificed in the name of the greatest good for the smallest number. The smallest number consisted of Magness and Malone.

Once TCI's balance sheet was cleaned up by the loans from HBO and the pension funds, Malone created a new kind of stock, Class B, with ten votes per share, most of which ended up in the possession of Malone and Magness. *The Wall Street Journal* found the manner in which much of the stock was obtained worthy of comment.

"Beginning in the early 1980s," *The Journal* reported, "the company initiated a dizzying series of complex transactions that ultimately had TCI pay the two a huge share of the company's supervoting shares, enabling them to tighten their control over the company. . . . The dealings, in part, involved the swapping of several cable franchises around Salt Lake City among four companies with similar names, two belonging to the executives and two to TCI. TCI ended up acquiring some of the franchises from Messrs. Magness and Malone, paying them in super-voting shares . . . even though TCI had owned them in the first place."

Complexity, like simplicity, had certain advantages. For one thing, it was almost impossible to tell what Malone was up to until he had done it. For another, complex transactions had a wonderful way of throwing off pursuit. When the dust had cleared, Malone and Magness owned only about 11 percent of TCI's stock but controlled 60 percent of the Class B, which gave them voting control of the company. TCI vigorously and repeatedly denied *The Wall Street Journal* version of events. *The Journal* stood by its story. Nothing else happened. Within the limits of the law—or within the limits of the law's officers to comprehend what was going on—Magness and Malone retained total control of TCI, and TCI became a very difficult company to understand.

Malone began to buy pieces of other cable companies, but he did not buy enough to trigger the regulation that required him to report the holdings on his balance sheet. He entered into strategic alliances with other cable systems like Taft Broadcasting; like a pair of corsairs, strategic allies sailed in company until it suited them otherwise, searching for loot. Malone, Magness, and their executives bought still other cable systems on the cheap, held them for a while, and sold them to TCI at a handsome profit. If there was a hole in the legal net, Malone would usually find it.

In complexity, there were many other advantages. TCI was almost impervious to a hostile takeover—the favorite business maneuver of the decade—because almost no one could figure out what TCI was worth and Magness and Malone could overrule any decision of their stockholders or board of directors. It was still possible to pay interest rather than taxes, but now it was possible to pay interest in an entirely new way. In addition to the alliances and investments, TCI spun off parts of itself, declared them to be independent companies, made certain that the letter of the law was obeyed, and retained a piece of the action for itself, all of which enabled Malone to fashion protective barriers he called "water-tight bulkheads." The spin-offs and controlled companies could enter the credit markets and borrow money without adding to TCI's indebtedness. If a spin-off or a controlled company failed, TCI lost no money. And no matter what happened, TCI could write off the cost of the investment. It was all quite beautiful, but nothing was quite as beautiful as the spectacle that met Malone's eyes after the great franchise wars came to their inevitable end. He had prudently stood aside, devoting his energies to turning TCI into a cat's cradle that only he and Magness understood while continuing to expand by little bites. Now it was time to move in and take his cut. The pickings were rich.

WHEN THE RACE TO THE CITIES WAS OVER, THE NATION was littered with broken and ailing cable companies. Something that started as a real estate grab driven by greed and technological fantasy ended up looking like Stalingrad—and Malone, who had bided his time and hoarded his cash, could pick and choose among the fully built, brand-new, heavily discounted systems that could no longer live with the consequences of their owners' delusions. When Heritage Communications, the company that bought Warner Amex's Dallas franchise, was threatened by corporate raiders, Malone bought control of the operation after a two-hour meeting and a handshake that cost him $1.3 billion. It was the largest amount of money he had ever spent, but Dallas was a bargain. Malone was nothing if not consistent; he had always been a bottom fisher, and he had never seen a bottom as richly populated as the one he encountered now. He picked up a second large franchise for a second billion dollars and made his selections among the smaller fry. He could dictate his terms, and he did. Between 1973 and 1989, he closed 482 deals, an average of one every two weeks; by 1988, he had bought more than 150 cable systems, most of them at fire-sale prices. At the decade's end, TCI was the largest cable company in America, with more than 11 million subscribers in forty-eight states—one-fifth the cable-viewing populace. Thanks to Malone's investments, TCI indirectly reached 39 million more, and according to one dauntingly complex analysis, the value of TCI stock had risen by a staggering 91,000 percent. TCI became one of the darlings of Wall Street, and the financial community was converted to the gospel according to Magness, as explained by Malone. A company that almost never made a profit and never made a large one, that piled debt upon debt to grow larger and larger, that threw off a huge amount of nontaxable cash— the figure was approaching $1 billion a year—and that was almost impossible to understand—that company was the company of the future, as Malone had prophesied. It was perhaps inevitable that he began to confuse himself with a force of nature.

"When you're driving plate tectonics," he said, "you're going to squeeze people's tails."

And squeeze them he did. TCI paid a small copyright fee to the owners of the movies and programs it plucked out of the air, but it continued to pay the over-the-air stations nothing for most of the signals it rebroadcast. While the more popular of the cable-specific programming services were finally able to extract a tariff because of their very popularity—a viewer's must-see cable channel, like HBO, was a cable operator's must-have cable channel—TCI received an immense discount based on the size of its audience. On a per-viewer basis, TCI paid HBO 90 cents. Smaller companies paid $5, and the cable programmers regarded Malone's insistence on massive discounts as little short of extortion. They had not yet surmised their strength. When Malone demanded his discounts, they either yielded or felt the kiss of his lash.

When MTV tried to raise its rates, Malone dusted off the tactics he used earlier on ESPN and announced that he and Ted Turner would create a rival rock video channel. MTV caved. When Turner tried to raise the rates for CNN, Malone hooked up with NBC to create a competing twenty-four-hour cable news service. The deal unraveled when NBC decided it couldn't live with Malone's idea of the rates TCI would pay for a news service. Malone's larger purpose had been served, however. He had shown Turner who was boss. And soon, he became Turner's boss in the most literal possible way. It was Malone who led the rescue party that saved Ted Turner from himself. Turner seemed to amuse him.

WHEN TURNER, THE OBSESSIVE SAILOR, WON THE America's Cup in 1977, he celebrated by getting drunk and climbing under a table—on television, at his own news conference. In his headquarters, he assembled a collection of hats, including a wizard's pointed cap and an Indian war bonnet, which he sometimes gleefully wore during his interviews with the press, of which there were many. *Time* magazine memorably called him the Mouth of the South, a man who said anything that was on his mind even when the thing on his mind was a little bizarre. He developed—and seemed to revel in—a reputation as a public lush, a shameless womanizer, and a borderline nutcase. At Turner's direction, a videotape was prepared, to be played over WTBS when the Russian missiles came over the Pole. It featured massed bands and an American flag.

Malone seemed particularly amused by Turner's liberal political notions—"like providing free cable TV for the homeless," said Malone indulgently. But although Turner often seemed badly in need of adult supervision, there was one thing about him that aroused Malone's open admiration. Ted Turner was the most gifted and successful programmer in the history of cable television.

In 1980, when Turner announced the start of CNN, his twenty-four-hour Cable News Network, many took it as a sign that he had finally and irrevocably taken leave of his senses. CNN was a very basic service. Its second-rate announcers specialized in a rip-and-read approach to the news: show some footage, describe it by reading (poorly) a couple of words ripped off the telex machine, show some more footage. Turner's detractors called CNN the chicken noodle network.

Clearly, Turner was doomed. To create CNN, he mortgaged every business he owned. In its first year, CNN lost $20 million. ABC and Westinghouse, with bottomless pockets and a nationally known news staff, had joined together to create their own twenty-four-hour service; when ABC and Westinghouse hit the airwaves with their star reporters, their many captive outlets, and their sophisticated packaging, Ted Turner would meet his richly deserved fate. Fifteen years later, CNN had 68.5 million viewers. The ABC-Westinghouse news service did not exist. Turner piped CNN into hotels and airports. He beamed it into the heavens, bounced it off a satellite, and took it international; by 1989, CNN was operating in eighty-six countries. It was still a very basic sort of news service, but its vacuum-cleaner approach meant that if its news was basic, it was also extraordinarily thorough. When the leaders of the world wanted to find out what was happening in the world—and, sometimes, in their own countries—they tuned to CNN. CNN, going away, was the single most valuable product in the history of cable television, and no one else had anything remotely like it. Still, Turner couldn't rest. Once, ending a meeting with some CBS executives, he was heard to mutter, "I'm going to own you boys. I will." He seemed to be in his cups—with Turner, it was sometimes hard to tell—but within his limits, he was a man of his word. Like John Malone, Turner had begun to confuse himself with a force of nature.

In 1985, he offered to buy the network for $5.4 billion that he did not have. Instead, he offered stock and junk bonds. Senator Jesse Helms of North Carolina also spoke of raising money to buy the network for the purpose of silencing its liberal newscaster Dan Rather. CBS, reacting as though it was surrounded by rednecks and unable to tell the difference between them, allowed itself to slip into the control of the financier Laurence Tisch, a decision that was soon bitterly regretted in the broadcasting and especially the news studios. Turner, for all his many failings, knew how to run a television network, and Laurence Tisch did not.

Next, Turner decided to buy a movie studio. Although many people had come to question his sanity by then, it was an entirely rational move; Steve Ross, for eminently sound reasons, had bought a cable company. Unfortunately, Turner bought the wrong movie studio. In 1987, he raised $1.4 billion and purchased MGM, a company with an illustrious past, a troubled present, and a dubious future. MGM also owned *Gone With the Wind*, the movie that had always been a lamp unto Turner's feet. Unfortunately, Turner couldn't afford to pay $1.4 billion for a damp squib of a movie studio. Others, including John Malone, were making audacious corporate purchases then, but there was an art to it that Turner had not grasped. An ideal takeover target of the 1980s had a lot of money in its till, a large and unused line of credit, assets that could be sold, or all three. Separately or in combination, they could be used to pay off the purchaser's debts and legal bills, provide operating capital, and sometimes reward it with an enormous amount of essentially free money. MGM had none of them. When the end arrived to the most terrible year in Turner's life, his house had burned down, his wife had sued for divorce, he was finally the proprietor of the movie of his dreams, and he was broke.

Although Malone seemed to like Ted Turner as much as he liked anybody—they went sailing together, a rare sign of Malone's favor—

he assessed the situation in the light of his usual self-interest. If TCI intervened and saved Turner Broadcasting, there was one very large possible downside: Ted Turner's life expectancy.

It was a subject that often made bold and outspoken men behave like superstitious peasants who believed that speaking the name of something made it so. People were afraid that something might "happen" to Ted. "If he were hit by a bus or shot by a jealous husband . . . ," Malone mused, but even John Malone trailed off before he reached the end of the thought. Turner was the son of a suicide. As Kurt Vonnegut once remarked, sons of suicides tended to feel that life lacked a certain zing.

On the other hand, there was a very considerable upside to Turner's difficulties: CNN and superstation WTBS with its valuable in-house sports franchises, especially the Atlanta Braves. It would never do for Ted's immensely lucrative creations to fall into the wrong hands, and Malone had no doubts about whose hands those were: "Someone like Rupert Murdoch or Time Inc.," he said. That would never do. TCI would have to rescue Ted Turner from the consequences of his folly.

With TCI contributing the largest share, Malone put together the consortium of cable companies that bailed Turner out with $568 million. TCI bought 21 percent of Turner Broadcasting, Time was allotted 17 percent of the action, and Turner was kept on a strict allowance; any expenditure of more than $2 million had to be approved by his stockholders. Of these, TCI was far more than the first among equals. Malone could easily play Turner and Time against each other while earning Turner's gratitude by posing as his friend. He had acquired a veto power over everything Turner did (Time also had a veto), he had acquired an opportunity to make all sorts of mischief (Turner, unlike Malone, could buy a television network; cable operators couldn't own networks, but broadcasters could), and Malone's options remained pleasingly open. He owned the largest piece of the most successful programmer in the business, and a shaken and subdued Ted Turner referred to him in terms usually reserved for the deity. "John Malone," Turner said, "is . . . John Malone."

Actually, Malone had been quietly accumulating pieces of programming services for years. None of them had Turner Broadcasting's stature, but they had their uses.

ONCE AGAIN, HE BOUGHT A LITTLE OF THIS AND A LITTLE of that until, almost unnoticed, he owned a lot of something. In 1979, he had invested $180,000 in a new service, Black Entertainment Television, and eventually owned 22 percent. He saved the Discovery Channel from bankruptcy and wound up with 49 percent. TCI owned 18 percent of Pat Robertson's Family Channel, 29 percent of the cable shopping service QVC, half of American Movie Classics, and 60 percent of the Prime Network, the largest grouping of regional sports programming on cable. When the programming investments were added to the off-the-books cable investments, the number of people sitting in the glowing circle of Malone's electric hearth was huge.

The reason for buying into the programmers, explained Malone, was to provide his viewers with quality television. This noble and altruistic motive aside, however, owning pieces of his programmers gave him five bites of an immense apple.

TCI received the usual steady and recession-proof stream of income from its 11.2 million subscribers. Owning pieces of programmers provided a second, indirect stream of income in the form of advertising revenues, and although these were not large—no single cable television channel delivered a mass market to the advertisers, unlike the over-the-air channels of the broadcasting networks—their cumulative impact was considerable. CNN was available in 55.3 million homes, WTBS in 54.7 million, Turner Network Television—the new service begun with Turner's high hopes restored and Malone's paternal blessing—reached 47.8 million, and Headline News 42.8 million. The numbers were 51 million at the Discovery Channel, 49.8

million at the Family Channel, 30.6 million at QVC, 27.9 million at Black Entertainment, 27 million at American Movie Classics, and 22.1 million at Prime. True, advertisers did not buy households; they bought the number of people who actually tuned into a show, but the spread of the TCI investments meant that a large number of people were watching something owned by TCI during the lucrative prime viewing hours. A small but pleasing portion of the resulting revenues reached the corporate treasury in the form of dividends, the real payoff came as the cable programmers prospered and grew in value, and TCI was well on the way to the sort of vertical corporate integration pioneered by Rockefeller and Carnegie and perfected by Henry Ford. TCI owned major waterworks, it owned the largest pipeline in the country, and it seemed only a matter of time before it owned a major movie studio, further tightening its grip on the audience. Last and occasionally best, ownership of programming services gave Malone a stick with which to beat other, non-TCI programmers if they betrayed signs of independent thinking at dealmaking time.

For example, when the popular and award-winning Learning Channel went on the block, Discovery (49 percent TCI) made a bid of $31 million. The Lifetime Channel, partly owned by Viacom, offered $50 million. Outbid in a fair fight, TCI then took a second look at the Learning Channel and made an unhappy discovery: the Learning Channel was no longer as good as it had been, and TCI had made a narrow escape. In fact, the Learning Channel had become unworthy to appear on many of TCI's cable systems, and TCI, always committed to providing its viewers with the highest quality of television, took it off. Without access to TCI's almost 12 million subscribers, the Learning Channel was no longer worth $50 million. Lifetime withdrew its offer, TCI soon noticed that the Learning Channel's virtues had been restored, and the Discovery Channel returned to the scene with its original and now winning $31 million bid. Everyone was happy now, except for some of the Learning Channel's former owners, who took TCI to court. Their case was thrown out. Under the rules of the game, no cable system was under an obligation to carry a cable program it didn't want. To the cable industry, the lesson was clear. John Malone could be beaten in a fair fight, but John Malone did not fight fair.

IT WAS STILL THE SAME OLD TCI, UNMELLOWED BY ITS wealth.

In what resembled a bad joke grown tiresome with ceaseless repetition, Malone continually announced that a new and friendly TCI had made the Damascene discovery that it didn't treat its customers very well. Henceforward, he promised (and promised), TCI would answer its phones, its repairmen and installers would keep their appointments, and service interruptions would be repaired in the blink of an eye. Nothing much happened. Malone continued to milk his systems, and now that he was in the big time, it didn't seem to matter how large his milked systems were, or how large his customers' elected representatives otherwise loomed in the eyes of the nation.

"Because of its size," Robin P. Charleston, Chicago's cable administrator, told Maggie Mahar of *Barron's*, "Tele-Communications can enforce its position. So far, they've done an excellent job of construction. But when we raise a problem about interpreting agreements, they respond with formal action—up to and including lawsuits. I have to take that into account." Mahar wrote that Charleston said this "carefully." Malone, it seemed, had Chicago in the palm of his hand.

Yes, it was great fun while it lasted. Although Malone was a private person, he was not averse to holding court and issuing decrees in the form of friendly suggestions. When Sumner Redstone, the New England theater operator, took over Viacom in 1987 and became a billionaire, he made the obligatory trip to Englewood and received Malone's blessing. When ESPN believed it had a chance to buy the rights to all the games of the National Football League, Malone advised against it. To take the favorite league in the public's favorite sport off free over-the-air television would not be astute, he said.

People would scream and so would their politicians. ESPN bought only some of the games. It was hard to believe that a day of reckoning was at hand, or that a gleefully vengeful ESPN would be its messenger.

TCI, WITHIN NARROW LIMITS, MAY HAVE BEEN THE company of a certain kind of future. It was not, however, a company of forever. There was a limit to how long Malone could play the game he'd chosen. In order to reap continued benefits from accelerated depreciation and interest payments, TCI had to buy more cable systems with yet more borrowed money, piling debt upon debt. Here, something called Buffett's Law, named for the celebrated Omaha investor Warren Buffett, came into play. As designed by Malone, TCI was a self-limiting phenomenon.

A company that grew larger and larger by acquisition rather than internal expansion had to buy larger and larger companies. Although there were exceptions to the rule, it no longer made sense for TCI to buy small cable outfits and small programming services, because small cable outfits and small programming services did not produce the desired result of larger and larger tax-extinguishing write-offs. Sooner or later, Malone would run up against the last remaining antitrust barriers of an increasingly libertarian government, or else he would simply run out of things to buy. Before that point was reached—and unless TCI found something else to do for a living—Malone was also likely to meet himself coming around a corner and collide with his doppelgänger in a shuddering crash. As TCI strode more deeply into a shrinking marketplace, and if it failed to develop a new strategy, it would inevitably begin to buy companies that competed with each other. Malone would go into business against himself, and the situation would become absurd. If Malone continued to rely on debt, it could also become dangerously absurd, especially if Malone either faltered or became overconfident. There was a psychological limit to how much money he could borrow, although no one knew where it was. Something—government action, a change in the financial marketplace, a new economic philosophy—would make his creditors nervous, his money would become expensive, and it would eventually dry up. It had happened often enough before. There was also a practical limit to how much he could borrow. If, for some reason—government action, a change in the television marketplace, a blunder—TCI's cash flow could no longer cover the payments on its debt, it would have to borrow money to repay its creditors, piling debt upon debt. If adverse conditions were not reversed, the story could have only one ending. Financial engineering based on borrowed money was not a strategy of forever, no matter what Malone said. TCI was a short-term winner, and the financial community—Wall Street especially—always loved a short-term winner. But short-term victory was also a self-limiting phenomenon. As was the sort of monopoly Malone had fashioned for himself.

It is a well-known, invariably forgotten lesson of history that would-be monopolists like Malone are usually great and vocal fans of market forces until they actually become monopolists, whereupon—like the government regulators Malone so thoroughly despised—they begin to make the rules to suit themselves. The more rules they make, the more hides they fry, the sooner an inevitable reaction occurs, usually when a crack appears in the monopolistic facade.

A crack had begun to appear. Slowly at first, and then with gathering speed, Malone began to need the programmers more than they needed him. If Malone hoped to thrive and prosper, he would have to get out of the financial engineering business and enter a whole new line of work. He would have to get into the television business.

Although cable television had come to resemble a utility—when many people moved into a new home, they automatically called to have the gas, electricity, and cable hooked up—it was plagued by a glass ceiling. By 1989, the country was almost completely wired; to continue its expansion—to expand as an industry, as distinct from the expansion of a single company like TCI—cable had to expand its audience in the areas where the coaxial pipe was already laid.

This was no easy task. In the systems where cable achieved its best penetration, no more than 60 to 65 percent of the homes subscribed to cable. Moreover, despite the fact that most systems—except a number of the ones controlled by Malone—now offered dozens of channels, most people still watched only a handful of them with any regularity, and they were always the same ones. To keep the audience (and its elected representatives) happy, it was essential for a cable operator to offer the must-see channels, most notably MTV and ESPN. A cable operator without MTV and ESPN was a cable operator in trouble. When Peter Barton stepped into his office on New Year's Eve 1989 and found the ultimatum from ESPN, TCI was a cable operator in trouble. The long free ride was over, and the days of the king were numbered.

The timing was impeccable. For the nation, the financial community, the cable industry, and TCI, the end of the phenomenon known as the 1980s coincided almost exactly with the chronological end of the decade. Its like would not be seen again, or not very soon. There was only one major bit of unfinished business. The last great merger of the 1980s slipped across the finish line just before the rules changed. Time Inc. had decided to run away with the circus.

TAKING A BREAK FROM JURY DUTY ONE DAY IN FEBRUARY 1987, Nick Nicholas, the new president of Time, called Steve Ross from a pay phone in the New York State Court Building on Foley Square. Ross invited Nicholas to his Park Avenue apartment. Nicholas immediately went. As the story is told, the fate of his jury duty is unknown.

When Nicholas, the acerbic son of a submarine captain, was named to his post in July of the previous year, he found himself at the pinnacle of a company that no longer had any clear idea of why it had been placed on earth. Neither did anyone else. In the eyes of many, Time had become just another company, more fallible than most; it was no longer a national institution. It was no longer very clear what Time did for a living—its magazines accounted for only 15 percent of its business—or how it figured in God's plan, a question that would have been unthinkable in the days of its founder, Henry Luce.

Twenty years after his death, Time Inc. had become the sort of company that Luce would have hated to the very marrow of his being. From 1923, when he and his equally young partner, Briton Hadden, created *Time* magazine, until Luce's death in 1966, he was in the business (although he did not regard it entirely as a business) of delivering a product (although he did not call it a product) that hit the bricks every Monday morning.

It was beyond question that the enterprise was supposed to make a certain amount of money. As editor-in-chief, Harry Luce was entitled to a comfortable life, but on a more urgent level, he required a healthy flow of cash to attract talented reporters to his banner, pay their salaries, and provide them with the budget they needed to do their jobs. The purpose of the exercise was to inform the American people of the world around them, change it if necessary but in a way congenial to Harry Luce, and if possible make it into a far, far better place. Paradoxically, the brilliant monster Harry Luce was one of the most gifted newsmen of his day. And as it happened, Harry Luce was not overly fond of television.

Indeed, it is not going too far to say that he despised it. The man of the middle with the golden brow looked at television and saw no redeeming features. In the early days of the new medium, he could have owned an entire network—a fabulous money machine even then—and he decided to pass. He thought, and said, that his corporate neighbor Bill Paley, whose CBS was located just up the street, had "cheapened American taste with his entertainment junk." He was also not overly fond of the movies. Luce could have owned MGM or MCA, the home of Universal Studios, and again he passed. Owning a studio, he wrote in a blistering memo, would create "conflicts in the fields of taste and standards." He might consider buying a horse or dog track, he added, but "anesthetizing people" was not his line of work. Television, if anything, was even worse. It not only knocked out the brain, but it was addictive. (Quietly, Luce's Time owned five television stations. He professed to deplore them because he couldn't control the mindless content of their broadcasts, but he kept them anyway. A foolish consistency, he might have said, is a hobgoblin of little minds. The stations were sold in 1970, four years after his death.)

Luce had not been indifferent to corporate growth, but when Time Inc. became a publicly traded company, he made a point of never knowing the price of the stock. By the late 1980s, his successors thought of little else. It was not an unusual preoccupation. The decade's corporate raiders and academic theorists had persuaded the world that nothing about an American company—what it made, what it did, what it proposed to do tomorrow—mattered as much as the price of its stock. Luce's constituency had been his readers; the readers were not the constituency of his successors, and unlike John Malone, they had not arranged things to do as they pleased. If they did not satisfy their stockholders, their jobs were doomed, and the flaccid magazines lacked the necessary glamour, dynamism, the enduring charm of novelty, and the promise of riches beyond the dreams of avarice. Television had them all. For the first time in its history, Time Inc. was run by men who owed their jobs and wellbeing to the very business the founder had despised as addictive, trivial, and unworthy of the attention of a serious-minded man.

J. Richard Munro, the popular chairman, had served four years as publisher of *Sports Illustrated* but made his mark by turning a profit in the once despised television subsidiary. Nicholas J. Nicholas, Jr., the short-tempered and unpopular president, had spent time in the magazine division (as a financial expert, not as an editor) but had won his spurs as Munro's hatchet man. The hatchet had largely been wielded in the direction of the man who had made possible the bright corporate future, Jerry Levin.

LEVIN WAS THE SORT OF MAN WHO SEEMED TO HAVE NO second act in his life, but who nonetheless was given repeated opportunities for an encore. With his invention of modern cable television, Levin had solved one problem and solved it brilliantly, but he seemed stumped when it came to the question of what to do next.

Thanks to satellite transmission, HBO was now available nationwide. Levin began to cycle the channel's offerings over a twenty-four-hour period, a sound idea if HBO, now concentrating on movies, had enough movies to offer. It didn't. Viewers soon became bored with HBO, and a bored HBO viewer was far more dangerous than one of Malone's angry cable customers. An angry but addicted cable customer had nowhere else to go. A bored HBO viewer simply—and easily—discontinued the service.

Nick Nicholas, brought in over Levin's resentful head to clean up the situation, fired underperforming executives and executives who got in his way, straightened out the Manhattan cable operations, and persuaded the parent company to buy the 90 percent of ATC—a major cable operation that a drifting Time had wandered into, wandered out of, and wandered into again—that Time did not own. With HBO, despite its persistent lack of variety, Time was the largest cable programmer in the country. With ATC, purchased in 1978, it was the owner of the second-largest cable system after TelePrompTer; ATC had 2.1 million lucrative customers in thirty-three states. The combined video operation was handed back to Levin, who proceeded to place Time's once sterling reputation and, eventually, its entire existence at risk.

First, Levin managed to lose $130 million in subscription television and videotext. It seemed a small matter, easily excused. Time was new to large-scale television operations, and even the august *New York Times* had dropped a bundle in the videotext fiasco. Next, he failed to tell the magazine division something it badly needed to know. This was not a small matter.

One of the more troubling aspects of the cable business was something called the churn: in any given month, between 2 and 5 percent of the viewers would cancel their subscriptions. HBO's subscription TV had been churned into oblivion; the ATC cable systems were continually churned. The problem, the magazine division decided, was a lack of information: people did not know what was on cable. *TV Guide* published some cable listings, had the in-house skills to publish many more, and could be bought for $900 million. Time passed on *TV Guide*. (It was later sold to Rupert Murdoch for $2.8 billion, and the Australian-born press lord did not regret his decision.) Instead, Time decided to undertake the largest new-magazine launch in American history. The publication, conceived in 1981, would be called *TV-Cable Week*. It would tell everybody in the country what was on their cable system and abolish the churn.

There were many reasons for the resulting catastrophe. Chief among them were the laws of physics. Although there would soon be more computational power in a musical greeting card than existed on the entire planet in 1950, there still wasn't enough reasonably priced computational power in the known universe to satisfy *TV-Cable Week*'s rapacious diet for information. The magazine would be sold to the viewers of hundreds of different cable systems. *TV-Cable Week* would therefore have to ship hundreds of customized editions, each with its unique listing of the nightly fare. For the listings to meet Time's standards for accuracy and clarity, *TV-Cable Week*'s computers would have to be programmed with the plot synopses of every television-available movie and every video rerun. There were thousands of movies. There were thousands of reruns.

To write the synopses, freelancers were hired. When the synopses were written, they were copy-edited. When the synopses were finally ready, the computers were incapable of handling them. The descriptions of the nightly fare on hundreds of different cable systems had to be entered in the magazine in the old-fashioned way, by human beings using keyboards. In 1983, after five months of existence and twenty-five editions, *TV-Cable Week* folded. Time Inc., never very candid about its mistakes, admitted to a $47 million loss. The actual loss was estimated at closer to $100 million. It was the worst and most publicized disaster in magazine history. Until then, Time had a slightly shopworn but still potent reputation for infallibly understanding the magazine marketplace. The reputation was now lost, never to be regained.

For a reason far less complex than the laws of physics, Jerry Levin could have stopped the fiasco in its tracks. *TV-Cable Week* was distributed by the cable systems whose listings it carried. If the magazine were to have the faintest ghost of a chance, it was vital that Time's ATC lend its support. ATC had no intention of doing any such thing, and Levin knew it; the people at ATC thought the idea of a weekly cable magazine was seriously nuts. But although Levin attended a number of *TV-Cable Week*'s strategy sessions, he did not tell his colleagues that *TV-Cable Week* was doomed. Instead, he was busy driving Time Inc. down the road to bankruptcy.

There was a much simpler way to deal with the churn at HBO: if the pay service offered a wide variety of movies, it would stop boring its customers to the point of cancellation. In alliance with CBS and Columbia Pictures, HBO founded a new Hollywood studio, TriStar Pictures. Unfortunately, Levin's team either forgot something about filmmaking or had never known it: it cost a great deal of money to make a movie. HBO neglected to place a prudent limit—or, for that matter, any limit at all—on the amount of money it would invest in TriStar's films.

"We revised it," Fay Vincent, then head of TriStar, told the reporter Connie Bruck. "We had to. It was an open-ended lien on Time's treasury." If the open lien had continued, there would soon have been no money in Time's treasury at all, and there was no way to undo the damage that had already been done. In all, HBO paid $1 billion for movies that should have cost the company half as much; the movie *Ghostbusters* alone set HBO back by a staggering $36 million. It was true that *Ghostbusters* was a huge hit, but it was also beside the point. Most movies, no matter how much they cost, were not hits. Most movies, no matter how much they cost, made very little money or no money at all. And because of

Hollywood's curious bookkeeping, hit movies also—officially—made no money.

Once again, Nick Nicholas was brought in to clean up the television operation. If there was any single reason for Nicholas's persistent ill humor, people around the company began to say, the reason was Jerry Levin.

Levin was not fired—he was, after all, the man who had put HBO on the bird—and he did not quit. He said he intended to stay at Time until his work was done. Just what, exactly, his work was, he did not say. He was given a seat on the board. He was promised the vice-chairmanship of the company, a position with no clearly defined duties. He was made head of corporate strategy. In effect, he was told to go sit in a room and think deep thoughts.

While he was doing so, Nick Nicholas hit upon the solution to all their woes and found the key to a dazzling future. Time would merge with Warner, and it would become an entertainment colossus.

STEVE ROSS WAS READY TO DEAL.

In 1983, as he was working his way through the Atari disaster, Ross received a visitor at his East Hampton estate. Rupert Murdoch was an amiable, soft-spoken man with an Oxford education and a cultivated mind. He was also the only competitor in the world John Malone actively feared, although Malone was on excellent terms with his own inner Napoleon. Malone, with his stranglehold on one-fourth of the cable viewers in America, could dictate terms to NBC, CBS, and ABC, but Murdoch could not be reached.

Murdoch owned two-thirds of the newspapers in his native Australia. In Britain, he owned two tabloids with enormous circulations and the venerable *Times* of London, which no longer resembled the *Times* of old; it also sold a great many more newspapers. In America, Murdoch owned—among other things—the *Chicago Sun-Times*, the *New York Post*, *The Village Voice*, and *New York* magazine. He was keenly interested in television, although not in cable systems. Murdoch regarded cable systems as ruinously expensive and costly to maintain.

In Europe, he controlled a satellite that covered Britain and much of the Continent; it was, the British Home Secretary conceded during question time in Parliament, "technically illegal." In British publishing circles, the fact that Murdoch's influential newspapers were loud in his praises of Prime Minister Margaret Thatcher while his favorite prime minister allowed him to operate an illegal satellite were not regarded as separate events.

Like Luce, Murdoch believed that American culture was destined to rule the world. Unlike Luce, and for his own profitable purposes, he defined American culture as popular entertainment; his European satellite had an almost insatiable appetite for American films and television shows. To guarantee a regular supply of raw material, Rupert Murdoch badly wanted a film studio, and Ross owned one.

Steve Ross did not impress him. Here was a man, Murdoch reported in amazement after their meeting, who lived like Midas while his company was in the midst of a $400 million crisis. Murdoch was further scandalized that Ross had actually taken a vacation when he should have been attending to his affairs. During their three hours together, Ross spent much of the time teaching Murdoch how to play Atari video games. As Murdoch was leaving, he mentioned that he planned to buy some Warner stock. He hoped Ross wouldn't mind. "Be my guest," said Ross.

Clearly, the man was a hopeless lightweight. Murdoch immediately launched a raid on Warner's stock. Parrying deftly, Ross was soon in touch with Chris-Craft, a company that manufactured powerboats, owned television stations, and served as the investment vehicle of its proprietor, Herb Siegal, a former Hollywood agent. Once everyone had been maneuvered into position, Chris-Craft owned 14 percent of Warner's voting stock, the vanquished Murdoch was $40 million richer, and Ross, who had never been able to bring himself to fire anyone, had found the ideal person—Herb Siegal—to rejuvenate his shaken company while Ross avoided all blame for the ensuing bloodbath. To a man with a hammer, everything is a nail. To Steve Ross, every lemon was an opportunity to make lemonade.

As the film studio and the music business began to boom again, Ross gradually reduced the number of board seats Siegal controlled. He increased his own paycheck; by the late 1980s, Ross regularly took home $14 million a year, one of the largest executive salaries in the country, while he continued to reduce the powers of the man who had made it possible. Ross suggested that Siegal should take his profits and go away, something Siegal, driven to distraction by Ross's version of a greased-pig race, was perfectly willing to do provided he was paid enough. The call from Nick Nicholas was a gift from the gods. Buying out Siegal would be no problem. Taking control of Time would also be no problem. The people at Time were already convinced that they were taking control of Warner, and they would be encouraged in this delusion.

Unlike the people at Time, Ross never wrote anything down on a piece of paper he could not destroy. Nobody had ever seen him read a book. He knew nothing about the magazine business. Dick Munro, Time's chairman, hadn't seen a movie in years. Time knew something about the film industry, but most of its knowledge revolved around its inability to do anything but fail in the business. Time's management was conservative, rigid, parochial, and condescending to people who were not the legatees of a high calling. Warner was Jersey City, City College, and BBQ: Brooklyn, the Bronx, and Queens. In most major respects, Time and Warner were roughly as similar as Bulgaria and Norway, but there was one area of the corporate landscape where Time and Warner were very much alike. Both were large players in cable television. In cable, the merger and the meeting of minds would be seamless, the possibilities great.

"We were in no-man's-land in cable," said Ross. "We were too small to be large and too big to be small." With the addition of Warner's systems, Time's cable operation would become a much larger second-largest in the land, able to challenge Malone's TCI for dominance. Ross would once again be a contender. To raise money, he had sold Viacom two channels originally developed for Qube, Nickelodeon and MTV; at Viacom, they proceeded to make Sumner Redstone a great deal of money. Now Ross would have HBO, one of the most valuable of all cable properties, finally living up to its potential. In cable, Warner and Time were a perfect match. Everywhere else, the accomplished and charming Steve Ross—with considerable assistance from his counterparts at Time—took his new partners to the cleaners.

Harry Luce, when his very considerable blind spots were set aside, was a man who knew what he did not know. Late in life, he tried LSD, to find out what all the fuss was about. As his successors merged with Warner, there were a great many things they did not know, but they seemed unaware of the gaps in their knowledge. Ross could have enlightened them, but they never asked him.

Ross could have told them that in Hollywood the film studios were the kings and the television operations were the vassals. When Ross spoke to Bob Daly and Terry Semel, the executives who ran Warner Brothers, he spoke to them as equals—and then only because he was chairman of the company. Daly and Semel were not going to take orders from Time, which didn't know how to make movies. Neither did Ross, but, like Harry Luce, Ross knew what he didn't know.

Ross could have told Time many other things. For example, he could have told Time that the record business was no place for a gentleman. Not only did record companies tend to know the same kind of people that parking lot companies knew—the kind of people who provided a steady flow of customers for another of Ross's early businesses, funeral homes—but Warner music was about to become heavily involved with gangsta rap, a musical genre whose obscene and racist lyrics, combined with the tendency of its stars to get indicted for things like murder, would soon cause national outrage.

When Ross went to Hollywood, he dined with Clint Eastwood

in opulent surroundings, lavished presents on Barbra Streisand, provided the talent with free corporate jets and free Acapulco vacations, and let the music and film operations run themselves—just as they ran themselves when he was not in Hollywood. The people at Time weren't interested in any of this. Nor were the Time people much interested in what Ross would do when he finally walked in the door. They wanted to do a deal, a huge, stockholder-pleasing deal. They wanted to place Time on the corporate map of the 1980s and harvest riches beyond the dreams of avarice, in some as yet unspecified way.

Jerry Levin, Time's resident genius and chief of strategic planning, attended to the details of the merger that interested Time and did not exceed his instructions. Oded Aboodi, an Iraqi Jew born in Israel, who did not officially work for Warner and was known as Ross's Rasputin, attended to the details that interested Ross. Of these, there were two. Ross was approaching the retirement age of sixty-five; how long would he remain with the company? And what would his titles and duties be? Unsatisfied with the response, Ross left the table vowing never to return, wept over what might have been but could not be, and was coaxed back by an anxious and forgiving Time. In February 1989 the deal was done. The companies would merge in a painless, tax-free exchange of stock. No money would pass from hand to hand. Ross would become chairman, yielding the position in a few years to Nick Nicholas. Ross would then proceed to pasture and enjoy his twilight years. Many people, including the people at Time, believed that this would actually happen. Their number did not include a man named Marty Davis.

From his office high above Columbus Circle, Paramount Communications chairman Martin Davis had watched the goings-on in Rockefeller Center with mounting interest. His company, founded by the late Charles Bluhdorn—known, not in a friendly way, as the "mad Austrian"—and formerly called Gulf+Western, had once owned a wildly diverse collection of companies that manufactured everything from automobile bumpers to mattresses. Davis had sold them all and pared the unwieldy company back to its core enterprises: the Paramount movie studios, the publishing house Simon & Schuster, and part ownership of a cable network. By 1989, the renamed Paramount Communications was sitting atop an immense mountain of surplus cash.

When Davis looked at Time Inc., he saw the same thing Ross had seen: a plumbing system. In Paramount Studios, Davis already owned a waterworks; Time's huge cable system would provide him with the pipes. He had a shrewd notion of what Ross was up to: despite what the press releases said or Time might have believed, Ross was getting Time for free. If Davis intervened, he could accomplish one of two things. Either he would seize Time for himself or he would force Time Warner to accumulate a huge amount of debt to repel him, crippling a dangerous competitor. In June, two weeks before the Time and Warner stockholders voted on the merger, Davis made a bid of $10.7 billion for Time, cash on the barrelhead, $175 a share, later raised to $200.

In Time's offices on Sixth Avenue, pandemonium reigned. In Warner's offices on Rockefeller Plaza, calm prevailed. Unless steps were taken, the immediate future was remarkably clear. The Time stockholders, who would make precisely nothing from the painless, cashless Time-Warner stock-swap merger, were certain to take Davis's money. Fortunately, the solution was equally obvious. Time would go to its bankers and buy Warner with $14 billion in borrowed money; a cash transaction would not require stockholder approval. Ross was agreeable. He was now buying Time with Time's own money, and if the revised deal went through, Ross and his stockholders would receive an extremely gratifying sum. The Time stockholders would still receive nothing.

Ross insisted on a further provision. No matter what happened— if Davis succeeded, if another buyer entered the race and offered even more for Time, or if Time was somehow able to escape its tormentor—Time still had to pay $14 billion for Warner. Time saw nothing strange about this, perhaps because its captains weren't thinking very clearly. The situation, Nick Nicholas exulted, was like "being strapped to a rocket that just left Cape Canaveral."

Time borrowed the money. After a journey through the Delaware courts and loud angry cries from its disenfranchised stockholders, Davis was repulsed. Time and Warner finally became Time Warner. Ross was its chairman. Nicholas was its president. The merged company was $16 billion in debt.

SIX

John Malone and the Laws of Physics

PARAMOUNT STUDIOS, AS IT HAPPENED, HAD ALSO AT-tracted the attention of John Malone. Whether he liked it or not, he was finally in the television business—the ESPN episode had taught him that, if nothing else—and the television business brought with it certain new requirements. He owned a huge pipeline. He needed a waterworks.

Malone's programming investments couldn't do it for him, exten-sive though they were. Not even the talented and now financially recovered Ted Turner could. Cable channels, although they had come to occupy an enormous amount of space on the home dial, still ap-pealed to niche audiences—on most cable channels, on the best nights they ever had, less than 1 percent of the viewing public. To make real money in the programming and production business, Malone required a whole new kind of programming and production vehicle.

True, cable—taken as a whole—had seriously chipped away at the viewership of the networks—there were four of them now, with Murdoch's Fox finally up and running. But the networks still owned the only mass television audience in the land. As a cable operator, Malone was forbidden to own a network—if push came to shove and the economics ever made sense, he could always use Turner as a stalking horse—but there was another and perhaps better way of getting into the television business. A movie studio was also a television studio, producing shows that reached the double-digit audience that was beyond the grasp of the cable channels. If Malone owned a movie studio, he would be able to take much larger bites from a much larger apple.

He could produce television shows and sell them to the networks for a fee—if the show was successful—that could be enormous. He would own the rebroadcasting rights and make a second pile of money. If another cable operator, such as Time Warner, picked up the program, he would be paid a royalty, a third source of income. TCI itself would be in an ideal position to negotiate substantial discounts, charge the viewers its usual rates, and make even more money. Naturally, TCI's studio would also produce films for theatrical release, and the whole cycle would begin all over again. He would own a film library and rent it out. He could do the same thing abroad. Rupert Murdoch was right. The world was mad for American films and television.

Steve Ross owned a movie studio. Murdoch owned a movie studio. Viacom's Sumner Redstone did not yet own a movie studio, but he owned a major television studio. Viacom's *Cosby Show* had made hundreds of millions, perhaps billions. It was a stupendous business.

Unfortunately, Malone knew nothing about it. For years, he had exercised his talents elsewhere, and he readily admitted that nobody at TCI was remotely capable of running a film operation or programming service of any kind. He would have to buy a studio, and the choices were limited. Sony owned Columbia and had bought TriStar, Matsushita owned MCA, and neither Japanese company was in a mood to sell. Disney, so recently the sick man of Hollywood, had become stunningly successful and was also not for sale. Malone visited Paramount and, he said, "jokingly" offered Marty Davis $70 a share for his company. Mr. Davis had other fish to fry, but he and Malone kept the line open. Malone entered into talks with MGM/UA, the studio that had briefly broken Ted Turner's spirit and bankroll. MGM was the new and very sick man of Hollywood, but the talks came to nothing. Malone kept looking.

OTHERWISE, IT WAS BUSINESS AS USUAL AT TCI. MALONE had celebrated the last years of the 1980s by doing what he had always done, buying cable systems. He paid $380 million for the operations of Jack Kent Cooke, who had brought the first big money into cable and recognized an opportunity to cash out when he saw it. Malone also paid close to $3 billion for control of United Artists Entertainment, a cable and theater operator that was not connected to the film studio of the same name; Malone briefly became the largest owner of cinema multiplexes in America. He also had his eye on the telephone business.

When the FCC announced in the late 1980s that it would not be entirely unfriendly if the telephone companies went into cable—in part because the commission wanted to give Malone some competition—Malone looked danger in the face and laughed. "All I want to know is," he said, "when are they going to let me provide telephone service? I could lay fiber optic faster than the telephone companies— they've got unions coming out of their ears." His father always said he had a big mouth. By all indications, Malone really did believe that TCI could become a telephone company, one of the cable industry's long and elusive dreams. His cash flow was still immense, the press repeatedly proclaimed his genius, and he still confused himself with a force of nature.

He paid the ESPN ransom and passed on the cost to its subscribers; Malone was averse to eating money he regarded as his own. If he had left it at that, everything might have been well, or at least different. His subscribers had already taken an enormous amount of Malone's guff, and no champion had stepped forth. Nor did a man who confused himself with a force of nature believe that the politician had been born who could lay a glove on him.

Malone tended to ignore the fact that the politicians he so detested hadn't walked into the Senate from the street, seated themselves at some empty desks, and announced that they represented, say, the state of Tennessee. Like many of his fellow conservatives, Malone seemed to view the government as something *out there*, an intrusive and alien force that existed solely to deliver the mail, protect him from the Russians, and prevent him from making all the money he was entitled to. The nation's 50 million cable customers, by contrast, appeared to be a hopelessly addicted bunch of powerless if sometimes annoying peasants who seemed to believe they were entitled to cheap television. As yet, no one had turned the restive masses of unsatisfied cable customers into a political constituency. In time-honored American fashion, this required three things: the writhing maiden fastened to the railroad tracks, representing the viewers; the hyperbolic villain, who gave himself all the best lines; and the stalwart hero with features of wood. In the absence of a single one of these elements, no political constituency could be formed. If John Malone had only kept his mouth shut, it might never have happened.

ALBERT GORE WAS SOMETHING OF AN ENVIRONMENTALIST, a bit of a techno-dweeb, and happened to be a senator from Tennessee. Around the time Malone was ordered by ESPN to put up or shut up, Senator Gore discovered that the good citizens of the Volunteer State had developed a huge problem with their cable companies, remarkably few of which Malone owned. For the senator and the king of cable, the paths of duty were clear. The senator, a man in search of an issue, was required to show fight. The king of cable, who had many more stockholders than himself and Bob Magness but seemed to forget the fact, was required to remain above the fray, display a lofty and impartial visage—and forcefully agree with Senator Gore, whereupon (if the history of the cable industry was any guide) nothing of any importance would happen. It wasn't in him.

Cable rates had risen all over the country, but nowhere in the country had cable rates risen as high as the ones in Tennessee, where they rocketed into the stratosphere for reasons that had remarkably little to do with television.

It is an axiom of economic booms that, as they approach their final stages, hot properties begin to sell at prices that defy the laws of reason and gravity. In the late 1980s, few properties were as hot as cable systems, and the cable systems watched by the people who elected Senator Gore were the hottest of them all. As Wall Street stood by with wheelbarrows full of extremely expensive money, eager entrepreneurs snapped up systems as though they were worth their weight in rubies—or, in the case of Tennessee, platinum. And when the entrepreneurs woke up the following morning with terrible, throbbing headaches, they arrived at a typical entrepreneur's deduction: the people who were going to pay for the consequences of the entrepreneur's stupidity were going to be the entrepreneur's new customers. In Tennessee, the customers did not agree, and word of a golden opportunity soon reached a receptive ear on Capitol Hill. One man's hot property had become another man's hot issue.

Subsequent events bear a resemblance to the old Yiddish folktale about God's twelve secret emissaries to Earth. No one knows who they are. They can be anyone at all—a homeless beggar, a golden-haired little girl, or an elected politician who sounds like a neurotic computer—but if a person harms a hair on an emissary's head, that person will soon find his household plumbing infected with the plagues of Egypt and the Almighty's war chariots drawn up on his lawn in battle array.

In attacking the new cable barons of Tennessee, Gore was performing constituent service. Constituent service meant that Gore was supposed to attack a man named Marty Pompadur. It was a seriously rattled Marty Pompadur, after all, who had bought the hot properties in Tennessee and woke up with the terrible, throbbing headache. Remarkably few people had ever heard of Marty Pompadur. To his delight, however, Senator Gore discovered that many people, some of them rich and a few of them powerful, had heard of John Charles Custer Malone. Gore's subsequent actions will surprise no student of American democracy.

Throwing red meat to his new audience of potential contributors and helpmates, Gore announced that Malone was the leader of the cable Cosa Nostra. What this had to do with the deplorable situation in Tennessee was a trifle obscure. Gore's enemy, as it was now Malone's agreeable task to point out, was a guy whose name sounded like a bad haircut. But Malone believed he was driving plate tectonics, and red meat was also bait.

"He called me Darth Vader . . . ," Malone said. "You can't win a pissing contest with a skunk, so there's no point in getting involved in that kind of rhetoric," added the man who just had. He sounded hurt, personally hurt. "They just don't have to be so personal about it."

It did not seem to occur to him that, no matter how much money he had, he was just a cable guy who had made an awful lot of enemies and remarkably few friends. Nor did his calculations seem to entertain the possibility that the man he had just called a skunk (he also called Gore a nut) would soon become Vice President of the United States.

It was true that no man, not even John Malone, could predict the future with any accuracy, but the prudent man took thought of likely possibilities. When it came to politics, Malone was not a prudent man. And there was much at stake.

The laissez-faire and devil-may-care Reagan administration had abandoned government regulation of cable television's rates. At the moment, TCI could charge its customers whatever the market would bear, and charging whatever the market would bear was important to Malone's version of TCI's ongoing prosperity. As long as cable rates continued to rise, TCI could borrow increasing amounts of money at favorable prices. If cable rates were to stabilize, borrowing cheap money would become more difficult. If cable rates were rolled back, the situation at TCI could become nasty; not only would borrowing money, any kind of money, become even more difficult, but it was possible that revenues would no longer cover the interest on the existing loans. As Malone often said, cable television was a creature of the government, and in America any government policy—such as the nonregulation of cable rates—could be reversed if a large enough constituency assembled. Senator Gore, the man with whom Malone had picked a gratuitous fight, was assembling a large constituency.

How it would all play out, the future would tell. In the meanwhile, the last years of the 1980s were a time when the script of John Malone's life underwent a drastic revision. ESPN had called his bluff. He and the future Vice President of the United States, like two angry drunks encountering each other in a darkened barroom, were locked in an embrace as comical as it was deadly. At this fascinating moment in his career, it was possible—probable, even—that Malone had never heard of Woo Paik. Outside a small corner of MIT and an equally small corner of the cable manufacturing business, almost nobody had ever heard of Woo Paik. He was the next somebody who was going to invent the next something that would once again change the industry forever. Provided Malone and the other cable guys could figure out how to make it work.

IN 1988, A SMALL SAN DIEGO OUTFIT CALLED VIDEO-Cipher—soon to be sold to General Instrument—suddenly realized that it had a huge and perhaps fatal problem on its hands. The Japanese had invented something called high-definition television, and they were once again marching on the American marketplace.

This, in itself, did not immediately alarm the people at Video-

Cipher; the company developed components for backyard satellite television dishes, a profitable but distinctly marginal part of the television business where the fearsome Japanese did not compete. After a little thought, however, the people at VideoCipher realized that there was horrible danger here. The HDTV signal was huge, much wider than the normal satellite broadcasting band. If HDTV became the new broadcasting standard in America—and few people doubted that it would—every backyard satellite dish in the country would become worthless. Backyard satellite dishes were already large and expensive. The new dishes would be enormous and very expensive. Almost nobody would buy one of them. VideoCipher's entire business was based on backyard dishes; it would be destroyed. There had to be a solution, some way around the problem, some way to compress the HDTV signal. The chiefs of VideoCipher asked one of their best engineers, a Korean émigré named Woo Paik, to find out what it was.

It was a situation that had its origins in technology, ego, and logic. The Japanese had invented HDTV, starting in the 1970s, as another example of their newfound world-beating industrial prowess, but they had also invented it to make a pot of money. Once HDTV was perfected, every television set in Japan would have to be replaced. The next step was obvious. If Japan could successfully export HDTV and take the world by storm, every television set in the world would have to be replaced, and the Japanese would manufacture many, most, or possibly all of them. High-definition television, unlike the previous leap forward into color television, was an entirely new kind of television.

A motion picture could be shown anywhere on earth, because the equipment was standardized. Television was not. America and Japan employed a format known as NTSC, which variously stood for the National Television Systems Committee or Never The Same Color. NTSC television used 525 interlaced lines. Most of Europe used PAL television, for Phase-Alternating Line, originally a superior format because the owners of color sets didn't have to continuously fiddle with the knobs. France, the Soviet Union, and some former French colonies used SECAM, for Séquential Couleur Avec Mémoire or Something Essentially Contrary to America. PAL and SECAM deployed 625 lines. But no matter what the system, existing television was based on the finest technology of the 1930s; the standards for American television broadcasting had been written in 1941. The screen of a television set was modeled on the screen in a Depression-era movie theater. Modern wide-screen movies had to be cut, pasted, and sometimes reshot before they could be presented for home viewing, and the introduction of color in the 1950s had been nothing but a quick and extremely expensive fix. The 1941 standards were not changed. Color was simply painted over something that remained, underneath, a black-and-white image. HDTV changed all this.

A normal television image was the equivalent of a movie shot on 16 millimeter film. The much clearer, more vivid theatrical motion picture was shot with 35-millimeter film, a standard the Japanese sought to equal or better by doubling the number of lines painted onto the television screen. They also made the screen wider and narrower, like a contemporary theater screen. The picture was remarkably clear, and to the casual eye it appeared to be almost three-dimensional. It was also completely incompatible with any television set in the world. And there was more. Because the new electronic technology of HDTV was as good as or better than the old mechanical and chemical technology of Hollywood filmmaking, the Japanese could replace every camera in Hollywood, and because HDTV was transmitted by cheap, efficient broadcast waves rather than the vastly expensive Hollywood system that delivered clumsy reels of film to American theaters, the Japanese could finally crack the American stranglehold on one of the two major industries (the other was aircraft manufacture) that had proven impervious to attack. They owned the HDTV technology, they were poised to manufacture the necessary equipment, and for the first time they had a compelling reason to take over a big hunk of Hollywood and run it themselves. Or so they thought.

In 1989, Sony paid $4 billion for Columbia Pictures, a turkey of a studio that hadn't cut much of a swath for decades. The more cautious Matsushita followed shortly thereafter with its $6 billion purchase of MCA, the home of Universal, a studio as venerated as Columbia was reviled. The payoff, it seemed, was just around the corner. From the perspective of Hollywood, however, the situation looked very different. Like the city councils that had watched the cable companies parading before them with open wallets and hats in hand, Hollywood took stock of the newcomers and a single word formed in the film capital's collective mind: prey.

Five years later, Sony took a stunning $3.2 billion write-down on its Columbia studio, which meant that the company had managed to lose $3.2 billion in what had seemed a surefire investment. Shortly thereafter Matsushita, always a company to upstage its rival, sold most of Universal to the Seagram distilling company and fled screaming back to Osaka, bleeding copiously from every pore. The Japanese had no idea how to make American movies, and they had hired Americans who either took them to the cleaners or burned haystacks of their money. Elsewhere in America, HDTV did not fare a heck of a lot better. To the television broadcasters, HDTV looked like the worst idea since the electric fork.

The huge HDTV signal occupied five normal television channels. Many broadcasts would be crowded into the high-number and least desirable part of the dial, there would be far fewer channels, and many broadcasters, unable to obtain space, would go out of business. Next, because HDTV was an entirely new kind of television, the surviving broadcasters would have to spend billions on new equipment at a time when they had significantly less money. Among many other problems, HDTV reached the viewers from a satellite. This was fine in Japan, where there was only one broadcaster, NHK, and NHK made its money from license fees paid by viewers, but it was not fine in America, where the broadcasters made their money from advertisers. In America, local broadcasts were not permitted on satellites. And without local broadcasts, many local advertisers would abandon the medium or reduce their expenditures; the American television industry was being invited to shrink, spend immense amounts of money, and turn their backs on thousands of companies that paid their bills. Last, every viewing household in the country would have to spend many hundreds or thousands of dollars to buy a new television set. No one knew for certain how the viewing public would react to this news, but the prognosis was not good. From an economic point of view, HDTV made no sense whatever. It looked like suicide.

At this point in the proceedings, however, the Motorola Corporation introduced a concept called Land Mobile, and the whole game took on a strange new form. From the broadcasters' point of view, Land Mobile was horribly dangerous. Unfortunately, Land Mobile, unlike HDTV, made a great deal of sense.

Led by Motorola, the users of land-based mobile communications systems—police and fire departments, ambulance services, air traffic controllers, and pizza parlors, for whom Motorola manufactured most of the radios—approached the FCC with a simple and compelling idea. Their sector of the broadcasting spectrum was crowded, many of the available frequencies were noisy, the mobile communications business was growing, and there was one sure way to serve the public good. The television broadcasters were sitting atop a wide band of empty spectrum, had absolutely no use for it and never would, and Land Mobile needed it badly. This argument gave the television broadcasters a lot of trouble. For one thing, it was true.

A number of the television channels in the desirable very-high-frequency band—numbers 1 through 13 on the dial, prime beachfront property in industry parlance—were protected from signal leakage by empty channels that functioned like windbreaks. The Land Mobile people wanted these channels for their own use. Higher up in the spectrum, in the ultra-high-frequency range—everything above 13—the landscape slowly deteriorated from middle-class suburbs to burned-out slums, at least from the broadcasters' point of view. The deeper into UHF territory they went, the harder it was to broadcast a reasonable television signal. Much of this property, too, was both vacant and usable by mobile communications. The Land Mobile people quite reasonably pointed out that the television broadcasters weren't using any of this empty land, had no plans to ever use it, and it was urgently needed for lifesaving radio transmissions. The FCC was inclined to agree. The broadcasters hit the ceiling.

Although the broadcasting spectrum was owned by the American public, a curious policy had prevailed for decades. If a prospective broadcaster could prove he was well capitalized and if he promised to serve the public interest—a concept flexible to the point of invisibility—he would receive a broadcasting slot for free, provided no competitive bidder arrived with even more money and even more heroic vague promises of public service. Once a broadcaster received a slot, he usually occupied it forever if he kept his nose clean and didn't lose his shirt—and here, too, the definitions were extremely flexible. By and large, a secure position in a desirable part of the broadcasting spectrum was a license to coin money. Cable was already a proven threat to this golden livelihood; cable, although divided into a myriad of tiny niches, had already stolen a third of the audience. Now Land Mobile had appeared with its entirely reasonable proposal. Land Mobile wasn't threatening to take away the audience, at least not directly. But Land Mobile confronted the broadcasters with a danger whose name they dared not speak.

Land Mobile transmissions might cause interference, causing even more viewers to migrate to cable, and this could not be allowed to happen. Far worse, it might finally occur to the government that broadcast spectrum was worth something, a very great deal of something, and the government would begin charging rent; once the battle was joined, the debate could easily—and horrifyingly—head in that direction, with possible consequences that were unthinkable.

Moreover, America, an emotional country, had fallen into one of its irrational moods, and the broadcasters were not exempt. Many of them seemed to have convinced themselves, in the mystical way of such things, that their right to the spectrum had been bestowed by God himself. It was theirs, by jingo, and they would fight. Unfortunately, their cupboard was depressingly bare of armaments.

They weren't using the empty spectrum. They didn't need it, they didn't want it, and they had nothing to put on it. At this point, visions of HDTV began to dance in the broadcasters' heads. The seductive, crystal-clear images of HDTV gobbled up an enormous amount of spectrum. Without the empty spectrum, now threatened by the eminently reasonable arguments of a bunch of police departments, pizza barons, and a radio manufacturer, the broadcasters could not bring the miracle of HDTV to the American people.

The broadcasters still had no intention of bankrupting themselves by adopting high-definition television, but there was no point in telling the public servants that. Everything now depended on persuading the government that the broadcasting industry panted for HDTV as the hart pants for the water-brook. Later, they could declare the experiment a failure—or, better yet, premature—and chuck the whole thing.

HDTV sets and technicians were imported to Washington. Demonstrations were given. The FCC was remarkably unmoved, bad news for the broadcasters. But the broadcasters had also attracted the attention of a number of legislators, none of whom knew the faintest useful thing about electronic engineering, and the legislators made a delightful vote-getting and nation-saving discovery of the sort that is manna in the political desert. In its present form, HDTV was Japanese. "This," announced Senator Gore, "is the Battle of the Bulge for electronics!"

It is difficult now, at the remove of a decade, to remember the intensity of American emotions on the subject of Japan in the late 1980s. Japanese VCRs were sledgehammered into useless scrap on national television by people who resembled everybody's mom and grandparents. A few luckless Japanese-like people, who almost invariably weren't Japanese, were killed because they looked Japanese. Loud maledictions rent the air when the Japanese bought Rockefeller Center and the Pebble Beach golf course. It occurred to almost no one, least of all the Japanese, that the Rockefeller family had just sold the Japanese investors the second-best thing to a very large bridge.

For a time, it was very hard to think clearly about the Japanese. As it happened, it was also very hard for almost everybody but the broadcasters to think clearly about HDTV. HDTV was the wave of the future. Unless the country could invent and manufacture its own form of HDTV, the American economy was doomed. So, back in the real world and to the broadcasters' delight, was Land Mobile. Choosing their psychological moment with care, the broadcasters pressed their advantage.

In 1987, they petitioned the FCC. In the interest of eviscerating their bottom line, enraging their advertisers, and dismaying their viewers, the broadcasters asked the commission to grant each of them, free, an entire second television channel, the better to pass a miracle they had every intention of strangling in its crib. The following year, a very worried VideoCipher asked Woo Paik to save the company from certain ruin.

PAIK, KOREAN BY BIRTH, MIT BY EDUCATION, WAS A large, amiable, and confident man, methodical and hard to excite. It never seemed to occur to him that he couldn't solve a problem, and with HDTV, the problem was clear: to receive HDTV in its present form, the backyard satellite dish would have to be at least twenty feet in diameter. The solution was equally obvious. Working alone or with a few picked associates, Paik would have to invent a new form of HDTV.

VideoCipher was a small part of a much larger company, tucked into the lower left-hand corner of the country. Nobody else had the remotest idea of what Paik was up to, including his old friend Jae Lim—they had been the only Koreans in their class at MIT—who now headed the Institute's Center for Advanced Television Studies. Lim, too, was attempting to invent a new form of HDTV. He had a small staff of graduate students and almost no money to speak of. In their occasional calls back and forth across the country, Lim told his classmate about the almost insurmountable difficulties he faced. Paik had always been a much better poker player than Lim. He listened, but he did not mention his own work.

Lim's relatively impoverished Center for Advanced Television Studies (CATS) had begun to receive funds and equipment from Nicholas Negroponte's Media Lab. The ambitious Negroponte was steadily building his empire. Unlike Lim, he had plenty of money, a staff of well-paid computer experts, and access to very expensive state-of-the-art scientific apparatus, some of it donated. He had everything Lim needed, including the requisite vision. Given Negroponte's considerable abilities as a propagandist and his deep pockets, it would have been child's play for him to place MIT at the cutting edge of television research.

For once, Negroponte had seen the future with accuracy as well as his customary and forceful clarity. His chance had come, his chance to place the Lab on the cutting edge of science, to participate in a future whose arrival was imminent, and to silence, perhaps forever, the critics who had begun to say that said the Lab was not a serious undertaking, that it was run by an egomaniac playing with his toys while gulling his contributors out of bales of money. He blew it.

It was possible, Negroponte insisted, to digitize a television signal. He had shrewd doubts about HDTV and eventually came to scorn it, but there was no doubt in his mind about the future of television. Digital was the way to go. Like so many of the things he said, it was not a popular view among—in this case—people who knew a great deal about television signals. Digital television, a CBS executive told Congress as late as 1990, defied the laws of physics. Another industry figure flatly stated that digital television would arrive around the same time as the antigravity belt. There were a number of sound reasons for thinking so.

Television, like radio, was based on an analog signal that mimicked the light waves and sound waves that brought sight and hearing to the human eye and ear. To digitize the signal meant that the electronic image would be converted into binary code, the code could be converted into a stream of electrons, and the electrons would be sent to a television set, which would decode them and display a picture. It was theoretically possible—it did not, in fact, defy the laws of physics—but there was a seemingly insurmountable reason for not doing it.

Digital television required vast computational power at the broadcasting end to encode the digital signal, and it required an equally vast amount of computational power at the receiver to decode it. Even if such a thing could be done, the cost would be prohibitive if not ridiculous. With customary optimism and flair, Negroponte and the Media Lab proposed to solve the problem by making it even more complicated. The answer, they said, was digital compression.

COMPRESSING THE INFORMATION FLOWING THROUGH A telecommunications system was at least as old as the telephone, when Thomas Alva Edison invented the word "hello" to settle the hash of Alexander Graham Bell—who preferred "ahoy!"—while solving once and for all, in a neat and economical manner, the question of what someone said when he picked up the receiver. Many years later, Claude Shannon of Bell Labs, the father of modern information theory, took up the question again.

Digital technology, Shannon reasoned, would allow whole sections of a binary signal to go missing while it was being transmitted. It was not necessary to send, for example, an entire well-known word, phrase, or name. Instead, it would be possible for the software at the transmitting end to send the letters M-I-K-Y-M-O-U. The software at the receiving end would fill in the blanks. Shannon, writing in the late 1940s, had been a little ahead of his time, but Negroponte believed the time had finally come.

The Media Lab proposed to take Shannon's theory and apply it to television images. With digital compression, a broadcaster would send, say, a picture of two people conversing in a room. Afterward, it would only have to send a fraction of the image. Unlike analog television, which re-sent the entire picture of the room thirty times a second, the compressed digital image would be like a picture hung on a wall. The room would be painted on the television screen, and the transmitter would send a new image only when someone or something moved, the lighting was altered, or the camera changed its position. As much as 90 percent of the actual scene would be missing from the signal, and the eye would not detect it.

Because the compressed digital signal was small and tight, as many as four or six or, theoretically, thousands of signals could be sent down a broadcast channel, a coaxial cable, or a fiber-optic filament where only one analog signal had fit before. The size of the signal would vary with its content; in the words of the digitally literate, a compressed digital signal was "scalable." Because of its rich visual images and complex action, a movie like *Schindler's List* would require a great deal of digital real estate, but a talk show, with its single set and limited motion, would not. While transmitting a talk show, a broadcaster could use the same channel to send even more digital signals, for paging services, for radio and telephones, for anything that could be converted into binary code.

Because a digital signal was very quiet while an analog signal was very noisy, the buffering channels—the windbreaks—could now be used for transmissions. Because a digital stream of electrons was identical with all other digital streams of electrons except in size, it was possible to use the progressively more difficult frequencies at the higher end of the broadcast spectrum as though they were ordinary television, telephone, or data channels. The airwaves, once a scarce resource, would become a mother lode—to use another buzzword, a "communicopia"—of clear, crisp, easily usable signals. Using the same technology, the terrestrial cable companies would find that their coaxial cables had been turned from garden hoses into fire hoses. But there was, as usual, a catch.

Digital compression required even vaster computational power. Moreover, technological breakthroughs that looked great on paper and performed superbly in the lab had a way of not working very well, or at all, in a workaday environment where people spilled beer on things. Once again, it looked as though Negroponte and the Media Lab were looking at a remote possibility and seeing an immediate certainty. But Negroponte and the Lab were not only on the right track, they were actually ahead of the curve. The problem could be solved.

In the MIT Center for Advanced Television Studies, the impoverished Jae Lim, working on his own version of HDTV, had caught a glimpse of the solution and believed he knew his way to it. All that was needed, it seemed, was to combine Lim's skills and insights with the vaster resources of the Media Lab, its backstopping computer scientists, and Negroponte's powers of persuasion, and the Lab would have its moment of glory. Thanks to the farseeing vision of its founder and the genius of Jae Lim, the Media Lab would invent digital television. Which was where the next error crept into the data.

The American corporate sponsors of Lim's CATS, although close with their money, insisted that it was an American effort for the benefit of American engineers and the advancement of American television. Moreover, Lim, a naturalized citizen, was an ardent nationalist. Negroponte, by contrast, insisted that everything done under the auspices of the Media Lab had to be shared with the Lab's corporate sponsors—and, in the case of digital television, CATS would have to share its secrets with the Japanese. Sony, a large contributor to the Lab, was mentioned. The American sponsors of CATS were adamant in their refusal, and Lim, the nationalist, was unmovable. Whatever Lim came up with belonged to America. Digital television was not invented at the Media Lab, and Lim didn't invent it either.

THE LEARNING CURVE HAD BEEN STEEP, BUT IN SAN Diego, Paik finally had his arms around the problem. He hadn't known what a modem was, and he had to look up the word in a dictionary. His thinking, however, paralleled Negroponte's and Jae Lim's. In order to solve the satellite dish problem, he decided, Video-Cipher would have to invent digital television. Then he would have to compress the signal. He was given a lab, ordered to drop everything else, and assemble a team. The survival of the company was at stake.

IN WASHINGTON, WHERE NOTHING WAS KNOWN OF THE desperate—or, as far as Paik was personally concerned, calm and methodical—events in San Diego, a contest was underway at the FCC. Any company or institution that thought it could create an HDTV system was invited to step forward and compete, provided it could meet certain requirements. Entering the race would cost each contestant $175,000, nonrefundable. There would be an equally nonrefundable $200,000 testing fee as the FCC determined the quality of the entry. There was a daunting requirement: somehow, the huge HDTV signal would have to be modified to fit down the pipe of a single existing television channel, a feat that was likened to squeezing an elephant into a bathtub.

On June 1, 1990, the number of contenders had been reduced from fourteen to seven, among them Japan's NHK, Bell Labs, and MIT's forlorn and bankrupt CATS. The Japanese system was still pure analog television. The others had produced versions that were mostly analog but contained some digital software and components. Meanwhile, laboring in obscurity in San Diego, Woo Paik and his scratch team had invented compressed digital television. At Video-Cipher, a question arose: now what were they supposed to do? In all probability, the company had been saved by a radical and unexpected breakthrough dreamed up by a guy working down in the basement, but it was a broadcasting technology. VideoCipher and its parent, General Instrument, were hardware companies, not broadcasters. The companies hesitated.

At the last possible moment, Paik's system was entered in the

Washington contest, and almost immediately the nation's editorialists were thunderstruck with glee. The Japanese, after spending at least a billion dollars and almost certainly much more, had been decisively defeated. Analog HDTV was hopelessly obsolete. American ingenuity, coming out of nowhere like Spruance's outnumbered carrier planes at Midway, had carried the day. In 1990, when an American technological advance was combined with a resounding Japanese defeat, it was hard to remain calm, choose one's words with care and tact, and understand what had actually happened.

The reality of the situation was neither so neat nor so clean. Many unanticipated years would pass—the better part of a decade, in fact—before digital HDTV would be ready for over-the-air broadcasting. But Paik's system seemed to work just fine on cable television, where it would allow many hundreds of new channels. In the cable business, HDTV was, at best, an afterthought, but the promise of an immediate payoff appeared to be enormous.

If it could be made to work as advertised, digital television would enable the cable companies to steal a huge march on the broadcasters, and the Wired World would become reality at last. Digital television gave John Malone one of the best ideas he ever had: once he had carefully prepared the ground, he could sell TCI for an immense amount of money and make himself a billion dollars. It also gave him the worst idea he had ever had in his life: once he had prepared the ground, and if he was unable to sell TCI for an immense amount of money, he would actually have to install digital television on his systems, or try to. In the meanwhile, he decided to buy Paramount Studios even if Paramount didn't want to be bought. Where Paramount was concerned, he had been a nice guy long enough.

SEVEN

The Shark Goes Fishing

THE YEAR 1990 WAS NOT KIND TO JOHN MALONE. THE government was no longer indifferent. Wall Street was no longer his happy and contented friend. These two events were not unrelated. One was temporary, and the other was not.

All the old rules were changing, but Malone did not change with them. In most important ways, he and TCI were still the same as they had been in the 1970s, except that they cut a much wider swath, were a little older, and were considerably more disliked by a far greater number of people. He was still the king of the hill; his cable systems were the largest in the country. He still had no movie studio, but he was soon observed in the vicinity of Sony Pictures and MCA. Clearly, his ambitions along those lines continued to burn brightly, and further developments were expected. He still had his reputation as the smartest guy in the business and on occasion he could still move with his former adroitness, but as the new decade began, a kind of entropy set in. It was not that his rivals grew smarter; it was as though he began to lose points off his intellect the way others lost hair. Like the Roaring Twenties, the Roaring Eighties had ended abruptly as though on cue, and Malone could not adapt.

IN WASHINGTON, THE FORMERLY DEDICATED FREE marketeers of the Bush administration gazed upon the accomplishments of their predecessors and experienced a well-mannered, carefully disguised, and extremely bad moment. The debt-fueled buying spree of the 1980s, the savings and loan calamity, and the ensuing collapse of the real estate market had hollowed out whole sectors of the national economy. For the first time in sixty years, the country was experiencing a free-falling deflation and no man knew how it would end. Three of the largest banks in the country—Citicorp, Chase Manhattan, and Bank of America—were arithmetically insolvent, which meant that three of the largest banks in the country were broke. A genuine, old-time depression was possible—not one of the mild, painful, but easily managed recessions that had prevailed since the reforms of the demonic Franklin Roosevelt, but a full-bore, mouth-of-hell collapse from which the country might not recover for a decade and the reputation of the Republican Party would almost certainly not recover until everyone now living was dead.

It had happened before, the last time the banks were broke. Suddenly discovering unexpected virtues in the wisdom of their fathers, the members of the Bush administration decided that they hated debt. In the language of the flowers, debt was called leverage, and the members of the Bush administration decided that they especially hated highly leveraged transactions, called HLTs. The members of the Bush administration made their feelings known to the banks. Malone and TCI lived on highly leveraged transactions. He was not amused.

"They just came in with a very broad definition, okay, of what an

HLT is, that looked entirely at historical balance sheets," he complained, "and didn't look at all at the basis upon which media loans are made. In media loans, the balance sheet is meaningless. The government is fishing for tuna and catching porpoises." It was hard to believe the 1980s were dead, or that someone might have been seriously wrong.

There was an easy solution, a very old one. While Malone waited for the government to come to its senses, he borrowed his money in Europe, the traditional resort of an American company with a terrible balance sheet. But even after the government recovered from its fit of nerves, there was only a marginal improvement in the situation. Malone had to cope with an unfriendly Wall Street, and Wall Street, having suddenly changed its mind about how the world ran, refused to change it back.

Wall Street no longer loved him; with the arrival of a new decade, Malone's repeated lessons and home truths about cash flow, depreciation, and borrowed money were no longer operative. In a time of bear markets and financial retrenchment, Wall Street had experienced one of its periodic Great Awakenings.

The Street had never understood TCI, but previously its inhabitants had taken their own blank incomprehension as a sign of Malone's enduring genius. After all, the guy said he was making a lot of money. Now, in cheese-paring times, the Street badly wanted to know how much TCI was actually worth, where it was going, and what it would do when it got there, and the few clear figures it could shake out of Malone's boxes-within-boxes were not encouraging.

TCI's indebtedness was somewhere in the vicinity of $9.5 billion, and Wall Street had rediscovered a truth more timeless than Malone's facile explanations: debt was something that had to be repaid, and TCI's ability to repay its creditors was shrinking toward the vanishing point. Back in 1980, when Malone began a buying spree that made him the gatekeeper of his industry, TCI generated ten cents for every dollar of its capital. In 1989, the year of the ESPN ultimatum, TCI generated three cents. Here, the newly alert and gingered-up financial analysts found something they understood, although it had been staring them in the face for years. Unless Malone did something and did it soon, TCI was locked in a debt-upon-debt cycle. To repay his loans, he would have to borrow money, and he no longer had much of a cushion. Wall Street was no longer amused by John Malone. When Wall Street was not amused, the credit markets were not amused. When the credit markets were not amused, they charged more for the use of their money. With Malone trapped in the loop of a debt-upon-debt cycle, the more money he borrowed, the more it would cost, and the end would be in sight.

It was amazing what the financial analysts could find once they buckled down to work. Malone had certainly bought a lot of things over the years—his purchases were one of the many reasons he had recently been the darling of the Street—but most of them also came equipped with heavy loads of debt. Moreover, as far as the analysts could figure out, Malone's investments made TCI no money at all. In fact, the investments actually lost TCI money as the company poured in more cash to cover its new obligations. In the gospel according to Malone, this was all as it should be, and the real money would be made as the investments grew in value. Here, too, the news was not good. In 1988, TCI could have sold its media investments—at least the ones that could be found, counted, and were liquid enough to sell—for an estimated profit of $248 million. In the bear market year of 1990, the potential for profit had shrunk to $184 million. Perhaps it would recover, but Wall Street was not overly fond of surefire investments that betrayed a tendency to shrink.

Last on Wall Street's bill of particulars (but first in the minds of its countrymen), there was the business that TCI was actually supposed to be engaged in: supplying television to the masses. Only one-sixth of TCI's growth came from new subscribers to its existing cable systems. Two-thirds of the growth came from Malone's acquisitions, and the remaining 17 percent came from the periodic increases in the monthly cable bills. Malone had no new services that might attract the recalcitrant viewers—35 percent—who never bought cable, he would lose his ability to purchase viewers when he ran out of cable systems to buy, and Senator Gore had not gone away. The senator, having been handed his issue of nationwide importance and his obliging villain on a silver platter, had frozen on Malone's ankle like a terrier.

Senator Gore was no longer a one-man band. Many people, it turned out, were ticked off at their cable systems, even when their cable system wasn't TCI. Vote-getting national issues, like large and generous contributors, had a way of attracting the attention of politicians, and Gore's bandwagon was now thickly populated with suitably indignant legislators. The reregulation of cable seemed only a matter of time. With reregulation, TCI would lose its ability to increase its television prices at will. It was entirely possible that TCI would be ordered to lower them. TCI's cash flow could collapse, and the game would be up.

Still, Malone had some breathing room. The political situation could change. It was impossible to estimate when Malone would no longer be able to buy cable systems, but the moment had not arrived. All bear markets end; when the market kicked into reverse and the bull defeated the bear, the value of Malone's investments would begin to rise again. Unfortunately, all—or most—of his other problems would remain, including a problem about which Malone never spoke: a large number of his cable systems, milked of their money for years, were obsolete. Bringing them up to speed would cost hundreds of millions, if not billions, of dollars. Adapting them for Paik's new digital television would cost billions more. The money would have to be borrowed.

Malone could always let the matter ride, of course—he had let the matter ride for years—but there was no telling what Senator Gore, Congress's loudest technophile, and his growing number of allies would do. Malone found the solution in the place he always did: the very financial markets that would almost certainly kick the stuffing out of TCI, its aging systems, and its mounting debt. Through a creative use of the financial markets, Malone would abandon TCI to its fate.

When the bear market ended, TCI's programming investments—alone of just about everything it owned—would once again become hot properties. It would be a golden moment. Malone could get out of the plumbing business with a whole skin and a fat wallet.

THE RESULT WAS A MASTERPIECE OF LEGAL HUMOR. Malone gathered together most of his programming interests, spun them off into a supposedly separate company, and called it Liberty Media. One of his purposes, he said, was to make TCI's assets more comprehensible to investors. Another purpose, according to informed speculation, was to split up TCI before the government did it for him. His most obvious primary purpose, however, was the vast enrichment of John Malone, allowing him—if it became necessary—to lay rubber and go squealing off into the night, leaving his TCI stockholders in possession of a very large bag.

Once the spin-off was completed in 1991, Liberty was an independent company under color of law. Under color of reality, it was a well-hedged bet. Malone and Magness controlled it. TCI people ran it. It would be a simple matter for TCI to reabsorb it. It would be an equally simple matter for Liberty to go its separate way. And if John Malone had created Liberty to make TCI's former programming assets more comprehensible and attractive to investors other than himself, he went about it in a very odd way.

For starters, the Liberty prospectus—the document that described the deal and set forth its alleged benefits—was 337 intricate pages long, roughly ten times the length of a normal prospectus. Reading it was work, a very great deal of work, and far more work than many potential investors were willing to undertake, especially because only the most seasoned of potential investors could understand it without help, and most people could not understand it at all.

The deal was not a spin-off in the usual sense of the word. In a spin-off, an investor in the original parent company (here, TCI) receives a share, a number of shares, or a fraction of a share in the new entity to compensate him for the fact that an asset of the parent company has departed, but the TCI-Liberty deal was something called an exchange offer. In an exchange offer, an investor trades his shares in the old company for shares in the new one, reducing or eliminating his prior holding. In the Liberty deal, the TCI stockholders were invited to surrender 16 shares of TCI, a company most people didn't understand very well, for a single share in Liberty, a company that had been made almost impossible to understand. The principal beneficiaries were Malone and Bob Magness.

Anyone who managed to wade through the prospectus would have discovered that Malone and Magness intended to trade at least half their respective holdings in TCI, a company with a world of mounting troubles, for a substantial piece of Liberty, a company that now contained TCI's most desirable assets. For Malone and Magness, this was all well and good, but for the other potential investors, there was a very interesting catch. Liberty would issue only a small number of shares, and the shares were expected to trade in the vicinity of $250. The price, TCI explained, was justified by the extraordinary value of Liberty divided by the few fortunate souls who would be able to take advantage of the opportunity. Perhaps, but there was also an unfortunate fact that TCI tactfully chose not to mention. Most investors want to be able to sell their stock at a known or predictable price. With only a handful of shares trading in three figures, Liberty would be an illiquid stock—it would not trade vigorously or often, its posted price might have little or nothing to do with the price a share would actually fetch, and it might not be possible to sell it at all. Liberty was not the sort of stock most people wanted to own. It was, however, exactly the sort of stock John Malone wanted to own. Remarkably few people but Magness and Malone were going to buy into Liberty, a circumstance that perfectly suited Malone's purpose. His purpose was to play a lucrative game of three-dimensional chess.

Although he and Magness controlled TCI through the Class B stock, Malone actually owned only 1 percent of the company, a holding worth $28 million. Exercising his exchange rights, he traded half his stock and received 61,000 shares of Liberty, a holding that represented 8.5 percent of the new company. If the TCI stockholders had exercised all of their exchange rights, he would have owned 1 percent. But the nearly incomprehensible nature of the exchange offer, combined with the illiquidity designed into the Liberty stock, prevented the TCI stockholders from exercising all their rights. Malone was already ahead of the game.

At this point, things began to get even more interesting. According to Malone, he allowed himself to be persuaded to take the Liberty chairmanship. For reasons never properly explained, the TCI board was unable to fill the job in any other way, although it required only one day of work each week. Malone agreed to serve without pay and received an option to buy an additional 100,000 Liberty shares over the next ten years at a per-share price of $256. No sooner had Malone occupied his new position and received his options than he discovered a hitherto unsuspected problem, and he hurried to the Liberty board with his newfound concerns. For tax reasons, he said, he wanted to exercise all his options at once. The understanding board gave its consent—whereupon Malone began to turn himself from a centimillionaire into a near-billionaire.

The price of Malone's options was $25.6 million. To pay a portion of the bill, he sold Liberty his personal holding in the QVC shopping channel for $100,000. This was hardly a great sacrifice. Because Liberty had a large stake in QVC, because Malone controlled Liberty as its chairman, and because Malone was a substantial Liberty stockholder who was about to become an even more substantial stockholder, he essentially sold his QVC shares to himself. His outstanding bill now stood at $25.5 million, and Malone was just warming up.

In a second transaction, he sold Liberty 800,000 of his remaining shares in TCI—moving even more of his money out of TCI—for $12.5 million. Because Malone still controlled TCI, because Liberty was still a part of TCI in fact if not in law, and because Malone controlled Liberty, he had, in effect, sold himself another block of his own stock. He then gave Liberty a promissory note for his outstanding balance and set out to improve the situation further.

Malone now controlled 22 percent of Liberty. Because he had paid only $256 for each of his new Liberty shares and the market price had reached $330, he had also made a $7.4 million paper profit without stirring from his chair. But despite the marketplace reward that Malone had so effortlessly received, the Liberty stock continued to trade at a discount (when it traded at all) because a number of Liberty's programming companies were themselves illiquid: they were privately held, and the marketplace couldn't figure out what they were worth. With Liberty's encouragement, a number of such companies—including Black Entertainment Television and the Family Channel—suddenly saw a blinding light, issued stock, and produced documents describing what they did for a living, how they did it, and how much money they made, making themselves (and Liberty) much easier to understand. The timing was impeccable. The bear market was over and investors were mad for programming stocks. Liberty owned quite a lot of them, and they were all wonderfully comprehensible thanks to Malone's timely suggestion. It was now time for an inspired maneuver.

Thanks to the prohibitively high price of Liberty's stock, Malone had been able to effortlessly accumulate nearly a quarter of the company while reducing his TCI holding to a shadow of its former self, whereupon—through a mysterious exercise that can be charitably described as circular thinking—he stumbled upon an astonishing insight. The price of Liberty's stock, he concluded, was too high by an order of magnitude.

Making a mockery of all previous pronouncements on the subject, Malone split the stock 20-for-one, then 4-for-one, and finally 2-for-one, creating many relatively cheap shares of stock where only a few very expensive ones had existed before. Liberty was no longer an illiquid stock. By early 1993, Liberty's market value approached $3.5

billion, somewhere between seventeen and twenty times its value in 1991, and Malone's stock was worth somewhere between $600 and $840 million. Meanwhile, the market value of TCI, the company Malone had largely left behind, grew only two and a half times. If his fortune had remained concentrated in TCI, Malone would have been worth a beggarly $125 million. And still Malone was not done. If he was destined to leave the cable business—as increasingly seemed likely—he was determined to leave it as an even wealthier man.

THE VEHICLE FOR HIS NEW AMBITIONS WAS QVC, THE shopping channel Liberty controlled in partnership with Comcast and, just recently come aboard, Barry Diller, widely referred to as the most successful executive in recent Hollywood history. QVC's only competitor, the Home Shopping Network, had complained—and its owner had testified before Congress—that TCI had a policy of shutting HSN out of its cable systems, but the problem was neatly solved in 1992, when Liberty bought HSN and achieved something that resembled a death grip on televised home shopping. The marketplace loved clever Liberty all the more, and Malone's stake in Liberty became even more valuable. It also became useful.

Malone had always used his TCI stock as a private currency; the more valuable the stock, the more things Malone was able to buy, handing over private certificates rather than public ones. The price of a stock also resembled a real estate assessment; a company that issued valuable stock, like a company that owned a corner lot on the busiest crossroads in town, could borrow a great deal of money. With the newly liquid Liberty one of the darlings of a revived stock market, Malone was in a position to buy a movie studio without using TCI at all. By a happy chance, a variant of the same thought had occurred to Barry Diller.

AT NO PREVIOUS POINT IN A LIFETIME DEVOTED TO television and the movies had Diller shown any particular interest in or profound understanding of the sort of financial engineering where Malone excelled—Diller had made television programs and movies and made them very well indeed—but he was a man with a long memory.

At ABC in the 1960s and early 1970s, Diller had created the made-for-television movie of the week and otherwise exercised his creative genius, doing much to propel the network from a third-place also-ran into a powerhouse that took top billing while making a great deal of money for his chief, Leonard Goldenson. In the 1970s, he had turned Paramount into the hottest studio in Hollywood. In the 1980s, he had done much to turn the Fox network—at first, something that looked like a certain failure—into a going proposition, vastly enriching Rupert Murdoch.

After years of placing his talents at the service of others, Diller had sworn a mighty vow that he would never work for anyone else again as long as he lived. If he ran a company, he wanted to own it, as he owned a large piece of QVC, although QVC seemed to be a very odd place for a man of his talents and accomplishments. People had always stared at him when he lunched at the Four Seasons in New York, but after he moved his operations to QVC, they stared differently. The man who had invented the television movie, run up an unprecedented string of profits at Paramount, and created the fourth television network—a man who could have cut an independent production deal with virtually any studio in Hollywood—was the same man who currently spent his days peddling spray-on vitamins and cubic zirconium.

Diller didn't quite see things the same way. He had arrived at QVC only partly as a result of the blandishments of Malone and Brian Roberts, the young heir apparent of Comcast, the cable operator that owned the other big piece of the shopping channel. Diller was fascinated by QVC in the same way that he was fascinated by his new laptop computer, a Macintosh Powerbook. QVC ran itself with computers and telephones; QVC, Diller believed, gave him an opportunity to build an entirely new kind of television, a television that bore a certain resemblance to the visions of Nicholas Negroponte, although Diller was not overly impressed with Negroponte's Media Lab. Interactive television, Diller insisted, would be invented by trial and error, it would look nothing like the predictions, and Diller himself had only a vague idea of what it would be.

He could conduct many trials and make many errors at QVC. The place was a money machine. It would also enable him to do something else—with the help of John Malone, who controlled a second money machine in Liberty. Diller could get back into the old game, moviemaking, where he had already proved himself, and he would return as an owner.

History has not recorded how this idea came to him, but it was a timely inspiration. In truth, Diller wasn't very good at the home shopping business. QVC ran just fine as long as he kept his hands off it, but when he tried to create a new channel offering upscale goods more worthy of the Barry Diller of legend, it failed. Anybody who knew the home shopping business could have told him it would fail; upscale goods didn't sell on television. Despite the many intelligent things he had to say about it, Diller also made no strides in the direction of interactive television. But there was one thing he both understood very well and knew how to do. He knew how to make successful movies. Moreover, he had an ax to grind. There was an old score that needed settling.

MALONE STILL WANTED A MOVIE STUDIO, HAD NO IDEA how to run one, and by 1993 was in the middle of a small Hollywood adventure that left an increasingly bad taste in his wallet. He had used TCI to invest up to $90 million in Carolco, the studio that had produced a box office smash with *Basic Instinct* and gave Arnold Schwarzenegger his last entertaining role in *Terminator 2: Judgment Day*, a movie whose extensive use of digitized special effects had whipped the cyber-faithful into a froth of ecstasy, as though Carolco had invented Scotch tape or defeated Rommel in Tunisia. In exchange for the money, Carolco gave Malone the right to show its movies on his cable systems before theatrical release, an event that produced varying degrees of outrage and apprehension in the immense corner offices of the movie and theater industries; no network, no cable system, had ever been allowed to show a movie before theatrical release. Amidst the cries of outrage, it was temporarily forgotten that Carolco had an excellent reason to sell Hollywood's birthright for a mess of pottage. Carolco was on the ropes.

The studio never produced another movie that Malone wanted. In exchange for his $90 million investment, he got zip, the customary reward of most outsiders when they tried to buy their way into the game. It was back to Plan A—buy Paramount, or in any event do something with Paramount that would serve everyone's mutual advantage. By 1993, Malone had been in talks with Marty Davis for three years. And Paramount, unlike every other studio—no matter who happened to own them in 1993—had a long and fruitful history of outside ownership.

Starting in 1965, Paramount had been owned by Gulf+Western, a colorful and slightly shady conglomerate controlled by Charlie Bluhdorn, a colorful (literally: because of a combination of high blood pressure and atrocious temper, Bluhdorn was often the color of tomato soup) and slightly shady entrepreneur who had begun life as a refugee from his native Austria and become a millionaire by the age of thirty. When he acquired Paramount, a tottering and geriatric studio, he also acquired its marketing chief and public relations executive, Marty Davis, who became Bluhdorn's soul mate, right-hand man, hatchet man, and yes-man. Bluhdorn had the good sense to realize that he couldn't actually run Paramount and he seemed to sense that Davis couldn't run it either. Instead, he hired gifted studio chiefs and left them alone to work their incomprehensible magic—with the exception of those moments, never taken seriously, when he decided to entertain himself by going into his tyrannical-mogul act.

Hollywood was accustomed to executives who gnawed the scenery, although not many of them were the color of tomato soup.

As his first choice to run the studio, Bluhdorn chose Robert Evans, once the handsomest of the film colony's Golden Boys (he played a bullfighter in the film version of *The Sun Also Rises* and had his only starring role in *The Fiend Who Walked the West*, an event that was variously described as a miracle of typecasting or definitive proof that God had a sense of humor) and more recently a genuine whiz when it came to producing films. Under Evans's leadership, Paramount went from strength to strength with *Love Story*, *The Godfather*, *Rosemary's Baby*, and *True Grit*. He also, industry gossip insisted, developed a chemical dependency as large as the gross national products of several Central American countries, and he hit a bad dry patch just as the hellhounds of the Securities and Exchange Commission began to breathe down Bluhdorn's neck over some rather colorful irregularities in Gulf+Western's bookkeeping. Evans, who had nothing to do with Charlie Bluhdorn's accounting practices but also wasn't making money anymore, was invited to seek his destiny elsewhere.

He was replaced by the team of Michael Eisner and Jeffrey Katzenberg, with Diller in command. It was a world-beating combination. In 1977 and 1978, Diller's Paramount produced twenty profitable movies in a row, a hitting streak unmatched in modern Hollywood. During one seven-year stretch, Paramount made at least $100 million every single year; in 1984, it made $140 million. The year 1984, as it happened, was also the year Charlie Bluhdorn dropped dead in his corporate jet as it flew home from his estate in the Dominican Republic, a country Charlie Bluhdorn more or less owned. The party had been great while it lasted, but the party was over. Marty Davis was in charge.

In a series of maneuvers remarkable for the sheer improbability of their adroitness, Davis—a man widely regarded as a jumped-up office boy whose self-esteem had gotten the better of him—began to divest himself of Bluhdorn's unwieldy collection of unrelated companies, shrinking the company back to its core operations: Simon & Schuster, the New York publishing giant, and Paramount. But when it came to Hollywood, the place where Davis had spent all of his working life, his newfound magical touch abandoned him.

Davis decided that Paramount lacked the single quality that would bestow enduring greatness: the personal touch of Marty Davis, a man who had never made a movie. Moreover, his notion of the personal touch centered on a single large and festering idea. In Davis's view, it was essential for the immensely talented Diller to fire the immensely talented Eisner. Davis's reasoning on the subject was a trifle obscure; it seemed to have something to do with the fact that Eisner's compensation threatened to resemble his own, Eisner's growing ego seemed to make him think he was as smart as Marty Davis, and—most especially—Eisner's file of admiring press clippings. Henceforward, if there was to be any well-compensated, egotistical, and admirable person at Paramount, that person would be Marty Davis.

The rest of the story became an indelible part of the Hollywood playbook. Diller, dreaming of a fourth television network and already halfway out the door while laboring under the curious delusion that he was supposed to be running Paramount, refused to fire anyone and moved his act to Murdoch's Fox. Eisner and Katzenberg took a hike across town to Burbank, where, like exiled European scientists laboring over an atomic bomb, they worked tirelessly to turn Disney into an industry powerhouse. By 1993, it was all ancient history. But Barry Diller had a very long memory. He also had access to a great deal of money, and he had an ally—or so he believed—in John Malone. They both wanted to take control of the same studio.

For Malone, always ready to seize the main chance, the only question was how to do it. At first, he later said, his chosen instrument was Ted Turner, but Turner and Davis, their egos in ripping good shape, could not come to an agreement. Next, according to Malone, Davis offered Liberty 20 percent of the studio and, having gotten wind that Diller was prepared to make a move of his own, asked Malone to put a spoke in Diller's wheel. There are, as so often happened when Malone was involved in something, two entirely different versions of what happened next: Malone's and almost everyone else's.

In Malone's stated view, he was the very model of the modern ethical businessman. The rival version says that he was playing both ends against the middle. He knew very well that something was going on in Diller's mind, and he knew exactly what it was. Diller had asked the QVC board to authorize a raid on Paramount. Malone excused himself from the discussion on the ground that TCI was in discussions with Paramount. This had a very convenient result. Malone, who could have stopped Barry Diller, had placed himself in a position where he could not stop Barry Diller. He wanted Paramount, and he had wanted it for a very long time. If Diller launched a raid and succeeded, Malone would own a large piece of the place. If the threat of a Diller raid drove Davis into his arms, he would also end up with Paramount. In either event, Liberty, Malone's getaway car, would be enriched with a piece of one of the most desirable studio properties on earth. And by excusing himself from the discussions, Malone put an end to the risk that he would be forced to reveal a very large secret: if certain of his other plans matured, he was planning to leave everybody in the lurch.

MALONE, LIKE STEVE ROSS, WAS A MAN WHO LIKED TO have several strings in his bow. He and Magness still controlled TCI. They also controlled Liberty. Liberty had a large stake in QVC, which was planning a raid on Paramount. Malone had many bases covered. With the bulk of his personal fortune transferred to Liberty, Senator Gore and his congressional allies could no longer get at him in any meaningful way, and he had an excellent chance of pulling off a major coup in partnership with one of the most talented entertainment executives of modern times. It would not, however, be the coup of coups. That particular triumph would be accomplished if he could sell TCI itself, lock, stock, obsolete cable systems, and dangerously mounting debt, for tens of billions of dollars.

Selling TCI for vastly more than it was worth involved an act of prestidigitation unmatched since the British hid the Suez Canal from the Nazis in 1941—no easy task, it would seem. Fortunately, the very thing he needed to turn the trick had already been placed in his hands. It was Woo Paik's digital television. Nobody understood digital television very well. It would be Malone's agreeable task to instruct them. Then, wrapping himself in the mantle of the future, he would find his sucker. It would cost him very little—a certain amount of rhetoric from the brilliant king of cable, a few plausible actions that might cost TCI a little money. By the summer of 1993, with Diller poised to strike at Marty Davis, Malone was well on his way. He had been working on his new plan for over a year.

IN 1992, MALONE HAD ELECTRIFIED THE NATION—AND, most importantly, the nation's investment community, its press (the *New York Times* repeated his words on the front page), and its cable industry—by announcing the imminent arrival of the 500-channel world. It would be based, of course, on digital television. Cable would bring it to a waiting nation, with TCI in the van. Digital television would not merely be more television. Instead, it would be the information superhighway. There would be data services; the long anticipated—Negroponte talked about it constantly—convergence of the computer and the television set would become reality. There would be an entirely new form of cable-based telephone service. The Picturephone, for one, would finally become a ubiquitous appliance, although the Picturephone had utterly failed to take the country by storm as long ago as 1964.

The home viewer could customize his programming. Negroponte

would get his smart television set at last, and interactive television would become a fact. There would be other services and uses as yet undreamed of; digital cable television would be a boon to the human race. It was well known that Malone was no ivory-towered theorist or unwashed gearhead driven to the brink of madness by the elusive wonders of the digital domain. The John Malone who took his listeners to the mountaintop and showed them powers and dominions was a notorious cheapskate and an intensely practical man.

Moreover, the intensely practical Malone was speaking to a choir consisting of the financial community and the press, where true and useful knowledge about any technology more complex than a can opener was vanishingly small. Even so—or, perhaps, precisely so—in the press and the financial community, technological enthusiasm burned with a refiner's fire. Everybody read the press, and money talked.

With Wall Street dramatically alerted to the imminent arrival of the 500-channel world by the impeccably pragmatic Malone, the financial community's celebrated herd instinct immediately kicked in. A cable company that did not plan an interactive, 500-channel, digital future was not looked upon with favor, and there would be no financial reward for any cable company that said the whole idea was nuts. There was little danger of that. The dyslexic former lawyers, ex-ranchers, and retired garment salesmen who ran most of the cable business were a far cry from the steely-eyed, flint-hearted, ruthless robber barons—Edison, Carnegie, and Henry Clay Frick came to mind—who had built the great industrial empires of the past. Edison, Carnegie, and Frick knew how their technologies worked and they had skeptically examined a foundered horse or two in their time, but most of the cable guys had seldom seen a sky that was not blue, and Malone had just shown them the bluest of skies.

It was Qube all over again, with a significant exception. In 1977, there really was something called Qube, and it worked. In 1992, there had been demonstrations of digital television, but they were lab work and videotapes. Many of the key components of a digital cable system either were prototypes, prohibitively expensive adaptions of other technologies, or did not exist. The reality of the situation notwithstanding, the other cable operators were more than willing to join Malone in his headlong charge into a future he described as immediate and certain. Moreover, Malone instantly suited his actions to his words. Or so it seemed.

He ordered a million digital set-top boxes from General Instrument, the inventor of digital television. It had not, however, invented an inexpensive digital set-top box and neither had anybody else. Malone then suspended his order for a device that did not exist. With Cox Enterprises, he bought Teleport Communications, a rapidly growing Staten Island-based fiber-optics company that provided local telephone service to businesses in seven major cities, including New York, Chicago, and Los Angeles. Teleport was not heard from again. He began to rewire some of his systems—but by no means all, a fact that was frequently overlooked—with hybrid fiber-coax. The new digital television, he announced, would be available to his customers in 1995. He neglected to add that the new digital television would not be available to all or even most of them. With AT&T and US West, his closest ally among the regional telephone companies, he launched an experiment with video-on-demand—a simplified form of customizable television—in Littleton, Colorado, announced that the test had been an unqualified success because the viewers had purchased more video-on-demand than they did old-fashioned pay-per-view, and neglected to point out that the viewers spent significantly less for video-on-demand than they did for rentals at the neighborhood video store. He helped Primestar, the satellite television business in which TCI was a partner, convert its signal to digital. It was far easier to convert a satellite to digital broadcasting than it was to convert cable, a fact that somehow got lost in the shuffle.

When all was said and done, Malone had bought a small telephone company, created the appearance of vigorous action, effectively disguised TCI—the most technologically backward of the major cable companies—as the company of the digital future, and spent very little in the way of real money. In a seemingly unrelated, somewhat puzzling event, he also announced that TCI would reabsorb Liberty in a tax-free, $3 billion stock deal. Malone had found his sucker.

EIGHT

The Bell Atlantic Way

O N AN EVENING IN JUNE 1993, RAY SMITH, THE CHAIRMAN of Bell Atlantic, gathered his three top executives around a card table in the basement of his town house in Potomac, Maryland. There was much to discuss.

RAY SMITH WAS NOT YOUR AVERAGE TELEPHONE GUY. HE was an outwardly affable, quick-witted, and amusing man who was devoted to amateur theatricals, and he put on a highly credible performance when he appeared in corporate videos that extolled the boundless digital future. Other captains of the telephone industry, like AT&T's Robert Allen, appeared to be made of glass; Smith always seemed to be looking for a spot of fun. Other telephone chieftains, for their own strategic reasons, were interested in the cable business as an investment, sometimes a very large one, a hedge against the future, a source of new income, and an experiment. Smith also had reasons to be interested in the cable business, but the enthusiastic amateur thespian in him kept bobbing to the surface: he loved the whole idea of television, especially digital interactive television, as much as he hated corporate bureaucracy. He remembered the old Ma Bell days all too well. Corporate rules told you how to hold a pencil. Corporate rules told you when to go to the bathroom. Smith was not eager to return to the old days. Instead, he was very eager to get into the television business.

In origin, he was not a scion of the middle classes. His father had been taken out of school at thirteen and put to work in Jones & Loughlin's Pittsburgh plant. His mother was taken out of school at thirteen and put to work in a bakery. Throughout his childhood, young Smith's ambitions were fired by a woman who was determined that her son would never work with his hands. He was dyslexic.

Despite his handicap, he developed a poor man's romantic love of learning and a highly intelligent poor man's disdain for people who would not use their minds. For a young man of Smith's background, there were three reliable ways out of the Pittsburgh of the 1940s: the gun, the Church, and the telephone company. Smith chose the telephone company.

Working part-time, he took his engineering degree at Carnegie-Mellon, studied literature at Duquesne, and joined Pennsylvania Bell. In the old Bell System, it did not take much for a man to become identified as a corporate rebel with a creative mind, provided the rebellion and the creativity weren't unseemly or overdone. Once, unable to get his parking lot paved by Pennsylvania Bell, Smith paved it himself and sent his superior the bill, an incident that was long remembered for its boldness and ingenuity. On a later occasion, trying to get his office repaired, he scattered dead pigeons around the place, called in his vice president for a meeting, and soon inhabited a repaired office. When the AT&T breakup was announced, Smith gathered his co-workers in his office and led them in the cheer: "Free at last!" It was with feats like these that Ray Smith made his mark as both a corporate maverick and a man destined for greatness. The following year, he was named Pennsylvania Bell's president.

In his downtime, which was never abundant, Smith took up painting and threw himself into the amateur theatrical productions that he loved. He also wrote—an unpublished history of his family, an unpublished, unfinished three-volume autobiography, and five plays that actually reached the stage in the little-theater circuit, including his hit comedy *The Fetal Pig*. In it, four comfortable middle-aged men decide that, like the unborn creature of the title, they have never lived. In the play's central image, they realize that if they had to sum up their lives on the side of a milk carton, they would have nothing to say. So they decide to have adventures.

That was Ray Smith as he packaged himself for public consumption. But there was another Ray Smith. It was the Ray Smith, the new chairman of a telephone company that stretched from Erie, Pennsylvania, to Washington, D.C.—Bell Atlantic was the telephone company of the Pentagon—and north as far as Alpine, New Jersey, who became infatuated with something he called the Bell Atlantic Way.

"At Bell Atlantic," he told his executives, "you are absolutely forbidden to make a victim statement, such as you didn't have enough people to do the job or they didn't return your calls. I expect you to put your heart and soul into it. Come back with a halfhearted minimalist performance, and I'll send you packing."

Lifetime employment was a thing of the past at Bell Atlantic; Smith cut the payroll until it was the leanest and most efficient of the regional Bells. He humiliated executives who displeased him with blunt personal attacks at open meetings, constantly churned his top management, and for special people he devised special torments. Once, Smith ordered an executive to report to the Swarthmore Amphitheater, where the man encountered his employer striding the aisles, declaiming a customized version of *As You Like It*.

"As you know, John," Smith intoned, "all the world's a stage and we are mere actors upon it. John, your audience is not applauding."

If this sort of behavior filled his executives with zeal and made them as keen as mustard, it has not been recorded. Smith, however, was rather proud of himself.

Striving to abolish the conservative Bell System mind-set, he also began a series of seminars, originally taught the courses himself, and eventually had 60,000 employees enrolled in two-and-a-half-day workshops where, among other things, participants called out encouragement to a blindfolded employee as he tried to hit a target with a Velcro-tipped dart.

AT FIRST, FREED FROM AT&T'S SHACKLES, SMITH'S immediate predecessors in the chairmanship thought Bell Atlantic could make a tidy killing by selling telephone equipment. Like most of the commercial fantasies of the newly liberated regional operating companies, the strategy went nowhere. The old Bell System had introduced any number of products—Princess phones, phones shaped like Mickey Mouse, overengineered answering machines that could be dropped from the top of a nine-story building and survive the experience intact—but no one had ever been trained to sell them in a competitive marketplace, and the situation did not improve after the telephone monopoly was broken up in 1984. AT&T, unencumbered by its regional offspring, plunged into the computer business. The move seemed to make eminent sense. AT&T knew a great deal about computers. Unfortunately, it didn't know much about customers who were not the captives of a monopoly. Commenting on one of its computer products, a reviewer noted that it had a unique virtue. Because it was too heavy to lift, it was impossible to steal. Before AT&T finally threw in the towel, its computer business lost billions of dollars. Simultaneously, the newly liberated regional operating companies entered many new lines of endeavor—real estate, for example.

Almost invariably, they failed. The cut and slash of the marketplace was not congenial to the ex-lifers of the late Ma Bell. They were, however, very good at providing telephone service, and they were very good at defending their turf.

When he came to power at Bell Atlantic, Smith tended his hardware in the best tradition of the old Bell System—the Bell companies, whatever their other faults, had done a superb job of maintenance—but it was the software side of the business that called to him. He led the way in popular new services like Call Waiting and Caller ID, and he tried to turn his billing department into something resembling a credit card company; you could buy a refrigerator and put the payments on your telephone bill. But running a telephone company had one great drawback for a man of Smith's temperament. It wasn't very exciting.

When push came to shove, Bell Atlantic spent most of its time peddling POTS—plain old telephone service. It did not sell PANS—pretty amazing new stuff. Still, there was no denying that the POTS business was a remarkably lucrative undertaking. In 1992, Bell Atlantic posted a net income of $1.3 billion—larger than Malone's cash flow—and presided over a cash flow of at least $5 billion. (The actual sum—it could have been triple that—depended on how the accounting rules were applied.) Bell Atlantic had a lot of money lying around. Its credit rating was superb, and it had remarkably little debt. The stock market loved Bell Atlantic, and so did the large institutional investors. But Ray Smith, who wanted to be a hero, wasn't much of a hero to anybody but a bunch of financial wonks who were perfectly content to see him spend the rest of his days as though the past were prologue and the future would be identical to all the dull things that had gone before.

In the parlance of the marketplace, Bell Atlantic was a mature company. It wasn't going to take the world by storm with an astonishing new kind of telephone. It already had one, the Picturephone, and the public hated it. Cellular telephones were a hot product based on new technology, but the only other new thing about them was their mobility; otherwise cellular telephones did the same things telephones had always done. Smith aggressively invaded foreign markets—to New Zealand, where he paid $1.2 billion for the national telephone company; to Mexico, where Bell Atlantic set its sights on 26 million potential cellular customers and planned to spend $1.04 billion; to Indonesia, the fourth-largest country in the world, where, like everyone who entered the Indonesian market, he found himself in business with the family of General Suharto, the country's cunning old dictator—but these were not cutting-edge initiatives. They did nothing to redefine Bell Atlantic—except, perhaps, as a telephone company that was willing to drop a couple of billion bucks in foreign parts. They did not enter the world of the future. To Smith, the answer was cable television.

BY 1992, CABLE TELEVISION WAS THE ANSWER, OR AT least an answer of sorts, for most telephone companies. Few commentators seemed to know what the question was.

The telephone companies had long been interested in cable, of course. It was a second wire into the home, which had always made them nervous, and it was a likely pathway for digitized data and related services, which intrigued them. But the wonders of television itself did not much excite them. Although few nontechnical people realized it, wired telephones and wired television were two entirely different kinds of technology, and the telephone guys didn't know much (or anything) about television. Voice transmission they knew. Data transmission they knew. And there was another thing they knew: no matter what the lab boys said in their more expansive moments, bringing analog television into the home over the twisted pair of copper wires that still served most residential neighborhoods was pretty close to impossible in a real-world situation. The telephone companies did not bully and bluster their way into the television business. They were invited.

As cable rates rose during the deregulated 1980s, the cable-viewing public and their elected representatives cast around for some-body, anybody, who could provide friendly, reliable television at a reasonable price. The telephone companies were reliable and friendly; memories of the AT&T monopoly had faded. The telephone compa-nies possessed technical expertise, vaults bulging with money, and balance sheets unblighted with debt. Perhaps most intriguing of all, compared to the telephone companies the fearsome John Malone was a pipsqueak.

Sensing the spirit of the times, the telephone companies calcu-lated that if they were only allowed to, well, fool around with cable, they would create 1.46 million new jobs while adding $110 billion to the gross domestic product by the year 2001; such astonishing preci-sion gave the debate a certain air of scientific objectivity. At the very least, cable looked like a sporting proposition. The telephone guys wouldn't actually have to produce television shows. They could string some new wires, buy their programming the way the cable guys did, and make some money. It would also be a stick in the eye for John Malone, who had been mouthing off about getting into the tele-phone business for years, but there was no urgency about it. The telephone guys were interested enough to crunch some numbers—and General Telephone and Electronics (GTE), a telephone company that did not have to play by the same rules as the regional Bells, actually made a small test run in California—but there was no ur-gency about it. The telephone guys were still not overly excited by television.

In 1991, after five years of kicking the matter around (there was no real urgency anywhere), the FCC finally allowed the telephone companies to enter a business called dial-tone video. Because of its name, many people thought dial-tone video was television that ar-rived by way of traditional phone wire. To a degree, Ray Smith thought so, too, until he tried it. Still, it looked like a fine opportu-nity for the telephone companies, provided they wanted to seize it, until somebody actually read and pondered the new regulations.

The telephone companies could not enter the television business in their own service areas, which gave them two unattractive options. At great expense, they could build a cable system from scratch in an unfamiliar part of the country where the local regulators had not been coddled for decades, the way the telephone companies' familiar regulators had been. Building a state-of-the-art cable system from scratch would cost a huge amount of money with no guaranteed return. It didn't make a lot of sense. As an alternative, a telephone company could buy a cable company. Buying a small cable company would also make no sense and buying a large cable company would, again, cost a huge amount of money. On the face of it and under the existing rules, there was no reason in the world for a telephone company to go into the cable business as long as television was the only thing a cable system could do, but in 1991 television was no longer the only thing a cable system could do. Thanks to Woo Paik, a huge technological gulf separated the late 1980s from 1991.

In contemplating digital television, the telephone executives reacted in two distinct ways: either their thinking was cool to the point of cold calculation or it was warm to the point of delirium. Ray Smith was a warm man. Sensing an enormous opportunity, he immediately put Bell Atlantic's lawyers to work at chipping away the regulations that said what a telephone company could not do if it went into cable.

IN AN ANALOG CABLE SYSTEM, THE COAXIAL CABLE—LIKE the water main it resembled—brought the same programming to every house that hooked on. It was a passive system, and a simple one. In a digital cable system, the same coaxial cable could bring the customers interactive programming and new services. It would be possible for the home screens in every house on the block to show an entirely different picture with an entirely different purpose, and because the programming would be various—there would, presumably, be interactive games, services, and a movie library, unlike analog's simple stream of images—an interactive system would require electronic switches to route the varied programming to different homes and optical-fiber cable to carry the huge amount of data involved. The telephone companies had decades of experience with electronic switches and optical-fiber cable. Any telephone executive in an operating position knew more about switches and fiber op than any cable guy who ever lived, including John Malone, because a telephone system was by definition a switched, interactive system that carried huge amounts of data. Unlike analog cable, a switched, interactive, digital cable system had a singular quality that was not lost on the telephone executives. Any telephone company that built an interactive digital television system outside its service area had just built the backbone of a competing telephone system deep in enemy territory. It would be a bridgehead, easily seized, and Smith believed he had a shining example of just this future before him.

"England," he said.

In Great Britain, where large, American-style cable systems were the newest way of delivering television, a TCI-US West business alliance (and others) had already succeeded in piggybacking telephone service over their wires, as predicted. It was popular. It was giving British Telecom a run for its money. In Britain, it was possible for a rational and intelligent man like Ray Smith to believe, the future of modern telecommunications had taken tangible form.

At this point, however, rational calculation stopped and fantasy took its place. The British cable systems were spanking new with all the latest bells and whistles; they had been specifically designed to carry telephone traffic. Britain was a seller's market; its existing telephone system left much to be desired. By contrast, the existing American telephone system, as the American telephone companies never ceased to remind their customers and their government, was the finest in the world. The situation in the two countries was not at all comparable, although it seemed to be. In America, a commercially successful cable telephone system was a theoretical possibility, and history taught that theoretical possibilities had a way of going haywire. This did not seem to occur to anybody, including Ray Smith and John Malone.

Moreover, a number of telephone executives, their minds temporarily clouded by the technobabble of the digital age, managed to convince themselves that they could move into the interactive television business as easily as they paid for lunch with plastic. They were confident men, and they knew how to run the equipment. It was easy to forget that they were also men who had never, since the breakup of the old Bell System in 1984, diversified into any business other than telephones without making a hash of things. It was also easy to forget that a lot of the necessary equipment, including the all-important digital set-top box, hadn't been invented yet. Ray Smith, in particular, believed he could become a television mogul.

Smith was perfectly aware that Bell Atlantic knew nothing about the entertainment business. Then he forgot. Digital television looked like a lot of fun—good moneymaking fun that solved a couple of knotty problems.

For one, optical fiber was a wonderful thing and Smith's Bell Atlantic had certainly laid a lot of it, but optical fiber was also too much of a wonderful thing. If brought to an individual house or even a small neighborhood, it would provide the residents with a digital pipeline large enough to run a small corporation. Even if every citizen owned a fax machine, a computer modem, and became addicted to e-mail, there was no way to use all (or most) of optical fiber's remaining capacity—unless, that is, a telephone company could pump something like interactive television into the customer's parlor. Digital interactive television, related data services, games, and other video-based software yet unborn would fill up the unused capacity—and generate new revenue—quite nicely. Unfortunately, Bell Atlantic's optical fiber was laid inside its regional service area, where Bell Atlantic was forbidden to enter the television business, but Smith knew a camel's nose when he saw one. The FCC had allowed the telephone companies to go into television; it was now a matter of removing the restrictions. Smith put the company's lawyers on the case.

Smith was also aware that the Trojan horse of an out-of-service-area interactive television system would face formidable obstacles if he tried to turn it into a telephone exchange. Indeed, he would throw up the same obstacles himself if anyone tried to invade Bell Atlantic's territory. A Bell Atlantic-owned, out-of-service-area telephone system, piggybacked atop an interactive television system, would have to pass muster with the state regulatory body. The regional telephone companies, Bell Atlantic among them, had been cosseting and jerking around state regulators for years—after which, as a reward for good or inconspicuous regulatory behavior, it also hired them. A regulatory agency was widely regarded as a training ground for future and much more lucrative employment in the private sector. Unless a regional telephone company failed to maintain its system and began to gouge its customers, regulatory zeal was not called for, and the wise regulator did much to keep his future boss—and, not incidentally, a company that was also a large contributor to the campaigns of the elected officials who monitored his current bosses—very happy. By definition, an unhappy regional telephone company was a regional telephone company whose monopoly was threatened by a well-heeled competitor like Bell Atlantic. For Bell Atlantic, simply getting permission to offer out-of-area telephone service would be a huge job of work.

Nor would Smith's problems be over then. Next, he would have to persuade the regional phone company to hook up his upstart telephone subsidiary with the rest of the telephone system. Otherwise, he would own nothing but the electronic equivalent of some cans and a lot of string. In its own service area, Bell Atlantic was a doughty and tenacious warrior when it came to yielding an inch of territory, and it could hardly expect its former Bell siblings to behave any differently. Smith had been around telephone companies all his working life; he knew just how hard it would be. Nonetheless, and at every possible opportunity, he talked up the possibilities of telephonic digital video, a technology with a few tangible benefits—particularly in regard to the surplus capacity problem—and the promise of a large number of headaches. No high-ranking telephone executive matched his enthusiasm. As a visionary, he was the equal of John Malone. But Malone—like the broadcasters with their cynical embrace of HDTV—was playing a double game. So, according to all indications, was Ray Smith.

On the table in Washington was a bill designed to undo or revise sixty years of government regulation of the telecommunications business. If it was passed in appropriate and pleasing form, the regional telephone companies could get into the long-distance business and amass new riches beyond the dreams of avarice. To get such an invaluable law through Congress, it would be essential to invoke the newest conventional wisdom: the unlimited benefits the consumers would instantly reap from the miracle of competition. Unfortunately, the public and their legislators were not overly excited by the prospect of more competition in the long-distance business. The issue seemed to have been settled long before, with the breakup of AT&T. There was already plenty of competition for the long-distance dollar. But by a happy chance, there was almost no competition for the cable television dollar.

Thanks to Senator Gore and John Malone, a hostile public was very interested in the cable television monopolies, and a long section of the telecommunications bill was designed to break them. The designated trustbusters were Bell Atlantic and the other regional operating companies; they would be given unlimited access to the cable television business. If Smith could persuade Congress that he couldn't wait to clean Malone's clock by bringing the country the same reliable, friendly, and inexpensive television service that was the hallmark of his telephone business, the bill would almost certainly pass. With the new law in place, Bell Atlantic would then make its move on the long-distance business. After a decent interval, if the telephone-based cable television didn't work as advertised, the whole idea of Bell Atlantic's television business would be allowed to quietly wither away.

There was only one thing wrong with this ingenious scenario. Ray

Smith resembled a criminal mastermind who had become smitten with the vicar's daughter. Television called to him.

IN THE WASHINGTON SUBURB OF STERLING, VIRGINIA, Bell Atlantic built its house of tomorrow and threw open the door to the public. Such houses had long been a staple of corporate futurology, prominently featuring whatever technological fantasy that happened to hold the nation in its grip. The Westinghouse version at the 1939 World's Fair, for example, featured Electro, the mechanical man, and his iron dog, Sparko. Electro's mission was to lighten the drudgery of housework, Sparko's exact function was somewhat obscure, and the shape of the future was clear: thanks to the march of science, clanking androids would do the world's work, and humankind would be free to improve its mind and soul. The Bell Atlantic house of tomorrow was firmly in the mainstream of this great tradition. The television set in the kitchen could order the groceries. The television set in the family room could call up video-on-demand. The children's television set could call up games and homework materials. Television—Bell Atlantic television—would banish dull care, abolish boredom, and shape the minds of the nation's youth. But to Ray Smith, the house of the future was only a fragment of a grand design. Next, he spent some real money.

Well before any of the other regional telephone companies committed themselves to anything more than idle talk, Bell Atlantic poured an annual $40 million into the design of Stargazer, a video navigator that enabled the viewer to find his way around the services—the video library, the digital shopping mall, the game parlor, the home banking—that were soon to take the country by storm. Stargazer's logo was a smiling Sun that winked. By 1996 at the latest, Bell Atlantic promised, thousands of lucky Virginians and New Jerseyans would be pushing the envelope of the future from the comfort of their living rooms. But Smith could scarcely wait to inscribe his new biography—television magnate, nationwide telephone tycoon—

on the side of his milk carton. He had sought attention, and he had gotten it. In 1993, from stage left, there entered John Malone and his own company of the future, TCI.

MANY THINGS HAD COME TO A HEAD BY THE TIME SMITH gathered his lieutenants around his suburban card table on a night in June 1993. New threats had appeared, a new possibility had arisen, and it was time to remake the company in a bold new way.

US West, the regional telephone company based in the Denver suburb of Englewood, had paid $2.5 billion to enter a partnership with Time Warner. With the stroke of a pen, US West became the owner of a quarter of Time Warner's cable system, the second-largest in the country, and a quarter of Time Warner's movie studio, Warner Brothers, stealing a very considerable march on the other telephone regionals and, in particular, Bell Atlantic. To all appearances, US West had acquired the backbone for a national telephone, data, and advanced television system, and US West, like Bell Atlantic, knew more about switches and optical fiber than any cable company in the world. It also owned a large piece of the Warner library. This was serious. Under Jerry Levin, Time Warner was barreling ahead into interactive television, a billion dollars of US West's money was to be spent upgrading Time Warner's cable plant, and US West served an enormous geographical region just to the left of the center of the country. It took no great imaginative effort to see that US West could connect its telephone system to Time Warner's soon-to-be interactive cable systems. Operating on such a scale, it would be worth the partners' while—at least from the perspective of 1993—to do battle with the state regulators and the other regional operating companies. There was far more at stake than some cans and a lot of string. The chief of US West, not Ray Smith, would become a television magnate and a national telephone tycoon. If Smith's favorite telecommunications bill—in addition to conducting psychological warfare, he was lobbying heavily for it—became a law, it would be a certainty.

Meanwhile, Southwestern Bell had purchased two Washington-area cable companies for $650 million, dropping like a parachutist into the heart of Bell Atlantic's territory and, incidentally, closing a small historical circle; the two cable companies were the last television properties of Gustav Hauser, the man who created Qube for Steve Ross. If Southwestern Bell rewired the systems and tried to go into the telephone business, they would be dealt with in the usual way, with high-priced lawyers and sympathetic politicians. Still, the headaches of the future seemed to be arriving a little too fast for comfort.

Most troublesome of all was AT&T. The mother of all telephone companies planned to buy one-third of young Craig McCaw's cellular business for $3.8 billion and soon announced that it would buy all of it for more than $12 billion. Everything else—US West, Time Warner, and Southwestern Bell—was conjectural. They hadn't actually done anything yet but spend money, but the threat from the AT&T-McCaw alliance was immediate and real.

Young McCaw was a dyslexic and gifted entrepreneur from Washington State who had stitched together a cellular phone business that, although he had yet to show his investors a penny of profit, was now available to 35 percent of the population. When AT&T's bags of cash were added to the equation and Smith's favorite bill became law, it was possible—likely, even—that the operation would soon blanket the country. In other words, AT&T was back in the local telephone business, big-time and wireless, and it appeared that the long-anticipated battle for the local market was about to be joined at last. The outlook was uncertain but did not look good. In the immediate short run, however, Bell Atlantic and the other regionals stood to lose a big piece of their revenues. Bell Atlantic and the others charged handsome access fees to connect their local networks to AT&T's long-distance lines; routinely overcharging long-distance companies like AT&T, the regionals made $25 billion a year, a full third of their profits, from the access business. This income was now at risk. An AT&T cellular customer could tap into AT&T long-distance without going through Bell Atlantic or anyone else.

Nor was this all. The introduction of a new digital satellite telephone, the PCS, was imminent. The PCS was the basis, at least in theory, of a cheaper, clearer, and vastly more data-rich form of telephone service than the old analog cellular systems. Southwestern Bell and US West could cluster their PCS receiver-transmitters on their new cable systems—PCS ground equipment worked best when it was clustered—without Bell Atlantic's permission and without paying Bell Atlantic a cent in tribute. AT&T could use the McCaw cellular system to do the same. Bell Atlantic had billions invested in its land lines, and a large piece of its land-line business now appeared to be in danger. In theory—it was one of Negroponte's favorites—a PCS telephone didn't need land lines, and wireless mobile communications were the technology of the future. Even this was not the last of the apparent bad news.

AT&T was the largest manufacturer of telephone equipment in the country. It was also deeply involved in the race to create digital HDTV. AT&T could build and sell futuristic telephones equipped to receive the data services that PCS would soon make possible. Without putting a foot outside its corporate boundary, AT&T could also create the dreamed-of device that George Gilder, in another of the unfortunate neologisms that stalked the digital revolution like the Hound of the Baskervilles, called the teleputer. "It's a horrible word," said Ray Smith, but the long-discussed convergence of the telephone, the television, and the home computer seemed to be within easy reach, and AT&T would own the technology. Bell Atlantic and the other regionals were forbidden to manufacture telecommunications equipment.

Bell Atlantic was not without its own considerable resources and bold visions, but in the digital summer of 1993, Bell Atlantic's resources no longer looked adequate and its visions resembled a comfortable delusion. The company was larger than the entire cable industry—all the regionals were—but if AT&T and US West walked away with the future, its comfortable size would become history. Bell Atlantic had spent more than $40 million a year on its television business, but its television technology was designed to run over its telephone system or parallel it. The parallel system hadn't been built, and as Smith soon found in a New Jersey experiment, it was possible to bring a television signal into the home over the existing copper wires but you didn't want to; for one thing, a television signal on a copper wire offered the viewer a single television channel, not 500 of them. Bell Atlantic was in the cellular business and it would go into the PCS business. These businesses had to undergo dramatic expansion at great cost and in the teeth of vigorous competition; the outcome was in doubt. Most important, Bell Atlantic was fastened like Gulliver to the mid-Atlantic earth by its immense network of land lines. At its core, it was a regional telephone company whose principal business was under threat by AT&T and the march of wireless technology. It could become, at best and at great expense, a regional television company, an obsolete telephone company, and a niche marketer—a very large niche marketer, it was true—of advanced communications services. Bell Atlantic owned no cable systems and therefore possessed no ready-made base for its PCS receivers, no huge Trojan horse to sneak in a cable-based telephone system outside its service area, and no ready-made conduit to bring its Stargazer navigator, its video shopping mall, or its digital television to a national audience. Instead, US West did. Unless Smith acted quickly, he could end up roughly where he had begun, selling POTS—together with some very costly television—instead of PANS. He would have little to write on the side of his milk carton. Or so it seemed.

Fortunately, and as usual, there were a number of things seriously wrong with this scenario. Unfortunately, Smith gave no sign of being aware of any of them. Hidden agendas, personal ambitions, digital dreams, digital nightmares, they all looked the same in the digital summer of 1993. But there was one thing about the future that everyone seemed to forget. Unlike the past, it hadn't happened yet.

In only a few short years, AT&T would stun the industry by abandoning the manufacturing business. US West would be locked in an endless and paralyzing lawsuit with Time Warner. Southwestern Bell's Washington bridgehead still would be nothing but a couple of cable systems. Every telephone-based interactive television system was on the shelf, perhaps permanently. By 1997, only Pacific Bell and US West were still interested in the television business, and Pacific Bell was about to be bought by a renamed Southwestern Bell, which no longer was, very much.

There were a couple of other false starts and undelivered futures. The cable companies had decided that running telephone service over their coaxial land lines wasn't something they wanted to do for another half decade, if ever, and wireless telephony had proved to be a curious mixture of a hot product and a damp squib. Even in 1993, the way people used their cellular phones—and would undoubtedly use their PCS phones—was well known if anyone had stopped to think about it. The vast majority of mobile phone owners used their mobile phones when they were driving, when they were walking down the street, when they were at the beach or in a restaurant, or when they wanted to show off on the commuter train. When they were at home or in the office, they used land lines. There was no overwhelming threat to Bell Atlantic's core business here, and there was no great opportunity in cable-based digital television. As late as 1997, John Malone's 500-channel world kept right on not happening. But in the digital summer of 1993, with his top aides gathered in the basement of his suburban town house, Ray Smith was well on his way to grappling with the phantoms in his path—and achieving greatness—by spending $33 billion.

MALONE AND SMITH HAD MET OFTEN OVER THE LAST FEW years, the acerbic and quotable cable baron who spoke without notes or text and the witty and personable telephone guy who had seen the future and knew just how it was supposed to work. They were sworn hereditary enemies, Smith and Malone, cable and telephone, and the subject of their ongoing debate was almost invariably the same: just which of them, in the new digital-everything age, was going to eat the other's lunch? According to the story they later circulated, their true meeting of minds came at a 1992 conference in Aspen, sponsored by the common enemy, Rupert Murdoch. Malone and Smith realized that they were twin brothers separated at birth. Malone knew very well that Smith had a hidden agenda. He did not mention his own.

It was Smith who made the first move. In May 1993, he called Malone to explore a possible collaboration, perhaps an alliance like Time Warner and US West, perhaps a joint venture. There was a meeting at Smith's office, another at Malone's; by summer, things began to move forward. Bell Atlantic was given the code name Shamrock. TCI was Ireland. Smith traveled to Malone's home in Maine, where they went out on Malone's boat and engaged in Malone's favorite sport, dickering. When the anchor snagged a submerged telephone line, they dickered some more.

Malone, clearly feeling his oats, placed Smith in an odd position; he wanted Bell Atlantic, a company with an enviable reputation for customer service and a vaultful of money, to prove itself worthy of TCI, a company with $10 billion in debt, no revenue to speak of, and captive municipalities that feared and hated it in equal measure. In plain language, Malone wanted to sell his company, and he wanted more money than Smith was willing to pay. Smith, who wanted to buy Malone's company but not meet his price, found himself in the position of a man arguing with a Marxist in the years before the collapse of the Soviet Union. Malone, singing his old sweet song, had an answer for everything.

Malone argued that an immensely profitable company like Bell Atlantic was a stagnant company mired in the mistaken thinking of the past, whereas a company like TCI, invigorated by the ten-mile hike and cold shower of its vast indebtedness, was building a golden and dynamic future. Bell Atlantic's customers were happy, Smith replied. The battle for the future, Malone said, was not a popularity contest. The beat and response went on and on. Bell Atlantic owned many contented friends in Washington and knew where to buy more. The digital future was going to arrive no matter what the government did. Bell Atlantic's telephone network was already an interactive two-way system but Malone's cables were all one-way. True as far as it went, but there was no way you could pump 500 channels down twisted-pair copper wire. Bell Atlantic's system was well maintained at enormous expense. A pity, because Bell Atlantic's system was obsolete. Bell Atlantic had an advanced computerized billing system. A pity, because Bell Atlantic's system was obsolete. But, according to Smith, he and Malone didn't waste much time in such idle chatter. "John and I didn't talk in clichés," he said. "We're techies." And so they spent most of their time discussing the new technologies so dear to Smith's heart—and that Malone, carefully masking his hand, didn't have. Malone was willing to agree to many things—he especially agreed that he and Smith held the future in their hands—but he and Smith could not settle on a formula that would allow them to combine their companies.

Almost at the end of his tether, talked to a standstill for perhaps the first time in his life, and unwilling to meet Malone's terms, Smith determined to make one last try. The sticking point was not the price; it was the number of shares Bell Atlantic was willing to exchange for the revenues Malone was prepared to guarantee from his subscribers, and the deck contained a pair of possible jokers. If Malone was unable to deliver the promised revenues, the deal could unravel. If the stock market didn't like the deal and the price of Bell Atlantic's stock fell to a certain point, Bell Atlantic would not buy TCI, TCI would buy Bell Atlantic, which was not at all what Smith intended, and Smith was aware of the danger. "Yes," he said, "that would have happened." For the sake of both parties, it was important to bring Malone to heel and close the deal quickly. And Smith was aware of another danger. Even if Malone agreed to terms, he seldom saw a deal he didn't want to renegotiate to his further benefit. If Smith carried the day, it was possible that precious time would be lost, the situation would change, and the merger would have to be restructured or abandoned. And Smith hadn't been able to take a close look at TCI to assure himself that the company he proposed to buy was identical with the company he believed he was buying. Close scrutiny of TCI's operations and technology, the process known as "due diligence," couldn't begin until Smith secured Malone's agreement to merge. Nonetheless, Smith was determined to press on.

Alone, he met Malone at the Waldorf in New York. In the lobby, Smith ran into Barry Diller.

"Barry was having a bad hair day," Smith recalled.

Unaware that he was talking to the man who would blast his hopes of buying Paramount, Diller began to rave about the merger madness that had seized the entertainment industry. Disengaging himself, Smith moved to the elevators. To deceive any possible observers, he rode up to the floor of the Waldorf Towers just below the floor where the meeting was set and walked the rest of the way.

While James Dickerson, Bell Atlantic's chief financial officer, waited in the lobby, Smith and Malone haggled. Dickerson's repeated calls to Smith in the suite garnered the same answer: Malone would not budge. Then, finally, he did. Bell Atlantic had its terms.

On October 13, 1993, the deal was announced at New York's Hotel Macklowe. Bell Atlantic would buy TCI for $23 billion in special stock and another $10 billion in assumed TCI debt. Malone seemed genuinely relieved, or perhaps he found it hard to believe his luck. There was no denying that he was tired—his doctors were looking into it. Recently, in rare moments, he had let an occasional outsider glimpse a lonely man, a seasoned gunfighter longing to retire. And he had his wife to consider.

Once again, Leslie Malone was not happy with their life. Her husband worked banker's hours, lunched at home, and joined her after work at their favorite health club, but there had been a change since he picked his fight with Senator Gore. Her husband had been denounced on television and in the press. There had been letters and threats. The house was surrounded by a new security fence. Guards had been hired. None of this was to Leslie Malone's liking. The Bell Atlantic merger had come at precisely the right moment. Malone could pocket his billion and quietly withdraw from the limelight.

Smith would run the new enterprise. Malone would be vice-chairman with no clearly defined responsibilities. He joked that he had become a billion-dollar flunky; he hoped Bell Atlantic would find him a Philadelphia office he could use part-time. Perhaps, he said, his political enemies would drag him in a cage down Connecticut Avenue in Washington, pelting him with fruit as they rejoiced in his fall. Beneath Malone's rough exterior, Smith mused later, there seemed to lurk a sensitive man.

"Darth Vader, the king of the cable Cosa Nostra," said Smith. "I think all those names really got to him."

At times, Malone seemed to be composing his own eulogy. "I've been forced to become Mr. Outside and I don't like it," he said. "Yet, when you become legendary . . ." It was hard for an outsider to believe that Malone was ready to chuck it. Too many times before, the self-possessed, preternaturally calm Malone had suddenly whirled in his tracks, squeezed off a round, and added another notch to his gun. It was even harder to believe that cable television's most feared had come to the end of his tether.

As things came to pass, Bell Atlantic's James Dickerson found it especially hard to believe.

NINE

The Death and Rebirth
of an Illusion

JAMES DICKERSON, THE BELL ATLANTIC FINANCIAL officer who replaced Ray Smith as the man in charge of John Malone, was only forty-seven years old, but he was soon a very old forty-seven-year-old man. Like many another, Dickerson discovered that Malone's negotiating style seemed to have been drawn from the pages of a CIA handbook on prisoner interrogation. Its principal features were endless repetition, spatial disorientation, and sleep deprivation.

For Dickerson, dealing with Malone meant spending six days a week in a New York hotel, far from his home and family in Philadelphia. Malone wanted numbers, and when the numbers didn't satisfy him, he wanted more numbers. Malone wanted answers, and when he was displeased with the answers, he wanted other, different answers.

Above all—it was the entire purpose of the exercise—Malone wanted more money.

On some nights, Dickerson got no more than three hours' sleep as he lay in bed thinking obsessively about Malone's demands as columns of figures scrolled through his head, and the figures never added up. His appetite fell off; restaurant food no longer appealed to him. One morning, he felt alarmingly dizzy, so alarmingly dizzy that he packed his bags and went home. Dickerson had never been a tightly wound man, but when his doctor took his blood pressure, medication was prescribed. Dickerson announced that he was joining US Healthcare as a senior vice president. Malone was back in form. He had already taken the precaution of hanging Barry Diller out to dry.

IN SEPTEMBER 1993, JUST AS DILLER WAS PREPARING TO announce his triumphal return to Hollywood if Wall Street and the directors of Paramount were willing, Marty Davis demonstrated that he had not lost his ability to surprise. Paramount, it was announced, would enter into a friendly $8.2 billion merger with Viacom. The unpopular Davis had slipped the noose. In his place stood Sumner Redstone, a man whose admiration for Barry Diller had once been unbounded.

Redstone, seventy years old in 1993, was regarded as a figure of fun. He was excitable. When exasperated, he would sometimes smash the damp end of his cigar into his forehead. He actually seemed to believe that entertainment celebrities were interesting and important people. There were many stories about Sumner Redstone. All of them ignored a singular and central fact: Redstone had not become a billionaire by fishing through gratings for nickels. Sumner Redstone was always good for a laugh, but Redstone had been an adult when all the rest of them were children.

When he played tennis, a game that engrossed him to the point of obsession, he strapped the racket onto his maimed right hand and strode forward to battle as though the life of his firstborn depended on the game; in 1979, trapped in a burning hotel, he had climbed onto a ledge and held on until rescue, grimly counting to ten although his hand was on fire. In legend and perhaps in fact, he had been raised in a cold-water Boston tenement, the modern equivalent of a log cabin. He graduated from Harvard in 1944, spent his war cracking Japanese codes, returned to Harvard for a law degree, practiced as an attorney for the next dozen years, and eventually joined his father's small chain of drive-in theaters. Redstone took the business indoors, pioneered the multiscreen multiplex, and turned the company into National Amusements, the country's eighth-largest movie chain.

A liberal Democrat, he was one of the chairmen of Edmund Muskie's 1972 bid for the presidency. In his spare time, he taught law at Boston University. Meanwhile, he invested his money. He made $25 million when Coca-Cola bought Columbia Pictures, $20 million when Marty Davis took Paramount private, and $15 million from a shrewd play at MGM/UA. By 1986, he controlled just under a tenth of Viacom International, a company that owned television's evergreen comedy series, *I Love Lucy,* and *The Cosby Show,* the most popular and by far the most lucrative comedy of the decade, but it was a decade that was not kind to companies with valuable assets.

The dreaded Ivan Boesky soon lurked in the vicinity; Viacom paid $200 million to make Carl Icahn, another emblematic raider of the period, go away. Management attempted to apply a threatened company's favorite 1980s remedy, using the proceeds from a junk bond sale to purchase the outstanding shares, but the junk bond market fell into turmoil, management was unable to close the deal, and a rival group of investors appeared. Keeping his head and choosing his moment, Redstone bought the entire company for $3.2 billion at six o'clock in the morning after a sixteen-hour negotiating session.

"The next step is sleep," he announced. "The next step after that is to play tennis. Then I'll go to work."

He owned *Lucy,* he owned *Cosby,* he owned cable systems, and he owned Warner's inspired creations, Nickelodeon and MTV. An inveterate salesman who still called at three o'clock in the morning to check the ticket grosses at his theaters, Redstone loudly and gleefully repeated Bill Clinton's offhand quip that he owed the presidency to MTV.

Unlike his peers in moguldom, he was not overly impressed with interactive television, nor did his interest quicken when focus groups enthusiastically reported that they would use interactive television to vote in elections. Redstone knew all about focus groups, and he knew the dismal voting record of the American populace. He watched with interest as General Telephone and Electronics (GTE) set up an experimental interactive television service in El Cerrito, California, with the usual home banking, games, and video-on-demand. The service was offered to 7,300 citizens. Only 350 ever signed on. GTE gave up.

Working with a pencil stub on the back of an envelope, Redstone examined the results of TCI's interactive test in Littleton, and then he announced his findings.

"They boast that buy rates run about twelve times as high; that's for typical pay-per-view," Redstone said. "That sounds great, until you look at the dollars and cents. Translated, that means about one movie per household every two weeks. At $2.99 to $3.99 per movie, video-on-demand would hardly seem the engine of growth to drive the network of the future," he concluded dryly. "And I might add that those economics would not even come close to justifying the enormous cost of building the network of the future."

Still, he gave it a shot. With AT&T as his partner, he tinkered briefly with his own interactive experiment in Castro Valley, California, didn't like what he saw, and walked away, saving everybody a lot of money. As an old theater owner, he knew a secret as old as Sophocles: people only paid money to watch a show if they wanted to watch the show badly enough to pay money for it. It had been many years since people watched television for the sake of the technology. It had been years since people watched a specific network—CBS—for a specific reason: Edward R. Murrow's matchless news team and later Walter Cronkite. Those days were gone, perhaps forever. Programming, content, actors speaking lines that moved people to tears and laughter—these were the things that sold the tickets and got the ratings. Paramount served Redstone's purposes very nicely. He was a simple man who bought his suits off the rack, and he liked his business dealings to be straightforward. He had the money. He had received unmistakable signs that he would not be unwelcome. And Paramount, unlike digital and interactive television, not only had a proven track record; it was very easy to understand.

Like any self-respecting entertainment conglomerate of the 1990s, Paramount was organized according to an old-fashioned industrial model. The New York publishing arm, Simon & Schuster, provided the pig iron in the form of published stories. The stories were then sold to other movie studios or to Paramount itself, where they were converted into the gossamer and moonbeams of movies and television series. The writers provided the content, and the studios did the rest. Not every product succeeded, but that was the way of the world. Paramount had a large library of beloved films that could be thrown into the breach, mined for ideas, or cloned. The studio would be the crown jewel of Redstone's empire and the capstone of his career. He knew all about the bad blood between Davis and Diller, of course; everybody did. Redstone had always admired Barry Diller—as a showman after his own heart, but also as a man of integrity. Men of integrity did not meddle in the affairs of other men of integrity. Diller would not interfere. Redstone and Paramount had a done deal.

Unfortunately, Barry Diller was determined to reoccupy his vacated throne. Within a week, he entered the lists with a bid of $9.5 billion, far more money than Redstone's friendly offer and on far better terms, with Malone's Liberty providing $500 million. Wall Street was ecstatic. "This," announced one overjoyed investment banker, "is a signature deal, and it's a competitive deal."

It had been thin commons on the Street since Michael Milken

went to the slammer. On Wall Street, prudent times were hard times, and there was nothing the Street loved more than a bidding war. Bidding wars were like prizefights; while the gladiators sparred to put the other on the mattress, the people who got the payday were the people who whispered advice into the cauliflowered ear while manipulating the betting pool. In the Paramount fight, a good deal of the money was destined to come from Sumner Redstone's pocket, something Sumner Redstone understood all too well. Redstone was not ecstatic.

It would be years, if ever, before he spoke another civil word to Barry Diller. Perhaps worse in Redstone's eyes, Diller wasn't even his own man. He was someone's paid flack, and Redstone did not have to look far to discover who that man was.

"In the American cable industry," Redstone's lawsuit said, "one man has . . . seized monopoly power. Using bullyboy tactics and strong-arming of competitors, suppliers and customers, that man has inflicted antitrust injury on . . . virtually every American consumer of cable services and technologies. That man is John C. Malone."

John C. Malone, however, was no longer very interested in a situation he had done much to aggravate if not cause. His mind was on higher things. He was about to sell TCI and Liberty to Ray Smith and become a billionaire. Shortly after he and Smith made their merger announcement, Malone dispensed with Barry Diller. Liberty was no longer interested in the Paramount deal. The $500 million would not be forthcoming. Diller and Malone's old friends in Comcast were left to fend for themselves.

"We wish Barry Diller the best of luck," Malone said as he headed out the door. "He is the only person who can make it work. It's just a small investment . . ."

Malone was not quite done with Paramount, however. It would be a nice addition to the bill of goods he was selling to Bell Atlantic, and it would help him jack up the agreed-upon price. He went to Marty Davis and tried to cut a deal. He was unsuccessful. No matter. Soon, TCI would be no more, its debt would be somebody else's problem, and it would be left to the agreeable and well-connected Mr. Smith to deal with a small regulatory problem that the disagreeable Mr. Malone had done his level best to create. Senator Gore had become Vice President of the United States. The Vice President's childhood friend Reed Hundt—a man who shared many of his views—was appointed chairman of the FCC. With the considerable assistance of John Malone, the FCC had been handed a new weapon, and if any reason had been lacking to use it, Malone's TCI had managed to provide it with one. Malone had many uses for Ray Smith. Cable television had been reregulated.

HAVING DONE HIS INADVERTENT BEST TO BRING THE Cable Act of 1992 into existence, Malone had done his best to head it off before it came to a vote. Ever-rising cable rates—there was considerable debate over whether they had risen by 14.5 percent or 30 percent since 1987, but no one could deny that they had risen—were necessary, he explained, to enable companies like TCI to bring their customers the new set-top boxes, the 500 channels, and the information superhighway. The nation was unmoved by his argument. Part of the reason could be found in the TCI-served city of Evansville, Indiana.

In Evansville, TCI tried to persuade the city council to oppose the reregulation of cable. The alternative, TCI said, was stratospheric cable rates. A visibly angry city council announced that it supported the legislation. TCI claimed that it hadn't been trying to blackmail anybody. Nobody believed it.

The 1992 Cable Act gave the FCC—rather than, as before, the more pliable municipalities—the power to set cable rates. In the industry, a sullen muttering said that no one, including Al Gore, had done more to bring about the sorry state of affairs than John Malone. The FCC, in turn, ordered cable operators to lower their subscribers' bills by 10 percent, with further rollbacks possible. TCI, an unpleasant company shaped in the image of a man who couldn't seem to shut up, seemed to have learned nothing and forgotten everything as it laid plans to take advantage of the new situation.

In a memo to his underlings, a TCI executive vice president named Barry Marshall pointed out that while the Cable Act reimposed government control over rates, there was a hole in the law, and TCI was going to drive straight through it, hard and fast.

"Transaction charges for upgrades, downgrades and customer-caused service calls, VCR hookups, etc., are now vital revenue sources to us," Marshall wrote. By raising its service fees, TCI could make up close to "half of what we're losing from rate adjustments"—a sum that TCI had previously estimated at between $140 and $160 million. To be sure, Marshall remarked in what passed at TCI for empathy, the customers would undoubtedly gripe. "It will take a while, but they'll get used to it," Marshall continued. "The best news of all is we can blame it on reregulation and the government now. Let's take advantage of it!"

After the document found its way into the hands of the press, TCI admitted that "the tone of one portion of the memo was regrettable." That sort of thing would now be the province of Ray Smith, a master of public relations and an expert in customer service. Malone would be well out of it—provided, of course, that getting out was what John Malone intended. With Malone, as Barry Diller discovered, everything but his wife's happiness was contingent, and Malone's past behavior abundantly demonstrated that not even his wife could stop him if he took an idea into his head. As Bell Atlantic's Dickerson soon discovered, Malone's signature on a document was also contingent.

To Malone, a signed memorandum of understanding was a signal that the time had come to renegotiate everything in his favor. It was likely that many things would happen before John Malone entered the ranks of the nation's billionaires, and many things did. For once, Malone's considerable and infuriating talents played him false.

———

TO RAY SMITH, IT WAS THE BEST OF ALL POSSIBLE worlds. He had gone one-on-one with the fearsome Malone and had emerged triumphant, on his own terms, with the largest merger in American history. Under Smith's inspired leadership, Bell Atlantic would sail fearlessly into the digital future while laying the ground-work for the largest land-line, cellular, and PCS telephone system in the country if not the world. As the press never ceased to point out, the wires of the combined companies would run past the homes of 22 million Americans. It was with a high heart that Smith dispatched—finally—a Bell Atlantic team to closely examine Malone's Potemkin Village, and it was with a high heart that he laid his plans.

The combined companies, Smith announced, planned to spend at least $15 billion to ramp up the Bell Atlantic–TCI systems over the next five years. By 1995, Bell Atlantic–TCI would deliver advanced television—for starters, video-on-demand, cable telephones, and that world-beating, irresistible device, the Picturephone—to more than a million homes. By the following year, it planned to have telephone networks in thirty new cities. By the turn of the century, it would have invaded territories that would give it a potential 40 million new customers, 8 million homes would receive advanced television, and Bell Atlantic, Smith predicted, would begin to make "real bucks." There was more: the two companies would bring advanced informa-tion services into 26,000 public schools, initially for free, later at a modest monthly charge. It is possible—even probable—that Smith actually believed all this, at least in those first heady autumn days when the world seemed to lie at his feet. But as time went on and farseeing announcement succeeded farseeing announcement, Smith increasingly resembled a man whistling past a graveyard while Ma-lone, in the role of cabdriver, tirelessly dickered about the fare. Bell Atlantic had heard from its stockholders and its scouting party, and the news from the real world was not good.

THE PROPOSED MERGER HAD GIVEN BELL ATLANTIC'S stock a pleasing bounce in the marketplace, but a number of professional money managers had a pretty fair idea of the actual condition of Malone's systems even if Smith didn't. Unlike, apparently, Ray Smith, a number of outside observers also knew how to count. Here and there, a number of still, small voices were raised, pointing out that Bell Atlantic–TCI made absolutely no sense whatever.

Smith had agreed to a deal that would cost him $2,350 for each of TCI's 13.2 million sometimes unhappy customers, who in turn paid an average of $25 dollars a month for their service. As Sumner Redstone might have remarked, the numbers simply didn't add up. The deal stood an excellent chance of eviscerating Smith's bottom line, draining his corporate coffers, and in all likelihood destroying his splendid credit rating. An investment in Bell Atlantic could become a speculation, hot one day and cold the next, depending how a frequently irrational Wall Street happened to feel about the company at any given moment, and Bell Atlantic's stockholders had not invested in it to speculate.

The pre-merger Bell Atlantic was one of the few remaining old-fashioned dividend companies. Its stock price never moved around by much, but the generous quarterly dividends arrived like clockwork, and they were better than money in the bank. Bell Atlantic was a fire-and-forget, widow-and-orphan stock. You bought Bell Atlantic, put the certificate in the safe-deposit box, and walked away without a care in the world, because your money was as safe as houses. It was for this reason that all of Ray Smith's chips were blue, at least until he and Malone plighted their troth. Other companies might crash and burn, still others might stumble, but good old Bell Atlantic was forever—in its traditional form, the company had been prudence itself. All that was now over.

Not only were the economics of the deal—at least from the point of view of the cautious investor—strange to the point of lunacy, but Bell Atlantic had no exit strategy. If, for some all too imaginable reason, Smith came to conclude he had bought a pig in a poke and he did not like the pig, no one else was going to pay $33 billion to take TCI off his hands; $33 billion was more than twice what everyone else thought TCI was worth. At best, Bell Atlantic could hope to sell off bits and pieces in dribs and drabs, hardly a dynamic and forward-looking policy for a company that had once dreamed of becoming the digital communications titan of the future. It would be years, if ever, before a scorched and staggering Bell Atlantic regained its former luster. On Smith's milk carton, he could write as his epitaph: he made a desert, and he called it peace.

But Smith had not entirely taken leave of his senses. Although he seemed to believe, with enormous optimism, that the future would take care of itself, he knew very well that Bell Atlantic's market value was intimately attached to the size of the quarterly dividend and the stability of the stock's price, and he proposed, in effect, to divide the new Bell Atlantic into separate financial entities cohabiting under a single roof. Existing Bell Atlantic stockholders would continue to receive their dividends as before. Malone, Magness, and the other TCI shareholders would receive a new class of stock that paid no dividend for five years. Five years was the amount of time that Smith and his people—or those of Smith's people who didn't think he'd lost his mind—calculated they needed to absorb their new investment; after five years, Bell Atlantic would return to its normal state of imperial solvency, and it would reap the rewards of its groundbreaking foresight. There were the customary three things wrong with this plan.

Although Malone had agreed to it, he didn't like it. The Bell Atlantic stockholders had never been asked for their opinion but they didn't like it either, and they almost immediately began to make their feelings known through the jungle telegraph of Bell Atlantic's daily stock price. It slowly but inexorably began to fall as Bell Atlantic's investors began to reduce the size of their holdings, and none of Smith's visionary pronouncements could stop the decline.

As a result, Bell Atlantic found itself caught in a financial trap of its own devising. In the deal Smith had cut with Malone, Bell Atlantic would assume the $10 billion in TCI's debt—a paper transaction—and pay the $23 billion balance, not with money, but with the special stock that paid no dividend for five years—a second paper transaction. The exact amount of the stock Bell Atlantic would have to give TCI's shareholders, including Malone, was based on a complicated formula, but one thing about the formula was simple: the less Bell Atlantic's stock was worth on Wall Street, the more special stock Bell Atlantic would have to fork over. If the downward trend continued, a point could be reached where Bell Atlantic would no longer be the purchaser of TCI. Instead, TCI would own Bell Atlantic. Provided, of course, that the merger went through as planned.

Ray Smith's mind was clearing rapidly. His thinking was further improved when his investigators reported back on the actual, as distinct from mythical, condition of TCI.

To say that progress was not TCI's most important product would actually have been a compliment, because it would have implied that a little progress, somewhere, was some small part of TCI's corporate life. The company's technological wonders—Malone's 500 channels, the cable-based information superhighway, the interactive television—were largely a product of rhetoric, smoke, and mirrors.

Bell Atlantic's scouting party detected few signs of the future's favorite telecommunications company. For years, Malone had been largely interested in his cash flow, and as long as his incoming cash held up, he had given little thought to the modernity of his systems or the composition of his audience. Almost half his customers were rural and thinly scattered. Bell Atlantic knew all about rural areas. A thinly scattered rural clientele occupied the last—the very last—service area a sensible telephone company wanted on its books because it was impossible to make any money there.

This might seem a small matter. Smith was not required, after all, to provide telephone service to any of Malone's customers, and the rest of TCI's cables ran through suburbs and cities where Bell Atlantic could make, as Smith might say, some real bucks once Smith's other favorite project, the new federal telecommunications bill, was written into law. So far, so good, but Smith was also betting his company on advanced television and data services, and TCI had never been equipped to deliver them.

TCI had laid almost no optical fiber, the essential conduit for any serious form of digital television. Few of TCI's back offices were equipped with the sort of computer systems that were essential to running a contemporary telecommunications network, much less the telecommunications network of Malone's bright predictions and Smith's dreamed-of future. When it came to the future, TCI was mostly talk, and talk—unlike TCI—was cheap.

For years, Malone had taunted Bell Atlantic and the other telephone companies about their obsolete networks and ancient technologies, but in reality Bell Atlantic was a technological powerhouse and TCI was not. At TCI, Bell Atlantic was going to have to spend billions to build a telephone network on some of the systems, and billions more before it could even begin to think about getting into the advanced television and communications business.

The situation was not exactly hopeless. TCI's service areas included the homes and offices of millions of desirable customers; it controlled the right-of-way—even if it didn't own the basic technology—of an information superhighway. But TCI was not worth $33 billion. A mistake had been made.

The price of Bell Atlantic's stock continued to decline. The December 15 deadline for closing the deal came and went, and no deal was consummated. From somewhere, the press learned that Malone was the cause of the delay. Nowhere was it suggested that Bell Atlantic had begun to stall for time.

IT WAS EVEN HARDER THAN USUAL TO FIGURE OUT JUST what John Malone thought he was doing. Normally, Malone had several balls in the air at the same time—parallel plans, alternate plans, trapdoors for the unwary, trapdoors for escape. Now, as far as anyone could see, he had none.

Not long before, he had been offered the chairmanship of IBM, a deeply troubled company. The position was his for the asking. But the chairmanship of IBM would mean returning to the East, a life of extensive travel, long hours at the office, everything he had given up to save his marriage, and with the exception of the security fence and the guards he felt compelled to hire, his life was organized to his satisfaction. Moreover, IBM would have meant leaving behind his investment in Liberty, because Liberty had been repurchased by TCI. Once he had sold TCI to Smith, retrieved his billion dollars, and dropped from public view, his life would also be organized to the satisfaction of his wife, and he would no longer be the Darth Vader of the cable Cosa Nostra. Ray Smith would be, if he chose to assume the role. Malone declined the position at IBM and painted himself into a corner.

Bell Atlantic had no exit strategy if the merger succeeded. Malone, surprisingly, had allowed himself only one strategy if the merger failed. The Bell Atlantic deal contained an unwritten penalty clause. If Ray Smith backed out, Malone was obliged to spend billions of dollars to build an interactive television system. With immense fanfare, he had staked his claim on the digital future, and if he suddenly announced that he'd been wrong or couldn't afford it, the stock market's punishment would be severe. Unless he sold the company, all other avenues were closed.

Paramount was now beyond his reach; the FCC had made it clear that TCI was not welcome, Malone had bid farewell to Diller, and Sumner Redstone was on the verge of winning the bidding war. In November, Malone looked in on Columbia, Universal, and Murdoch's 20th Century Fox, but another movie deal might queer the pitch with Bell Atlantic even if an opening existed. The studios were not for sale, and if he had to build an interactive television system on his own, he probably couldn't afford them. Nobody else was going to pay $33 billion for TCI. To achieve his goals—to please his wife, make his billion, and kick his way clear of TCI before the roof began to fall in—he had to sell TCI to Ray Smith. January 2, 1994, was fixed as the second deadline for closing the deal. January 2 came and went, and no deal was closed.

Malone seemed to be running on the inertia of an established habit that no longer served him well, haggling ceaselessly until every other eye glazed over, all other nerves frayed, and he was given what he wanted because it was the only way to make him shut up and allow everyone else to get on with their lives. But for once, Malone didn't hold the upper hand. The longer he delayed the proceedings and the deadlines came and went, the more Bell Atlantic discovered about TCI, and the more time Ray Smith had to think. Only a few months before, Smith had been in the palm of his hand. Malone was not a well man. Perhaps that was the explanation.

It was nothing serious, or so he said. Since the previous fall, Malone had been bothered by persistent flu-like symptoms that would not go away. His doctors suspected they were related to stress; Malone's immune system no longer worked the way it should. He had developed arthritis and walked with a limp, but he still set himself the usual grueling pace. Time—and his own infuriating tenacity— had always been his friend. He had never lost a fight in his life.

HE LOST. ON FEBRUARY 23, 1994, IT WAS ALL OVER WITH Bell Atlantic.

Two days before, Smith had announced that there was no way he was going to pay $33 billion for TCI. The new price was to be roughly $30 billion. A newly docile Malone agreed. Belatedly, Smith and his executives had become very unhappy with TCI's debt. They were deeply troubled by the price of their stock, down more than $20 a share from the October high. They had discovered that TCI was not a technological powerhouse. But if Malone had finally shown some flexibility, he still had an old grievance, and it had not been settled. He was unhappy with the stock he would receive. It was all very well to say that it was worth, on paper, a billion dollars. It hadn't traded on the market yet, there was a distinct possibility that it would trade at a discount, and instead of becoming a billionaire, Malone would be a mere centimillionaire. Earlier, he had confided to his associates that he believed the deal had only a 30 percent chance of success. With Smith and his executives perilously close to mutiny and Malone inclined to dig in his heels, the new agreement could come apart at any moment if outside events intervened.

On the morning of February 22, Smith sat down in his Arlington, Virginia, office, punched up C-SPAN on his television set, and learned that the FCC had reduced the cable companies' subscriber fees by another 7 percent. The previous rollback had only been partly successful. A third of the cable subscribers had actually seen their bills rise, and TCI's infamous memorandum seemed to reveal at least a part of the trick had been done.

Smith shrugged, left the room, and did not immediately return Malone's prompt call. Instead, he ordered his financial people to compute a new, even lower price for TCI. Hours later, he arranged a meeting the next day at the New York office of Skadden, Arps, Slate, Meagher & Flom, Bell Atlantic's outside counsel.

"You know what amazes me?" Smith said afterward. "There were only four people in the room that day, but there are at least twenty versions of what happened. It's like the movie *Rashomon*."

In the end, the two companies agreed—Bell Atlantic with a tactful and measured statement, TCI with a blistering diatribe—that the FCC action marked the end of their journey together. Bell Atlantic's latest and previously final offer, $30 billion in restricted stock and debt assumption, was no longer on the table. By TCI's own figures, the latest FCC rollback was scheduled to reduce its cash flow by another $144 million. Bell Atlantic estimated that it would cost anywhere between $15 and $20 billion to bring TCI up to speed and into the twenty-first century; a $144 million reduction in TCI's already reduced cash flow meant that the borrowing power of the combined companies had been reduced by $900 million. It was possible that Bell Atlantic no longer wanted to buy TCI very badly. It was possible that Malone no longer wanted to sell on anybody's terms but his own.

"He just kept reaching and reaching," an executive close to Bell Atlantic told *The Wall Street Journal*. But, given all the conflicting and mutually exclusive versions of the events in the conference room of Skadden, Arps, Slate, Meagher & Flom, it was impossible to discover just what, exactly or even approximately, occurred during the last merger meeting between Ray Smith and John Malone. Except for how it ended.

Malone and Smith pondered the situation for a while, then rose from their chairs and took the elevator down to meet the television cameras. The largest merger in American corporate history, they announced, was not going to happen.

Ray Smith finally got his new telecommunications bill out of Congress in 1996 and gradually abandoned the television business. Malone plunged onward into the digital future. And Jerry Levin actually built an interactive digital television system.

TEN

The Court of the Borgias

SIX MONTHS AFTER THE COLLAPSE OF THE BELL ATLANTIC deal in February 1994, Malone gave a celebrated interview to *Wired* magazine, a publication, partly bankrolled by Nicholas Negroponte, that was the house organ and influential voice of cockeyed digital optimism in its most virulent form.

Who, asked the magazine's correspondent David Kline, is building the information superhighway?

"Us," said Malone, matching his words to his audience while, not for the first time, ignoring a rather large amount of inconvenient reality. "We're building it. We've got 35 percent of the country done right now. By the end of the year, we'll be 55 percent done. And by the end of '96, we'll be completely done in terms of fiber and coaxed deployment—terrestrial network that is the superhighway. . . .

We're talking about something that is more complex than anything that's ever been designed, probably by close to an order of magnitude." He had never needed Bell Atlantic, he said, except for its political connections and its money. It did not occur to the correspondent from *Wired*—and, by all available signs, it did not seem to occur to John Malone—that he was talking through his hat.

IN THE DAYS IMMEDIATELY AFTER THE COLLAPSE OF THE TCI deal, Bell Atlantic's spokesmen had gone out of their way to say that Smith and Malone remained the greatest of friends—just a couple of guys, really—and that some sort of joint venture was still possible. No joint venture materialized. Bell Atlantic, slowly and inexorably, like a screen fading to black, lost almost all of its once vivid interest in the television of the future and decided to buy Nynex, the New York and New England regional telephone company whose service area was conveniently adjacent to its own.

THE HERD INSTINCT OF THE AMERICAN BUSINESS AND financial communities is a curious thing, at once powerful and fragile, like a bull made of glass. Sometimes the smallest thing—a cute little dog pulls aside a curtain, a child comments on the sartorial eccentricity of the monarch—can smash it to flinders. The collapse of the TCI–Bell Atlantic merger was such a moment.

Cox Communications and Southwestern Bell abruptly dissolved the $4.9 billion partnership they had formed, giddily, in the immediate aftermath of the proposed combination. Southwestern Bell, renamed SBC, proceeded with its own loudly trumpeted digital and interactive television system in Richardson, Texas, discovered that the citizenry wasn't remotely interested in interactive television, quietly built a regular cable system instead, and bought Pacific Bell. US West became far more interested in separating Time Warner from its existing cable systems—and buying others—than it had ever been in the television of the future. Truth to tell, a small US West television-of-the-future experiment in Omaha, like drunken brain surgery, had not met the company's expectations. And although Malone had spoken expansively of a project larger than the space program, he neglected to mention a serious problem with a component no larger than a textbook: the inexpensive set-top box. General Instrument, the company that invented digital television, was having the devil's own time figuring out how to manufacture one of them.

Malone still had his formidable reputation, and—just as a car going a hundred miles an hour could coast a long way after it ran out of gas—a formidable reputation had considerable staying power. "All roads," said a prominent media analyst, "lead to John Malone." Increasingly, however, the roads began to lead elsewhere.

While Malone was otherwise engaged, Redstone finally won the battle for Paramount; Barry Diller did not carry the day. But Diller was not down for the count, not yet, and TCI still owned 22 percent of his company. Curiously, Diller didn't seem to notice that Malone had already stabbed him in the back at least once. Anywhere Diller went, Malone went likewise. "I think," Malone said, rediscovering his protégé's virtues, "there's a lot of great things we're going to be able to do with Barry."

The next great thing was CBS. These were uncharted but promising waters. Since 1986, CBS had been controlled by Laurence Tisch, another immensely talented financial engineer who had made his first money in the hotel business, his second money in movie theaters, and his most recent fortune in insurance. Tisch, in whom the old American virtue of frugality burned brightly—he was a world-famous tightwad—knew and cared a very great deal about money and neither knew nor cared much of anything about television. He closed the network's CBS lab, where the long-playing record had been invented. He sold the profitable music division. He eviscerated the networks' news operation, once the finest in the industry.

Nothing seemed beneath his scrutiny. He closed his executives' private dining rooms. On the prowl for waste and redundancy, he made a study of the different kinds of stationery CBS bought and ordered reforms. He demoralized his employees, did not believe in the magic of show business, cared not a fig for new technologies, filled CBS's vaults with cash, turned the network into something that resembled a money-market fund, and did not seem overly concerned when the former Tiffany Network lost its grip on the viewers' affections. He was also looking for a way to cash in, and his network executives were looking for a way to get rid of him. When Tisch and Diller announced, on June 30, 1994, that QVC would merge with CBS and Diller would replace Tisch as chairman, the news was greeted with unfeigned delight that bothered Laurence Tisch not at all. Malone was similarly delighted.

On the face of it, it seemed unlikely that the FCC would allow Malone to own a piece of a television network, but it was possible that appearances deceived. As the prospective chairman of CBS, a deeply troubled national treasure, Barry Diller was the answer to a maiden's prayer, and Diller was Malone's latest sidekick. The FCC had previously given the predatory Rupert Murdoch a waiver to operate Fox, a network that otherwise appeared to be illegal, and Malone, unlike Diller, seemed to have the deep pockets CBS would need to extract itself from its dilemma. All the newspapers said he did, and the FCC knew approximately enough about high finance and sophisticated TCI-like pyramid schemes as the next fellow, which wasn't very much. Or perhaps the ingenious Malone would devise something that would legally give him a piece of the network while neatly sidestepping the FCC entirely. He had done it often enough before, although not recently. For example, he could reactivate Liberty as a legally independent holding company for programming assets, and there was nothing in the rules that said Liberty couldn't own a piece of CBS. The possibilities were various. Soon, however, they were also moot.

Ralph Roberts, the founder of Comcast, was a former haberdasher who got into the cable business when beltless slacks threatened his belt-manufacturing business; Brian Roberts, who ran Comcast on a daily basis, was his son. It had been Brian Roberts, perhaps even more than Malone, who had been instrumental in luring Diller to QVC to begin with, and Diller had come to view the younger Roberts as a personal friend. But the Paramount adventure seemed to cause the Roberts family to take careful thought about their investment and their partners. Malone, a longtime Comcast ally, had hung them out to dry on the Paramount deal, and he had planned to do them an even worse turn before the Bell Atlantic merger fell through: he had tried to turn TCI into an awesomely well-heeled competitor in every business Comcast owned or proposed to enter. Malone had decided that his old allies, the Robertses, should be offered an opportunity to die bravely for their country. In the interest of making himself a billion dollars while seizing control of cable's future, Malone had left Comcast to sink or swim on its own. Ralph and Brian Roberts, the old haberdasher and his son, had found the experience instructive. Malone could not be trusted to stand by an old ally.

Perhaps he really wanted Diller to take over CBS, perhaps he was up to something again, or perhaps both things were true, but Comcast would not be left holding the bag again. At the same time, it would be possible to teach Malone an instructive lesson even if it meant getting rid of Barry Diller.

The Robertses decided they liked QVC just as it was—selling spray-on vitamins and toaster ovens to the gullible and addicted— even if it meant, as it almost certainly did, that Barry Diller would take a hike. Comcast announced that it had no interest in owning a piece of CBS but that, to preserve an asset that was dear to it, Comcast would buy the parts of QVC it didn't already own. Barry Diller would not become chairman of CBS.

Diller, Malone discovered, was not exactly the easiest person to use as a Judas goat or a stalking horse; perhaps the Paramount experience had something to do with it. Malone said he would help Diller buy QVC, foiling the Comcast plan, but owning QVC no longer seemed to be high on Diller's list of life goals. Malone said he would help Diller prepare a new bid for CBS, but Diller, giving a convincing imitation of a man refusing to grab a lifeline, decided that CBS had become seriously overpriced. Malone, his generosity exhausted, joined Ralph and Brian Roberts in their buyout, preserving his interest in QVC and the devil take the hindmost. The hindmost was Barry Diller.

In February 1995, an angry Diller left QVC with $116 million in his pocket—a $91 million profit on his original investment of $25 million—and a familiar determination to let no man be his master. Unless, puzzlingly, that man was John Malone. For whatever reason, Diller seemed to believe that John Malone had bought his soul, and he took the reins at TCI's other shopping channel, HSN. And for John Malone, it was finally time to get into the television business.

Actually, he didn't have much choice. He was running out of wiggle room, and he had no one to blame but himself.

To attract a suitor in the form of Bell Atlantic, Malone had revived the old dream of the Wired World, this time with a digital twist, and although TCI was a maiden scorned, there was no going back. Digitized cable television was just about the only thing in the cable business that still attracted the favorable interest of Wall Street and the financial community, and the halcyon days of financial engineering were gone, perhaps forever. It was as though Malone had invented the Hail Mary pass and flummoxed everybody in his league until everybody learned how the trick was done.

With the Bell Atlantic dream turned to ashes and as CBS slipped from his hands, he took one last shot at the old way of doing things. TCI picked up the part of Heritage Communications it didn't already own, paid more than a billion in stock for a midsized operator called Telecable, and—now that peace had broken out with Viacom and Sumner Redstone needed money—agreed to fork over $2.3 billion for Viacom's cable systems, which gave him a considerable presence in San Francisco. Meanwhile, two of his affiliated companies picked up another 440,000 viewers in Pennsylvania and New Jersey. On its books, TCI now had more than 14 million customers, but the financial community was not amused. These were different times. TCI already had too much debt on its books, and now it had more. When Malone, like some Balkan warlord announcing his claim to lands and dominions firmly in the hands of others, revived his old dream of invading the telephone business, TCI's investment-grade credit rating—the only one in the cable industry—was yanked. TCI became a junk bond company; when it came to borrowing money, Malone's competitive edge was gone. Ceaseless expansion no longer worked, nor did bluster. Digital technology was the only way out.

On paper, it looked simple, so simple that the concept could be dramatized on an animated videotape for the instruction of the digitally thunderstruck press. First, you created an optical-fiber network to bring digital television and its huge volume of compressed data to the neighborhoods where the customers lived. Next, the existing coaxial cables brought the signal into the home along a right-of-way called the last mile. In the home, a digital set-top box decoded the signal, and both interactive television and the cable-based information superhighway were born. Malone calculated that a General Instrument set-top box would cost him around $500. Surely the customers would be willing to pay an additional $7 a month for their new channels and their interactive video-on-demand, effortlessly repaying TCI for the new devices.

But it looked even better than that. Malone carefully did not mention that a pending change in the law would allow him to charge his customers—including the rural customers who would never see a digital set-top box anytime soon, because it was economic suicide to bring land-based digital television to a thinly populated countryside—an additional fee to defray his costs. It would be tacked on to the regular cable bill. In other words, half of Malone's customers would pay for set-top boxes they did not have. And when somebody got around to inventing the satellite technology that would enable him to provide his rural customers with a form of digital television, his urban and suburban customers would provide the subsidy through their own monthly bills. Malone was planning to receive two huge, interest-free loans from his disgruntled and unhappy customers, and he would never have to pay them back. Cable looked like a wonderful business again.

Missing from this happy equation, however, were a number of inconvenient realities. When Time Warner, a much friendlier cable company, tried to charge its customers less than half Malone's projected monthly fees for modest new set-top boxes and modest new nondigital services, Time Warner's customers successfully rebelled. All across the country, a limit seemed to have been reached on how many new bells and whistles the viewing public would tolerate unless they were free. Malone's customers had put up with many things in their time, but the only way to test their mettle in the digital age was to throw them some new-style television and see how they reacted. Years began to pass, and no such interesting thing happened.

Set-top boxes were among the simplest components in a cable system. When General Instrument set forth to produce Malone's new digital boxes, however, GI discovered that they were remarkably hard to invent and, to everyone's shared unhappiness, even harder to manufacture. In the meantime, Time Warner had actually built a state-of-the-art interactive television system in Orlando, Florida, using immediately available, off-the-shelf components. Normally, this would be good news. Time Warner would test Malone's equipment for him. It would do his market research. It would spend vast sums of its shareholders' money, and Malone would reap where Time Warner had sown. But as Ray Smith had discovered back in one of his enthusiastic moments—in one of his many enthusiastic moments—something that worked just fine in the lab often worked very differently elsewhere in the world.

Jerry Levin, who had once been told to sit in a room and think deep thoughts, had been given new operating responsibilities at Time Warner. He was running the place.

HE SAT, SURROUNDED BY A SOLITUDE THAT SUITED HIM, in the chairman's office on the nearly deserted twenty-ninth floor of

Time Warner's headquarters at 75 Rockefeller Plaza. Although he spent other people's money with the sort of unstinting hand that gave a new meaning to the words "reckless abandon," he was not by nature an aggressive man. His conversation was both heavy and vague, dotted with words like "ineluctable" and sprinkled with phrases like "transforming transactions." His erudition and vocabulary had dazzled many a listener until, when the listener was finally alone with his thoughts in the hall, he suddenly realized that he hadn't understood a thing Levin had said.

His career at the old Time Inc. had been littered with one costly failure after another, hundreds of millions of dollars lost, the wreckage cleared away by other men who, unlike Jerry Levin, failed to prosper in the new Time Warner. One of his former superiors, Nick Nicholas, had said that Levin should never, under any circumstances, be allowed to run anything again, but Nicholas was now gone, like so many others. One by one, the people who stood between Levin and the chairman's desk had vanished from the scene, until only Levin was left. Daily, as he multiplied Time Warner's already crushing load of debt, as chaos spread throughout the corporate ranks, and as Levin happily led the company deep into a fabulously expensive form of interactive television that would never make a dime, it was expected that he would soon be gone. Instead, he remained. Like an aging, male Joan of Arc, he seemed blinded by his visions and deafened by his voices.

His favorite novel was Camus's *The Stranger*.

THE MERGER HAD NOT CREATED A WELL-OILED, smoothly running machine. Time Warner was a collection of immensely valuable, capably managed enterprises that individually made a great deal of money—even *Time* magazine, no longer one of the nation's essential publications, threw off profits of around $50 million a year, more than double those of its nearest competitor—but Time Warner as a whole was a chaotically managed company that made no money at all. Interest on the $16 billion debt was somewhere in the vicinity of $90,000 an hour, a figure that turned every divisional profit into a corporate loss. Nicholas, the chief architect of everything he beheld, seemed to have fallen into a trance. Levin seemed to have snapped out of one.

Levin was drawn to the Warner side of the company. Ross's romanticism found a compatible echo in his own mystical proclivities, and his love of complexity found its counterpart. Levin, the man in the double-knit suit with the nonmatching tie, also found that he rather enjoyed his new, Warner-style paychecks. He seemed to be in Ross's confidence, a privilege to which Nicholas was immune and Levin was not. And Ross, like Malone, was never so happy as when he was deep in a game of three-dimensional chess. Malone regarded business as a war to the knife, where the objective was to seize and hold territory. Ross regarded business as a hugely enjoyable pastime, played within the confines of his corporate family. No one ever saw Malone enjoy himself. No one ever saw Ross when he was not engaged in the pursuit of serious fun. Both were utterly ruthless men.

Unlike Malone, with his coldly logical mind, Ross thought of his company as an organism with fascinating dynamics all its own. For example, Nick Nicholas, his putative heir apparent, had outlived his usefulness with the completion of the merger. Nicholas would be stripped of his power and his friends, and then he would be shown the door. The beauty of the thing would be the completeness and inevitability of his defeat.

As a first step, Ross made the obliging Levin Time Warner's chief operating officer despite Levin's discouraging management history, cutting Nicholas off from the day-to-day affairs of the company. Ross also made a point of paying Nicholas a salary that was stupendous by the standards of the old Time Inc. Nicholas accepted it.

While Nicholas was being quietly removed, it was equally important to show the people on the Time side of the company their proper place in the new organization. Michael Fuchs, the temperamental Time executive who had finally made a financial and critical success of Home Box Office, was an ambitious man. Under his leadership, HBO had commissioned some memorable made-for-television movies, and to Fuchs the next step was clear. Because HBO had learned how to make movies, it would now make movies for theatrical release. With Ross's support, Bob Daly and Terry Semel, who ran Warner Brothers, informed Fuchs that they made the movies around here, not HBO, period and end of discussion. HBO did not make theatrical movies. Nor did HBO receive a discount when it showed Warner Brothers films. Nicholas did not spring vigorously to Fuchs's defense. In Michael Fuchs, Nick Nicholas had made a dangerous enemy, and Ross's plan took another step forward.

With the company $16 billion in debt, it was important to cut costs. This also had its uses. Nicholas unwisely accepted the task of debt reduction and compounded his folly by laying off 600 staffers in the magazine division. The people in the magazine division rightly regarded themselves as the only serious and responsible part of a company that was no longer serious or responsible. They watched as Ross paid himself a ducal ransom and Nicholas became rich from his new compensation. (So did Levin, but no one seemed to pay attention.) They were aware that Warner's seven corporate aircraft were at the beck and call of the Warner talent, who treated the planes as a private airline. They watched as Warner Music made ever more money by catering to the baser instincts of its audience. It was not lost on the magazine division that when Nicholas embarked on his cost-cutting campaign, it affected only one part of the company. The Warner air force continued to fly. Nicholas continued to pay himself an opulent salary. The record division continued to crank out products that were arguably dangerous to the mental health of their youthful consumers. Nicholas never seemed to grasp that the magazine people had the ears of their colleagues in influential news organizations whose publications were carefully read on Wall Street. The magazine people also had a way with words, and the word on Nicholas was very bad. If Nicholas, by some chance, were to be forced out of the company, there would be no catastrophically negative reaction in the financial community.

It was important to reduce the $16 billion debt itself; Time Warner's stockholders, unlike the stockholders of TCI, had not been indoctrinated with the gospel of debt and cash flow. Nicholas wanted to raise the badly needed cash by selling marginal cable systems and a large investment in a toy company. Ross didn't want to sell anything, and neither did Levin. Nicholas, who knew a thing or two about finance, quietly went to Wall Street, returned with $2.76 billion, and was not thanked. With the enthusiastic backing of Levin, who had no financial background, Ross detached Warner Brothers, HBO, and the cable systems from the company, placed them in a limited partnership called Time Warner Entertainment, fruitlessly scoured Europe for investors, and finally sold a 12.5 percent interest to Itochi, a Japanese trading company, and Toshiba, the electronics giant, for $1 billion. Everyone, including Nicholas, agreed that the Japanese had gotten a huge bargain. In exchange for a billion dollars in tuition, Toshiba and Itochi were allowed—encouraged, even—to examine Time Warner's cable business and learn its technological secrets at the very time that the Japanese, belatedly, were building cable systems in their home islands.

Nicholas was furious. The sole purpose of the new partnership was to raise money for Time Warner. The partnership had no business strategy and no other reason for existing, and it was impossible to predict the mischief that might be caused in the future; the partners—and anyone else who might be invited to buy into the deal—owned a piece of Time Warner's most valuable assets, and their actions could not be controlled. Ross and Levin, Nicholas insisted, had traded away an important piece of the company's crown jewels for a quick billion bucks. Nicholas was right on all points. Unfortunately, as Ross had foreseen, he was also powerless. He had alienated Michael Fuchs, HBO, and the magazine division. He had no support on

Wall Street. He could no longer stop Ross from doing anything Ross wanted.

Ross was a great believer in collegiality within his corporate family. It was therefore extremely fortunate that Nicholas's undoing was largely a result of his abrasive personality combined with his misguided actions, but there was one last flank to secure. Jerry Levin was Time Warner's third-ranking executive, and a man to whom Ross himself had given real power. Levin, unlike Nicholas, was susceptible to Ross's hypnotic charm, but Levin was not a stupid man. In a corporate power struggle, he would be either a formidable enemy or a useful friend. It was by a very happy chance, then, that Ross and Levin shared a common interest.

John Malone was an electrical engineer who had been forced by circumstances to take an interest in the technology of his own industry. Steve Ross was a former funeral director who loved the stuff. The Atari disaster had not dampened his enthusiasm. Woo Paik's digital television showed the latest way to the future. Time Warner—Ross and Levin—would reinvent Qube in a new and irresistibly improved form and take the world by storm. They would make pots of money and have a bang-up time.

JIM CHIDDIX, TIME WARNER CABLE'S VICE PRESIDENT for engineering and technology, thought he knew how to do it. A bearded bear of a man, he had dropped out of Cornell in his senior year and never finished college, went to Hawaii "for reasons that seemed very wise at the time," learned his trade on Oahu and in the Army, and became Time's chief engineer in 1986.

"Qube was a technology that let you put on a good show," he said on a winter afternoon in his Stamford, Connecticut, office, "but it didn't have much, really, for the consumer other than novelty value. Remember, Qube was before the microprocessor. The boxes in the home were extremely dumb. They could send back signals, but they couldn't do much else. When you pushed a button, the fact that you'd pushed that button was stored for a period of time in a very simple logic gate. The central computer would then call the names of all the boxes in the system and shout them out over an outgoing channel: 'Box number 1439-7, what's happening?' When your number was called, you would answer, 'Here I am, and by the way, button number four has been pushed.' It was technology that got a huge play in the media and a pretty short play in customers' homes."

The microprocessor would change all that, aided by fiber-optical cable and what Chiddix believed was his secret weapon, the same reliable old coaxial cable that Time Warner had used for decades.

Twisted-pair copper telephone wires were frequently likened to a garden hose. It could do some things very well, but it couldn't do much. An optical-fiber cable, by contrast, was like a fire hose; fiber op could do a lot of things. Then there was coaxial cable, the backbone of Time Warner's cable systems. Coaxial cable was considered obsolete when it was considered at all. In Chiddix's opinion, this view was dead wrong. There was, as the cable industry had realized for years, a tremendous amount of unused capacity on coax. Coax was a fire hose that acted like a garden hose. It could carry 150 analog channels, but no one had ever been able to figure out how to do it. Once again, the laws of physics kept getting in the way.

An analog video signal piped down a coaxial cable lost half its strength almost immediately and well before it traveled out of sight. The problem was solved by installing amplifiers once every 1,000 or 2,000 feet, creating another problem. The amplifiers acted like crimps in a hose, limiting the amount of programming that could be carried. Well in advance of the rest of the cable industry, Chiddix reasoned that if coaxial cable could be combined with optical fiber—which required remarkably little amplification—it would be possible to unclog the entire system. Optical fiber could be used for long-distance transmissions across a town or a region. Coaxial cable would do the rest. There were 864,000 miles of coaxial cable in the country, a huge and underutilized resource.

On paper—and, as it turned out, in practice—the solution was simplicity itself. In a cable system, a facility called the head end received and processed the video signal. Optical fiber would be run from the head end to a specific viewing neighborhood—the 500 or so homes called the last mile—that would receive their video signal through existing coaxial cable. The marching array of amplifiers would be eliminated, the crimp would vanish from the hose, and the purpose of the exercise was to multiply the number of analog television channels. Each house would receive 150 channels of television. The optical-fiber portion of the new network—called hybrid fiber-coax, or HFC—was digital, but it did not deliver digital television. That came later, with Paik's compression technology. Like James Watt—who repaired a pump and earned enduring fame as the father of the modern steam engine—Chiddix was attempting to make a quantum leap using existing technology, not invent a new one.

First, Chiddix and his engineers had to figure out how to deliver conventional analog television over a fiber-optical line. The problem was the lasers.

Traditional twisted-pair copper wire carried the human voice in the form of analog waves. An optical-fiber cable did not use analog waves. Tiny lasers no larger than grains of rice converted the human voice into the 1's and 0's of the binary digital code using rapid pulses of light or their absence. Like an analog telephone line, optical-fiber transmissions were narrowband, carrying a single form of freight—a digitized human voice or a string of numerical data—through a tunnel with a small diameter. A video signal was broadband, carrying human voices, moving images, their surroundings, the background music, and anything else that happened to be on the sound track. A video transmission required a wide tunnel with a very high roof. Here was another of the beauties of optical fiber. If you changed some of the components in the system, optical fiber became the necessary broadband tunnel.

"We did not want lasers that could turn off and on real fast, which is how you send ones and zeros," Chiddix said, "but lasers that could be modulated for much more complex information." Changes also had to be made in the telephone-based devices that translated the digital code back into analog waves for the coax to carry over the last mile. Tests in the company's Denver labs indicated that it could be done, perhaps in the real world. Using the leverage of the country's second-largest cable system, Chiddix invited manufacturers like AT&T to build him some equipment he could use.

Framed on the wall of his Stamford office was the first broadband laser transmitter ever made. It had cost $30,000. It was only a few years old, and it was obsolete. "It allowed us to change the entire topology of cable systems fundamentally," Chiddix said. Unlike TCI, where John Malone soon turned himself into the archetypical Texan with a big hat and no horse, Time Warner had made a significant technological breakthrough. Using existing components and a few new ones, a 150-channel network was possible.

To test the system, Time Warner rewired a 10,000-household neighborhood in the New York borough of Queens. The cost was around $110 per household, a reasonable sum in the cable business. As promised, the new system delivered 150 channels and a form of pay-per-view called near-video-on-demand. With near-video-on-demand, a subscriber couldn't call up a movie at the exact moment the subscriber wanted one, but because the movies were continually recycled over the many channels at short intervals, the subscriber could call up a movie very close to the moment he wanted to watch it. It looked like a gold mine.

It wasn't. Like so many of Time Warner's farseeing video initiatives, the Queens test occupied the cutting edge of practical television engineering and went nowhere fast—except, that is, as yet more fuel for the technological fantasies of Time Warner and everybody else. It had long been an axiom of engineering that just because you could build, say, a transatlantic tunnel, it didn't necessarily follow that you should. As Sumner Redstone had pointed out, there was a limit to the number of movies Americans would watch in their homes, and the number was very low. It also appeared that there was an absolute limit to the number of television channels the average American would watch for more than ten minutes a week, and the limit was rapidly approaching.

When an average of 3.6 channels were available to the American public, people watched an average of 2.6. When the average number of channels rose to 12.4, people watched an average of 6.2. When 29 channels were available, people watched 10. Specialized cable channels—MTV, the History Channel—drew specialized audiences that advertisers could target with some precision, but the audiences themselves were minuscule; a cable television channel was a spectacular success if it attracted 1 percent of the viewing audience. It was a niche market, and each niche was small. Broadcast television, by contrast, attracted a general audience, and the audience was very large.

Despite a serious if not grim erosion of viewers caused by cable's proliferating channels, the four major broadcast networks still attracted more than 60 percent of the viewing audience in the early 1990s and half of the audience in 1997. Advertisers understandably preferred a mass market, especially a mass market with many viewers in the nineteen- through forty-nine-year-old age cohort that advertisers identified as fanatical consumers. Network television, battered though it was, still delivered one. Cable television did not, and the more channels cable offered, the worse the problem became.

By blanketing the cable channels, an advertiser could reach around 40 percent of the audience, but only in tiny fragments, which was why the ads on cable resembled the ads on early broadcast television: they were ads for low-end, high-margin products like dog food and deodorant, endlessly repeated. Moreover, as the number of cable channels grew, it increasingly became a job of work for the viewing public to figure out what was on. In a world with Malone's 500 channels, the weekly *TV Guide* would be as large as the Baltimore telephone book; it would take a viewer forty-three minutes to surf through 500 channels. With Paik's compressed digital television, 1,500 channels was not an unfeasible number; with 1,500 cable channels, *TV Guide* would be as long as the Law of the Sea. Inevitably, the tiny audience watching any given channel would grow smaller still. This was no way to make a buck. Chiddix's 150 channels were a technological breakthrough and a possible harbinger of the future, but it was not a future that particularly interested the good people of Queens, who bore an uncanny resemblance to the good people in the rest of the country. Most people were not besotted with technology, and a great many of the others soon grew bored. When they watched television, most people wanted to kick back and relax. Most people did not want to wait a certain amount of time for a movie, accompanied by a certain amount of creative fiddling with their remote control. This was not kicking back and relaxing in the old mindless way, and it was the principal reason why pay-per-view had failed to take the country by storm. But the lessons of pay-per-view were lost on the chieftains of Time Warner. Ross and Levin were enchanted with Chiddix's new system.

Neither man was known as a great fan of the borough of Queens unless the Mets were playing at Shea Stadium—Ross's mother had spent a good part of her life denying that the family came from the outer boroughs—but Ross and Levin couldn't stay away from Chiddix's test bed. They came to admire it dozens of times, often in the company of their new Japanese colleagues.

Conspicuously absent was Nick Nicholas, the designated heir apparent and, not incidentally, the man who had repeatedly descended on Levin's money-losing television projects like an avenging angel. Nicholas had always had a problem with Jerry Levin. Now he had an even larger problem with Steve Ross. The time had come to take Nicholas out. Unfortunately, Ross had neglected to include an important element in his calculations. He was mortal.

In November 1991, Ross went home to die of prostate cancer. Two months later Nicholas went skiing in Vail. With Ross directing his forces from his deathbed and Levin working behind the scenes, the board of directors fired him. Nicholas, who had made one huge mistake and lost the will to fight, did not return to confront his tormentors.

Ross died a year later, on December 20, 1992. The world, it was generally agreed, would not soon see his like again. Jerry Levin, the last man standing at the top of the corporate hierarchy, became chairman of Time Warner. He announced that he would bet the company on interactive digital television.

CHIDDIX AND HIS ENGINEERS HAD ALREADY BUILT THE backbone of a digital television system in Queens, but no one had ever pretended that the borough of Queens possessed the sort of verve and panache that one associated with the introduction of a transforming technology. Instead, the interactive test would be conducted in Orlando, Florida, where everything would have to be built from scratch.

Orlando was the home of Time Warner's second-largest cable system, a city that had already seen the video future sputter and die no less than twice. Back in the days of Warner's Qube, Orlando had been the test bed for Time's own form of interactive analog television. The plug was pulled after Warner shut down Qube and no great damage was done. Orlando had also been one of the cities where Levin had introduced videotext and tried to make it go. The possible symbolism of these events was lost on Time Warner, nor did it seem to occur to anyone that Orlando—on paper an upscale version of Middle America, the target audience for interactive video—was not an ordinary American place.

Perhaps more than any other city in the country—with the possible exceptions of Las Vegas and Los Angeles—Orlando, Florida, was far down the road to an America where entertainment was one of the principal things that people did for a living. Orlando and its environs were the home of Disney World, Universal Studios Florida and its theme park, Splendid China, Pirates at Colossal Studios, Sea World, Ripley's Believe It or Not, Terror on Church Street, medieval restaurants with jousting knights, and, perhaps the ultimate theme park, the Kennedy Space Center. In Orlando, the aroma of fantasy was the smell of the paycheck and high-technology fun was the backbone of the economy. If interactive digital television was destined to attract an audience anywhere, Orlando would be the place.

Once the experimental city had been chosen, the first trick was to decide what the new marvel would do all day. The second trick was to get it up and running. The third trick was to decide what to do next.

Going all out, Time Warner decided to build a form of digital television that functioned like a giant VCR crossed with an ordinary television set, a video arcade, a personal computer, and a home shopping service.

Despite an abundance of tests that indicated precisely the opposite, there persisted a stubborn belief that video-on-demand was the way to make money out of interactive television, and Orlando would offer a lot of it. At any time, Orlando subscribers could call up a movie from the film library. They could pause it, they could rewind it, and they could fast-forward it. Viewing fare would include the old-fashioned analog channels that people still watched in their millions, but there would also be interactive video games that subscribers could play with other subscribers across town. In the future, there would be a news service that would (possibly) bring to life Negroponte's dream of a customizable information service while (perhaps) finally achieving some of the corporate synergy that still eluded a balkanized Time Warner. Time Warner's magazines, after all, published a lot of information. Somewhat lost in the equation was the fact that the magazines were not a video operation, Time Warner had no experience in video news and no video news operation, videotext had already failed, no television news operation made a significant amount of money—or any money at all—for anybody but ABC and CNN, and the viewing public had never asked for a flood of data to pour into its homes.

Last, there would be a virtual shopping mall occupied by, among others, the Sharper Image, Crate and Barrel, the U.S. Postal Service, a Dodge dealership, and a supermarket where a subscriber could pluck a virtual can of Campbell's soup from the shelf, rotate it on the screen, and read the label. Great things were expected from the virtual shopping mall.

Every year, Americans bought trillions of dollars' worth of goods. The home catalog business alone brought in more than $10 billion a year, and the two established television shopping networks, HSN and QVC, had combined revenues of $2.1 billion. A persuasive body of opinion said that the old brick-and-mortar stores of the central shopping districts and suburban malls were a doomed or seriously shrinking business. Visionary articles appeared in the press, describing how such stores might be forced to attract customers by turning themselves into theme parks. Here, the addictive nature of television and the wonders of interactivity seemed to play directly into Time Warner's hands.

In Orlando, Time Warner's subscribers would enter a virtual store, prowl the aisles and interact with the merchandise—by viewing the dazzling promotional materials, by ordering goods in precise sizes, colors, and quantities, by adding accessories—without having to hustle up a salesclerk, and then deal with the clerk's personal problems and the problem of out-of-stock merchandise. The virtual shopping mall, undoubtedly, was a killer app. It also seemed to solve an almost intractable difficulty.

It was already hard enough to attract quality advertising to the many channels of cable television. How, then, did you attract any kind of advertisers to interactive cable television, where the many channels became an immense number of channels and the viewer could interact with the television set by blanking out the advertisements altogether?

FOR MANY YEARS, TELEVISION ADVERTISING HAD BEEN impaled on the horns of a dilemma. Advertisers paid the network for an audience, but the most desirable audience, the one between the ages of nineteen and forty-nine, was the audience with the lowest tolerance for advertising. It was also an audience that was only vaguely measured, its size estimated by analyzing a handful of viewers who regularly reported their television habits, perhaps truthfully. Interactive television changed everything, although not for the better.

With interactive television, Nissan would know with uncanny precision the number of living rooms where an ad for its Sentra automobile was on prominent display. This was not the great idea that it seemed.

Nissan would not know who was in the room, whether the person in the room was awake and sober, or if anyone was in the room at all. There was no way of knowing that on analog television, broadcast or cable, either, but digital interactive television compounded an old problem even further. With the proliferation of channels, the fragmented audience would be even more fragmented. The number of living rooms where the ad appeared was certain to be small, perhaps minuscule. A minuscule (and, as always, conjectural) audience meant minuscule payments from the advertiser. Nissan's ads were very expensive to make. With a tiny audience, only some of whom were actually watching, it might make no sense to run the ads at all, no matter how compelling the content. But here the beauty of interactive television came into play. Interactive television could persuade people to watch advertisements, or so it seemed.

Nissan could reward viewers who watched its ads. If a viewer would agree to sit through, say, a fifteen-minute commercial, he would receive the right to watch a free movie. Moreover, the viewer would be required to keep his part of the bargain, punching a button on his keypad at certain points, signaling his presence in the room; no button, no free movie. Either that or a tiny television camera could be placed atop the television set and the viewer's presence or absence would be recorded. Cooler heads pointed out that television sets that negotiated with their owners or watched the watchers were not exactly a way for interactive cable companies or their advertisers to make a lot of friends. There had to be a more user-friendly way of selling things on interactive television, and there was.

In the user-friendly version, a television show, a movie, or a sporting event would be the sales medium. A viewer could use his keypad to click on John Wayne's boots, learn the name of a Western outfitter that offered exact replicas, and order them on the spot. Something similar could be done with James Bond's latest car. A test drive could be arranged. All the furniture on a movie set and any object or device touched or used by anyone in a regularly scheduled event could be similarly hot-keyed. Nikes, like John Wayne's boots, could be ordered directly off Michael Jordan's feet. In the calmer moments of the advertising visionaries, however, it was clear that the whole concept had to be thought through rather more carefully.

Hot-key merchandising looked promising for high-end goods like cars, haberdashery, and specialty merchandise—Nike shoes were a particularly torrid item—but it was unlikely to do much of anything for mass merchandisers like Procter & Gamble and its latest washday miracle. Even the most avid of consumers and technophiles were unlikely to click on a box of soap, and Procter & Gamble was the largest advertiser on television. The answer, it appeared, was Time Warner's virtual shopping mall.

Viewers could visit the Dodge dealership and the stores and view the commercials there, voluntarily. Mass marketing would be handled by department stores—Macy's was known to be interested—and the supermarket. The specialty shops would take care of the rest, and because Time Warner owned the virtual real estate, it would collect rent. Everyone would be happy, including the viewers. There was only one thing wrong with this happy scenario. There was a reason why there were only two major home shopping channels on television. Only a limited number of people wanted to shop on television. Their identities and their buying habits were known and easily discoverable. They were extremely unlikely to buy anything from the Sharper Image or purchase a Dodge Viper. And they were already John Malone's and Brian Roberts's customers.

———

As of 1988, some fifty shopping channels, a number of them backed by established names in retailing, had hit the bricks on the airwaves. Some thirty of them had failed. Telaction, the J. C. Penney service beamed at shoppers in the Chicago area, lost $20 million before the cadaver was sold to QVC.

"Whenever we flogged something on Telaction," said one of its former executives, "sales of the item went up in the stores on the Loop. We were in the business of providing free advertising for our competitors." By 1996, two channels, the Home Shopping Network and QVC, dominated the business.

HSN, the daddy of them all, came into existence when the enterprising owner of a Florida television station foreclosed on a bad debt, came into possession of 112 electric can openers, and decided to sell them on the air. The year was 1977. The can openers sold out, and the station owner decided he'd stumbled onto something.

As it evolved over the years, HSN came to resemble a cult, an addiction, a showplace of shallow family values, and a carnival booth. On-air sales personnel discussed their marriages and the births of their children. Registered viewers received birthday cards. Prospective buyers were invited to race the clock; in one of the oldest sales pitches known to man, merchandise was available in limited quantities and for a limited time only. If an item was hot, sales might run to $12,000 a minute. HSN picked up King James Bibles and microwave ovens in bulk, in distress, and in discontinuance, bought them cheap and sold them cheap. Many of the items on its shelves came from the shadowlands beyond the borders of respectable merchandising: spray-on vitamins, edible clothing. Cheap jewelry was a reliable best-seller.

The QVC channel, launched in 1986, was less frenzied and slightly more upscale, featuring celebrities like Diller's friend Princess Diane Von Furstenberg selling clothing and cosmetics named after themselves. At both channels, the core audience was remarkably similar to the congregations of video evangelists: middle-aged white women who watched compulsively, bought compulsively, and constituted 30 percent of a viewership that amounted to a scant 8 percent of the cable television marketplace. It was not an audience that would migrate to Time Warner's (or anybody else's) virtual mall anytime soon, or at all. Despite the best efforts of some of the finest minds in retailing, no other audience had ever been attracted to televised home shopping. Time Warner plunged ahead anyway.

"We announced in, I think, March of 1993 that we were going to do this, and that we were going to have it in operation by the first quarter of the next year," said Chiddix. "That was a mistake. That was way too fast. We didn't know enough to know it was a mistake."

The operating software, the video servers, and some of the other hardware were provided by Silicon Graphics, a company that had made its reputation by providing Hollywood with digitized special effects. The video switch, called an ATM—for asynchronous transfer mode—that made customized channels possible, was manufactured by AT&T. Time Warner bought the first commercial ATM switch AT&T ever sold. "I think it was serial number three," said Chiddix. Prototypes were notoriously expensive.

The set-top boxes were provided by Scientific-Atlanta. Whether each box cost $15,000, $11,000, $7,000, $5,000, or $3,000 was something that was never made clear. As designed, the entire system would crash if more than 20,000 viewers tried to order the same movie at the same time. In Orlando, there would be no problem; the Orlando experiment was scheduled to involve 4,000 viewers. But the system, provided Time Warner could make it work, was not exportable to New York, Chicago, or Los Angeles.

The electronics were elegant, but not for their simplicity; they had never been used to deliver video to thousands of homes on an hourly basis. Instead of a garden hose or a fire hose, the Orlando system resembled an infinitesimally tiny railroad based on a technology called packet switching.

With packet switching, information did not flow in an unbroken stream from a source to a destination. Instead, it was broken into bundles that were 53 impulses long. The leading impulse contained a time stamp and the routing information—the waybill. The remaining 52 impulses contained a small part of a much longer message—for example, a tiny fragment of a movie. The second bundle of 53 impulses might contain something entirely different, addressed to an entirely different location.

The computers at the head end lined up the packets and sent them on their way, the ATM switch read the waybills and routed them to their destinations, and after a certain amount of technological jiggery-pokery, the home television sets attached to the system received an uninterrupted video signal, although not necessarily the same signal received by the other sets in the system.

"We wanted Orlando to be interactive television, not just in the sense of allowing you to push a button and get a movie," said Chiddix, "but we really wanted to explore what American television could do. We had to have powerful graphics. We wanted every man to be able to manage all the choices we were going to put in front of him. We have customers who are functionally illiterate. Plus, we have customers who are intimidated by technology. We needed to be able to relate to them, to engage them and bring them in. And here we've announced to the world that we'll have this done in the first quarter of '94."

There was trouble with the navigation system. There was trouble with the set-top boxes. In the jargon of the television engineer, the toys kept smoking.

With Chairman Levin presiding over the festivities, the Time Warner Full Service Network was finally launched in January 1995, an event that was not treated as the triumph that Time Warner badly needed. Too much had been promised, all too airily, by Malone, by Levin, by the other apostles of the digital television age. The Orlando system was nine months late. A year earlier, Wall Street would punish any cable company that said it would not build an interactive television system. Now it punished any cable company that said it would. Time Warner had announced that it would send the Full Service

Network to 4,000 households. On opening day, the press gleefully reported that the number of Full Service households was five.

A year later, the system was up to speed and fully subscribed. The best-selling products on the virtual upscale shopping mall of the Time Warner Full Service Network in Orlando, Florida, were postage stamps.

ELEVEN

The End of Something Else

AT TIME WARNER, THE MAGICAL PERSONALITY OF STEVE Ross was sorely missed, but the ceaselessly inventive and devious mind of Steve Ross was missed far more. It was difficult to see how even Ross could have gotten the company out of a mess that was at least partly of his own making, but Ross had almost always found a way. Ross had been an enthusiast, but he had also been a cynic who knew how to blow something off when it had served its purpose or didn't work, just as he had blown off Qube. Jerry Levin was an enthusiast. Like the Bourbons, he seemed to have learned nothing and forgotten everything except that he had once invented cable television in its modern form and he was now the sovereign of the Time Warner empire. In the teeth of mounting evidence, he continued to dote on his Orlando experiment.

"I challenge anybody to say that video-on-demand isn't what the consumer wants," he said. "It's not that I'm some wild-eyed person who's lost in this technology that'll never be in the consumer's home. We decided to build the ultimate system. Everybody kind of pooh-poohs it because it's too expensive, but what we found is precisely what we expected. The buy rates are substantially better than any-thing that exists with primitive pay-per-view or near-video-on-demand. But secondly, more important to me, is that the consumer is not just stopping the movies, obviously to take a break; the consumer is fast-forwarding and rewinding electronically. People are going back-wards and forwards because they're obviously revisiting sections of the film. They're consuming it in an endearing way, and it's spectacu-lar."

In the Orlando version of interactive television, it turned out, digital compression had problems with clouds, wind, weather in gen-eral, and smoke. Ironically, smoke was one of the easiest things to portray on analog television; one of the first successful transmissions on electronic television had been a picture of moving smoke. Digital compression also had trouble with the color black. Many of the most prominent people on television happened to be black; when a com-pressed frame of Shaquille O'Neal, the basketball star, was frozen, O'Neal turned green.

Much of the equipment in Orlando was too expensive, too lim-ited, or both. No one could build an Orlando system in a major metropolitan area and expect it to either work or make money. As Sumner Redstone had pointed out, it made no sense to charge people pennies for something that had cost large bucks. It also made no sense to build an entire television system for 4,000 people when you could get most of the same test results with a bank of VCRs in a head house, a stack of videotapes, a bunch of kids with Rollerblades, and a few simple components. Time Warner and Jerry Levin had built a transatlantic tunnel and charged five bucks a ticket.

Elsewhere at Time Warner, things weren't in very hot shape, either.

ONLY A FEW MONTHS AFTER ROSS'S DEATH, LEVIN SOLD 25.5 percent of the studio, HBO, and the cable systems to US West, the huge regional telephone company headquartered, like TCI, in the Denver suburb of Englewood. It was a deal that did much to set off a brief but memorable chain reaction by stampeding Ray Smith in the direction of John Malone, but it had another, more enduring result. Time Warner was stuck with US West, the only regional telephone company that persisted in the belief that cable television—and especially cable-based telephone services—would carry it bravely into the future and enable it to seize the day.

Time Warner received $1 billion to upgrade its cable systems and $1.5 billion to reduce its debt, badly needed money at a crucial time, but an air of desperation seemed to hang over the whole affair. Only a few days before, the rumor on Wall Street said that US West was going to buy the entire company. Time Warner now controlled just 63 percent of the assets that provided two-thirds of its cash, and US West received a veto power over many of Time Warner's important actions. On the whole, it looked like the very best that Time Warner could have done with a very bad mess of pottage.

By 1993, Time Warner—only three years old—was a huge company staffed with highly skilled and resourceful executives who increasingly despised or pitied their leader. Warner Brothers was the most stable studio in Hollywood, reliably profitable, and it owned the franchise on the Batman films. Warner Music, under the guidance of the legendary Mo Ostin, owned a license to coin money, although a good deal of the money was coined by the music known as gangsta rap. Home Box Office, led by Michael Fuchs, was the premier cable channel in the country. The cable systems themselves were worth billions, and so were the magazines.

Time Warner also appeared to be drowning in debt. Its stock was underpriced in the market, creating unhappy stockholders and a bright opportunity for a plausible outsider with a mouthful of stockholder-pleasing rhetoric and a large bank account; Time Warner was one of the few large 1990s corporations still vulnerable to an old-fashioned, 1980s-style raid. The Time side of the company didn't like the Warner side of the company, the Warner side of the company didn't like the Time side of the company, and Time Warner was a mare's nest of hostile fiefdoms with a needlessly complex financial structure that spelled nothing but trouble and a technological strategy directed toward a goal that continued to recede over the horizon. Time Warner was like a forest afflicted with a serious but not yet fatal disease. There was money—a very great deal of money—to be made from cutting it down, sawing it into its component parts, and selling them to the highest bidder.

The threat from US West had been turned aside, at least for the time being, by forking over a substantial bribe and inviting the camel into the tent, but US West was not necessarily a reliable partner, nor was US West the only potentially destabilizing influence. Also circling in the water was Edgar Bronfman, Jr., president of Seagram, the Canadian distiller that owned a large piece of the Du Pont chemical empire. In an earlier life, the thirty-seven-year-old Bronfman had been a notably unsuccessful Hollywood producer, and it was said—known—that he wanted to buy a studio and get back in the game. Confronted with Time Warner's hastily erected antitakeover defenses, Bronfman was stopped in his tracks after acquiring 14.9 percent of Time Warner's stock, no seats on the board, and a very bad attitude. Courtney Ross, Steve Ross's widow, owned 2 percent of the company. The attitude of Mrs. Ross was also not good. The remaining stockholders from the old Time Inc., remembering how Ross and his people had been allowed to take them to the cleaners and contemplating the depressed price of their Time Warner holdings, were not in a forgiving mood. All available bets said Jerry Levin's days were numbered.

Despite the many unpleasant things that were said about him, the chairman of Time Warner was not a stupid man. Instead, he was a limited man with a curious and mystical bent. Ross, to whom he was endlessly compared and not to his advantage, had been the fox who knew many things. Levin knew one big thing, and he plunged stubbornly ahead. It was remarked that his persistence, if nothing else, was admirable.

He added another $3.3 billion in debt to the Time Warner bottom line, bought three more cable companies, and brought them into the corporate fold—but, wisely, not into the Time Warner Entertainment partnership, where they would have become immediately entangled with US West and the Japanese. Actually, there was much to be said for these acquisitions. If Time Warner hadn't been in hock up to its ears, if its investors and bankers had been in a kindly mood, and if its chairman hadn't been fighting for his corporate life, they would have been a splendid addition to the corporate jewel box.

The three cable companies were bargains; Levin had bought them at the bottom of a depressed market. Strategically, the acquisitions were sound. Time Warner's existing systems were more urban and less scattered than Malone's, giving the company a concentrated viewership, and the new cable systems tied the cable network even more closely together, an excellent idea if the company planned to enter the interactive entertainment and information business on a cost-efficient basis. Time Warner had long been the country's second-largest cable company, but with 12.1 million customers in thirty-seven states it now became the second-largest cable company by the smallest of margins. For all intents and purposes, Jerry Levin was the equal of John Malone. If Levin had been a different sort of executive and if Time Warner had been a different sort of company, all might have been well. Like every other cable baron in the early 1990s, Levin was also thinking hard about the telephone business. But for Time Warner—or for any other cable company—no big wins in the telephone business were coming anytime soon, or perhaps ever.

FOR TIME WARNER, THERE WERE NO BIG WINS COMING from anywhere anytime soon. Levin was like a man who woke up one morning to discover that someone had constructed a maze around him as he slept. His major corporate strategies—interactive television, telephones—would take unexpected years to play out, there was no guarantee or perhaps even likelihood of success, and in the immediate short run the initiatives had gone precisely nowhere. Levin's stockholders were restive if not openly hostile. There was no telling how long he would continue to enjoy the confidence or forbearance of his board. He had inherited a dangerous mess in the record division. The patience of Bob Daly, the powerful, respected, and above all highly competent head of the Warner Brothers movie studio, was nearly exhausted. Levin, one of his associates told *Vanity Fair*, had begun to squeak when he walked. In the affairs of some men, there was a tide. In the affairs of Jerry Levin, there was something that resembled a harmonic convergence. Where technology was concerned, he would tolerate many things, including an extremely bad press. But he would not tolerate a music business that seemed to be spinning out of control while blackening the company's name.

Properly managed, a successful music business could carry an entire entertainment company. It was an old axiom in Hollywood that a movie studio that owned a recording company was actually a recording company that owned a movie studio. Even more than films, popular musicians were a gift that kept on giving. Elvis went on forever, steadily making money from beyond the grave, and even a minor recording star was usually a reliable paycheck for at least a couple of years. But the recording business, as Ross could have said if anyone had bothered to ask him, was no place for the faint of heart, and in socially unsettled, puritanical times, a recording business that employed artists whose songs called for mayhem and rape was a political target as large as a barn. The future health and well-being of Time Warner's cable business depended on a government that already had a very bad attitude, and there were disquieting signs that Warner Music was likely to further sharpen the government's thinking, although not in a friendly or useful way.

In 1994 and 1995, Warner Music was hit by a kickback scandal, found two of its rap stars in jail and a third charged with murder, and was publicly denounced by former Secretary of Education William Bennett, Senator Bob Dole, and C. DeLores Tucker, chairwoman of the National Political Congress of Black Women, for unraveling the moral fiber of the nation's youth. Levin, suddenly a stranger to his closest associates, purged Warner Music of its top executives, including the sixty-eight-year-old Mo Ostin, who had turned a $100 million label into a $2.5 billion business. Forceful and focused management was not, however, Levin's style; if it had been, he might not have gotten into one or several of his current dilemmas to begin with. When he discovered that his forceful and focused actions were not rewarded with a chorus of praise, he tried to rehire Ostin. When Ostin refused to return, Levin gave Warner Music to Michael Fuchs, the forceful and focused head of HBO. Fuchs was precisely the wrong man for the job. Bob Daly and Terry Semel, who ran Warner Brothers, regarded Warner Music as part of their turf, and Daly and Semel did not like Michael Fuchs.

Fuchs was the Time-side television guy who had tried to make movies on his own. Fuchs had compounded his sins by investing HBO's money in Savoy Pictures, a Warner Brothers competitor. Now Fuchs was running the record company, and the studio chiefs were perhaps the only two people in Time Warner who could bring down Levin with a few telephone calls to the board.

Bob Daly was a former CBS executive who had long said that he would never return to New York. By certain signs, he began to make it known that perhaps the New York climate did not disagree with him after all.

IN JERRY LEVIN'S BURDEN OF WOE, THERE REMAINED TWO other pieces of unfinished business: the debt (which Levin had increased) and the company's irrational structure. He was able to buy Toshiba and Itochi out of the Time Warner Entertainment partnership at a handsome premium, but US West said it was perfectly happy with things as they were, and US West still owned more than 25 percent of Warner Brothers, HBO, and the cable systems. Still, the telephone company airily conceded, it might consider a revised role—it might even assume some of the Time Warner debt—if Levin would throw in the newly purchased cable systems and give US West complete control. It was almost as though Levin was being mocked.

As the autumn of 1995 approached, Time Warner's freedom of action appeared to be vanishingly small and the continuing tenure of its chairman was regarded as one of the great mysteries of American capitalism. The conventional wisdom said Levin absolutely had to raise a significant amount of money, buy his company some daylight, exhibit some backbone, and demonstrate a little of the competence that seemed to be in such short supply at 75 Rock. This was easier said than done.

Levin's corporate larder was almost bare. The magazines, so essential to the company's image of itself and its image in the eyes of the world, could not be sold. The only other large and marketable candidate was the company's part ownership of Turner Broadcasting. If sold, Time Warner's Turner stake might bring in as much as $1.5 billion in badly needed cash. There was only one thing wrong with the idea. Almost nobody wanted Levin to do it.

After a little thought and exploration, he hit upon an alternate plan. Time Warner would buy Turner Broadcasting, and it would buy Ted Turner. For all his eccentricity, Turner was a man of considerable charm and ability, just the sort of person to calm Bob Daly down. He was a media star in his own right, and he had redeemed himself in the eyes of Wall Street. He would draw attention from Jerry Levin, and the financial community would finally be pleased by something Time Warner did. Turner knew how to run a large television enterprise. As an added dividend there would no longer be any need for the dangerously ambitious Michael Fuchs. Levin would keep his job. It would cost Time Warner $7.5 billion, and it would be a transforming transaction.

By 1995, Ted Turner had lived three years longer than his father. He took lithium, a substance usually prescribed in cases of manic-depression, and perhaps it helped. Perhaps his business recovery and renewed success, too, had played their parts; there was no more talk of the door in his office that led to a fourteen-story drop.

Turner had bought the Hanna-Barbera cartoon studios, owned Yogi Bear and Huckleberry Hound, and founded the Cartoon Network. The MGM library became the basis of Turner Classic Movies. To the horror of cinema purists and the delight of Generation X, he colorized the black-and-white classics in his vaults; movies like *The Fighting 69th* now appeared in hues familiar to people who had grown up with Saturday-morning television. He had paid a billion dollars for two second-tier Hollywood studios, made movies—like *Gettysburg*—that were to his liking, and produced *Seinfeld*, the most successful comedy on television. CNN was available worldwide and offered a multitude of services: there was CNN for hotels, CNN for airports, and a CNN financial network. Time Warner had HBO, but in television, Turner seemed to be everywhere at once.

He was able to live large. He owned an island off South Carolina, a hunting preserve in Florida, and a Montana ranch where he maintained one of the largest privately owned bison herds in the world. He was married to one of the most famous and desirable women in America, the actress Jane Fonda. When the dashing Ted Turner and his beautiful wife appeared in the owner's box during an Atlanta Braves game, they were hailed as the First Couple of the national pastime. But Turner's accomplishments were small when compared to the undimmed ambition that still burned in his heart. Ted Turner wanted more, much more. He claimed that he woke up in the middle of the night crying out that he didn't own a television network. Ted Turner resembled a 1950s adolescent trying to persuade his parents that he needed a car. Everyone else seemed to have one. The parents in question were Jerry Levin and John Malone.

For the major media companies, no less than the major cable companies, 1994 and 1995 were the years of living dangerously. AT&T closed on its $13 billion purchase of McCaw Cellular Communications. Sumner Redstone paid over $10 billion for Paramount. Disney bought ABC for $19.2 billion. Edgar Bronfman, his dream of owning a studio undimmed, forked over $5.7 billion and picked up 80 percent of MCA. Turner, desperate to get into the game, made a run at NBC, received what he believed to be an encouraging response, and discovered that NBC wasn't for sale after all. Anyway, Time Warner didn't want him to buy it, and Time Warner still owned its veto.

Next, with the encouragement of John Malone, Turner decided to buy CBS, the prize that had once been within Barry Diller's grasp. CBS was definitely for sale; Westinghouse, a shell of a once great company, had entered a bid of $5 billion. But Malone, like an imp of mischief, seemed to have lost his once clear and resolute focus. Either that or he had decided to raise hell and see what would happen. Even as he urged Turner in the direction of CBS, he also seems to have encouraged Rupert Murdoch to snatch away CNN, although how this served Malone's purposes remained obscure. At another point, Malone seems to have urged Murdoch to make a hostile bid for Time Warner. Meanwhile, making his own contribution to a situation that resembled midnight basketball without the lights, Turner engaged Michael Milken, the disgraced junk bond king, and instructed him to raise $10 billion to trump the Westinghouse bid. Turner later admitted that the terms attached to the $10 billion would be a disaster for his stockholders—including Malone, who was cheering Turner on while trying to cut his legs out from under him. In any event, Time Warner was unlikely to allow Turner to buy CBS even if Malone succeeded in talking Murdoch into attacking Time Warner. And Turner himself conceded that buying CBS made no sense. Neither did much of anything else.

It was all very odd. Soon, it was also all very moot. Jerry Levin, a minnow among sharks, struck a blow in favor of his future employment and instantly clarified the situation.

ON AUGUST 19, 1995, LEVIN AND HIS WIFE FLEW TO Turner's Montana ranch. At a complicated moment in everyone's life, the Time Warner chairman had developed yet another problem, and time was of the essence. Troubling rumors had reached his ears that General Electric, the parent company of NBC, had taken an unwelcome interest in Time Warner. If the rumors were true and GE believed that Levin was still trying to sell Time Warner's stake in Turner Broadcasting, the electronics giant might charge from cover to stop Levin from doing something he no longer intended, and GE was capable of buying Time Warner without breaking a sweat. The situation had developed a whole new urgency. In Montana, Levin put his offer on the table.

On paper, Turner would be $2 billion richer, wealthier by far than John Malone. He would become Time Warner's vice-chairman with complete control of his former empire in Atlanta. Over the course of a five-year employment contract, his compensation could add up to an additional $100 million. Time Warner would no longer have an automatic veto over his actions and neither would anybody else, because he would control the part of Time Warner that interested him. On paper, Turner would become the second most powerful man in the combined company. In reality, it was possible that he could become even more than that. Turner took the deal. Everyone was happy, and no one was happier than John Malone.

Malone was in his element again, negotiating his own special deal after the ink dried, and because TCI owned 22 percent of Turner Broadcasting, he was able to assume one of his favorite postures: he owned a blocking position. For the moment, he was able to set aside the vexed question of digital television, the billions of dollars TCI was pouring into the ground with remarkably little to show for it, and the fact that General Instrument couldn't seem to manufacture something as simple as a damn set-top box. Once again, Malone was the troll under the bridge, and Jerry Levin wasn't going to cross it unless he paid the troll's fee.

Levin, trying to move things along, happily announced the completion of the deal on September 22. Malone, however, had a few more points to discuss. Malone's job wasn't on the line; Levin's was, and both Malone and Levin knew it. People who tried to put pressure on John Malone often likened the experience to a nervous breakdown that John Malone was not having.

Weeks later, he had what he wanted, or so he said: 9 percent of Time Warner's stock, tax-free and with voting rights ceded to Levin—unless Malone decided to take them back in the sort of maneuver Malone had long ago mastered. He and Turner became the largest owners of Time Warner, only a few points short of a controlling position. When the Time Warner directors met, 40 percent of the country's cable systems would sit down at the table. It was a situation filled with many intriguing possibilities. And as with the original Time and Warner merger, there was a question of just who, exactly, had bought whom.

TED TURNER HAD BEEN OFF THE LITHIUM FOR SIX months, or so he said. His associates claimed they saw no difference in his behavior. Neither did anybody else.

He likened himself to the financier Laurence Tisch, who had started out as a major stockholder in CBS, fired the chairman, and ended up running the place. "I'm used to being in charge," he told *The Wall Street Journal.* "I've been in charge for 33 years. Jerry's only been in charge for three or four. I'm a great believer in my own abilities. I think I could do just about anything."

His immediate task, he revealed, was to "crush Rupert Murdoch like a bug," hardly the remark of a man who expected to return quietly to Atlanta. Wearing a huge grin, he said much the same thing at the first joint press conference. Levin, hovering nervously in the background, seemed at a loss for words. In many ways, things had gone exactly as Levin had planned. In other ways, they had gone out of control.

Michael Fuchs quit. Turner took over the company's cable operations and was soon heard barking orders that were not politely phrased but made a great deal of sense. Daly and Semel took over the music company, were given Turner's studios, and fell silent. US West sued.

The Turner transaction, US West insisted, violated the terms of the Time Warner Entertainment partnership, although in ways that were not entirely clear to anyone else. US West said it had attacked Time Warner more in sorrow than in anger; the telephone company had been perfectly happy in the days before the dashing Mr. Turner appeared on the scene, and it was willing to be happy again if the dashing Mr. Turner disappeared. If pressed, however, US West said it would agree to get out of Time Warner's life in exchange for either $4 billion or 1.9 million of Time Warner's cable customers.

And at this fascinating moment, John Malone disappeared.

TWELVE

The End of the Affair

IKE MANY SPECTACULARLY SUCCESSFUL MEN, MALONE had made his money from a single, remarkably simple idea: the insight that he could sell a wonderfully legal, wonderfully addictive service, television, to millions of people, do it poorly, get away with it, pay no taxes to speak of, and persuade Wall Street that he was a genius. There were ample precedents for this sort of behavior, from Carnegie in steel to Gates in software, but perhaps no man so closely resembled John Malone as the first Henry Ford. The principal difference, of course, was that one of them manufactured a superb product.

In a long and occasionally evil life, Ford did many things, became many things to many people, and amassed an immense personal fortune. He created the first successful mass-production assembly line and seized a march on his competition that lasted a decade. He introduced the soybean to the American farmer, and he could lay plausible claim to the invention of the supermarket; the Ford mind was a fertile one. But everything in his life went back to his first, transcendent vision-brought-to-life, the people's car he called the Model T. It was Henry Ford's Philosopher's Stone. After the first Model T rolled off the line at Highland Park, everything Ford touched turned to gold, and a man does not willingly part with the magical implement even when its powers have begun to fade. For years, Ford refused to change the Model T.

In 1912, he returned from a trip to Europe and found that his associates had improved it. The prototype, gleaming with red lacquerwork, was ready for his inspection on the factory floor. Ford walked around the vehicle with his hands in his pockets.

"It was a four-door job," one of the witnesses wrote, "and the top was down. Finally he got to the left-hand side of the car that was facing me, and he takes his hands out, gets hold of the door, and bang! He ripped the door right off! God! How the man done it, I don't know!

"He jumped in there, and bang goes the other door. Bang goes the windshield. He jumps over the back seat and starts pounding on the top. He rips the top with the heel of his shoe. He wrecked the car as much as he could."

There was no further discussion.

Eventually, of course, Ford did improve the Model T. Like Malone, he adopted new technologies (Ford had once invented new technologies), but like Malone, he didn't improve his product enough, and he improved it too late. The Model T was the people's car of the past. The General Motors Chevrolet, with its electric starter, six-cylinder engine, hydraulic brakes, gas pedals, gearshifts, and advanced styling, was the people's car of the present.

There seems to be a twenty-year cycle to such things; the Model T had a hell of a run for twenty years, and so did Malone's TCI. Ford introduced his car in 1907. He finally shut down the production line in 1927, retooled, and built a whole new automobile, the Model A. The company never regained its momentum. In its heyday, Ford had manufactured nearly half the cars in the United States. Come to that, it manufactured nearly half the cars in the entire world. It never dominated its industry again.

In the Middle Ages, the only thing worse than being invaded by a hostile army occurred when your own army arrived to expel the invader. In modern business, it sometimes happens that the only thing worse than bureaucratic management and a lack of vision is a lone leader with a winning idea. John Malone's winning idea had been financial engineering, and it was no longer relevant to what the company was trying to do.

BY THE AUTUMN OF 1996—WITH THE BOSS NOWHERE TO be seen—TCI surveyed a landscape littered with the wreckage of its technological fantasies. The company's pride and joy, the new $100 million National Digital Television Center—reporters, never TCI's favorite people, were always given a tour of the studios in a converted Englewood warehouse—stood largely empty and unused. In 1994, TCI had paid $125 million for 20 percent of the Microsoft Network, the new on-line service from the Redmond, Washington, software giant that was certain to take the country by storm. In 1996, Microsoft returned the investment because the investment had been made in a technology that suddenly became obsolete. TCI had entered into a pilot program with Pacific Gas & Electric, using cable TV to monitor household energy consumption. A homeowner could watch his refrigerator and furnace on his television set. He could also set his burglar alarm. Qube and its imitators had done—or tried to do—much the same thing twenty years before. By 1996, TCI's home energy project had gone nowhere.

The list of unproductive ventures was long. TCI paid $13 million—later raised to $30 million—for a quarter of the Interactive Network, a start-up company with what appeared to be a red-hot technology that would take the country by storm. Using the Interactive Network's control unit, a viewer could play along with game shows like *Jeopardy!*, second-guess the coach at football games, unmask the killer on *Murder, She Wrote*, and compare his score with the scores of other, similarly equipped households. Qube had already done all that, too. So—in more sophisticated form—had Videoway, an interactive television service based in Montreal with viewers in a whopping 160,000 households. The average Videoway subscriber watched 8.5 hours of interactive television a week. Four of the hours were spent playing games. The remaining hours were spent consulting such things as astrologers and weather reports, or checking out the winning numbers in the regional lottery. This was not the high road to the big time; this bore an uncomfortable resemblance to a complete dead end, accompanied by mockery. But there was a measure of method to TCI's madness.

For one thing, the Interactive Network technology seemed to be the perfect vehicle for one of cable television's most cherished (but seldom mentioned) goals: the jackpot of home gambling. Potentially, home gambling was a business worth billions; it would reach the long-elusive mass market at last. Meanwhile, piggybacked on General Instrument's equally elusive set-top box, it would be a cheap and easy way of interacting with broadcast television as distinct from customized and expensive interactive services—to order John Wayne's boots, the revolutionary Veg-O-Matic, recordings of Rimsky-Korsakov's immortal compositions, or to schedule a test drive in a Nissan Sentra. TCI was not alone in sensing the potential of the Interactive Network.

NBC and Sprint, the long-distance company, poured in money. So did Motorola, the Gannett newspaper chain, and Nielsen, the television rating service. Negroponte loved it. Spending its investors' money like there was no tomorrow, Interactive geared up to roll out its product and seize the day. TCI continued to be a generous and helpful friend, especially when it appeared that Sony would come aboard with its new Game Show Channel, an ideal symbiotic product for Interactive's system. But when Sony withdrew from the deal, TCI appeared to take leave of its senses.

As the other investors watched in horror—the disappearance of large sums of money arouses powerful emotions—TCI inexplicably moved to seize Interactive's assets. There was little to be done; NBC needed TCI to launch its new cable channel, Motorola intended to sell TCI some set-top boxes as soon as it figured out how to make them, and Sprint had certain expectations that involved more than a billion dollars of TCI's money. Meanwhile, some TCI executives wanted to move forward with Interactive, others favored a rival technology that never panned out, and the words "power struggle" were used. This was extremely unusual. There had never been a power struggle at TCI, Malone had all the power and TCI had always been the extended shadow of a single decisive man. But Malone didn't seem to be around.

By 1996, thousands of Interactive's black boxes were uselessly collecting dust in a Silicon Valley warehouse. The company's phone was cut off, the handful of subscribers had vanished, and bankruptcy loomed. The surviving employees posed for a group photograph, fists aloft and middle finger extended. The picture, explained the company's founder, was a message to John Malone. Wherever he was.

All of these variously failed initiatives, however, paled to insignificance compared with the largest failure of them all, the invasion of the $200 billion telephone business.

DAVID BEDDOW, TCI'S CHIEF TECHNOLOGY OFFICER, knew very well that the land-line telephone business would not be a breeze when it failed to be a snap and perhaps Malone did, too; without Bell Atlantic's experience and deep pockets, the traditional telephone business was a mug's game, and Beddow was the first to say so. But telephone service no longer had to enter the home by

L. J. DAVIS

wire—and in 1994, three events converged that made it seem that riches beyond the dreams of avarice were once again within TCI's grasp.

The federal government had always given slices of the broadcast spectrum away, having first assured itself (if no one else) that the public interest would be served. Now it was decided to auction off slices of the broadcasting spectrum for money. No one knew what would happen. To its astonishment and delight, the government discovered that there was a pot of money to be made.

The land-line telephone business had long been regarded as a natural monopoly, and the experience of Time Warner suggested that it was a natural monopoly still. The cellular telephone business had been a duopoly; in each region of the country, the government granted only two licenses, one to the local telephone company and the second to an independent operator like McCaw. The cellular telephone business was still growing at a rate of 50 percent a year. But wireless digital telephones, at least in theory, were cheaper, clearer, and could offer a multitude of new services. Wireless digital telephones, at least in theory, could eat cellular telephony's lunch.

Wireless digital telephones would not work without access to the broadcasting spectrum, and if the government decided to sell the spectrum to the highest bidder, the government was no longer picking the winners and the losers. Anyone with enough money could buy the necessary spectrum, sell the marvelous new devices, charge connection fees, and clean up. When the new telecommunications law was passed and signed into law, the local telephone market would be up for grabs, at least in theory. At least in theory, TCI could hook up its land lines with the over-the-air digital signal, throw in a few switching systems, and make a deal with a long-distance carrier. TCI, having lost one golden opportunity to get into the game with the collapse of the Bell Atlantic merger, would be offered a second glittering chance. It would become a national telephone company. The government would not interfere—not even with TCI—because the government would also become rich. One of these predictions actually came true.

The first experimental FCC auction, for a minuscule amount of spectrum dedicated to paging services, brought in more than $200 million, an astonishing sum. Here, clearly, was a huge opportunity. The citizen tax revolt so skillfully exploited by Ronald Reagan was still in full cry. It was as much as a politician's reputation was worth, not indeed his place, to suggest that the populace should actually pay for the government services they demanded and expected. Now, with spectrum auctions, it seemed possible to solve many problems at once, painlessly, and at no cost to the voting public. The dangerous budget deficit left over from the Reagan years could be reduced to manageable size, and the voting public's cherished subsidies and entitlements could be salvaged. Like legalized gambling, spectrum auctions were the answer to a politician's prayer.

Before the end of the year, further experimental auctions brought in nearly $2 billion, some of which was actually paid. The FCC geared up to do some serious business.

TCI did not proceed on its own; for years, Malone had reduced his risk by entering new ventures in the company of well-heeled partners. Moreover, TCI had a problem. In the sections of the country it served with cable television, TCI was known all too well. In the rest of the country, it wasn't known at all. Although the prophets of the future had predicted that the age of giant corporations was irretrievably past, people still preferred to deal with giant corporations. Giant corporations spent billions of dollars to advertise their wares and create nationwide corporate identities as reliable and trustworthy friends of the nation's consumers. TCI, which was neither of these things, badly needed to join forces with a giant corporation.

AT&T wasn't interested. MCI was in the midst of a long flirtation with Rupert Murdoch. Among the nationwide telephone companies, only Sprint responded favorably, and Sprint proved to be a receptive listener.

The new partners made no little plans. Sprint and TCI formed an alliance called the Sprint Telecommunications Venture. Comcast, TCI's longtime and occasionally bemused associate, and Cox Communications, the cable company with the most modernized systems, also came aboard. Sprint owned 40 percent of the enterprise, TCI had 30 percent, and the junior partners took 5 percent each. Together, they would spend $4.2 billion to bring wireless PCS to twenty-five metropolitan areas with over 100 million potential customers. Like Ma Bell of old, the Sprint Telecommunications Venture would offer both local calling and national long-distance, and by the year 2000, the alliance happily predicted, it would own 18 percent of its local market and 5 percent of the wireless telephone business. But Malone and his partners, it seemed, just couldn't make it on the outside. Like TCI, the Sprint Telecommunications Venture was designed to lose a huge amount of money. The wireless network alone would cost $4.2 billion, revenues would be $6.9 billion, and the undertaking would bear the Malone trademark of huge debt, no profits, and no taxes. In the year 2000, the partners predicted, they would be in hock to the tune of $8.1 billion, and they were scheduled to post losses of $250 million a year. It was not explained why anybody thought this was a good idea.

Following the gospel according to Malone, the partners proceeded to spend money in order to lose money. In March 1995, the Sprint Telecommunications Venture paid $2.1 billion for twenty-nine licenses covering, among other cities, New York, Detroit, San Francisco, and Dallas–Fort Worth, the largest sum in the largest auction the FCC had held to date. TCI, bidding separately, picked up Philadelphia for another $8.9 million. None of this was stock or notes. The FCC demanded real money. With a firm step and a swinging stride, the partners marched into the future. Shortly thereafter, they decided that their map was wrong.

The Sprint Telecommunications Venture, it was announced in February 1996, would no longer offer local telephone service as a united front. If Sprint wanted its name on local telephone service, it would have to pay its pals. A national brand name was all very well in its place, but some things had gone wrong, and others had changed.

For one, converting a cable television system into a cable telephone system was turning out to be a lot harder than Malone had thought, and the projected revenues from Sprint wouldn't begin to cover the staggering cost. The coldly calculating Malone had badly miscalculated.

Meanwhile, the Telecommunications Act of 1996 allowed cable systems to resell the services of the regional telephone companies. In theory, it was a cheaper way of getting into the local land-line business—provided, of course, that the regional telephone companies decided to surrender a piece of their business without putting up a tremendous fight, the cable companies figured out how to bring the cheap dial tone to the customers' homes, and the customers rushed to embrace the untried new service. In reality, none of the foregoing occurred. According to outside analysts, it would take the cable companies somewhere between six and ten years to figure out how to become telephone companies. The bonanza—or, in the case of Malone and his partners, the opportunity to lose a lot of money—had been indefinitely postponed.

That was the bleak reality of the situation. The next great thing was not the telephone business after all. The next great thing was the cable modem and the Internet. Using modems, TCI and its cable partners could offer Internet services, and they were certain to take the country by storm. The country was mad for the Internet. Bill Gates's Microsoft, looking the other way, had been blindsided by the Internet and was struggling madly to make up for lost time. The cable companies could hook the public into the Internet right now—or in a while, as soon as they rewired their systems. There was no point in sharing the windfall with Sprint.

By the end of 1996, the partnership that had planned to become the next Ma Bell was trying to decide what to do with the rest of its life, John Malone had been missing for months, and Wall Street was far from pleased. The price of TCI's stock, heading steadily south like a thermometer on a cold day, was approaching $10 a share. If things kept on like this, TCI would soon be close to worthless in the marketplace.

IT WAS NOT THAT MALONE HAD LOST HIS TOUCH, BUT A man of Malone's narrow if considerable skills could thrive and prosper only when four conditions were met: when the government didn't know what he was doing, when the government didn't care what he was doing, when it still made sense to expand by making strategic purchases, and when Malone was in personal command of his company. By 1996, none of them applied. Slowly at first, and then with increasing speed, everything seemed to go wrong.

The Time Warner–Turner deal had gone according to someone's plan, but informed betting said that the plan wasn't Malone's. With the supposedly erratic Ted Turner installed in the Time Warner executive suite and the supposedly indestructible John Malone fading from the corporate landscape, Time Warner suddenly began to resemble the media powerhouse of Steve Ross's dreams. Jerry Levin was no longer much in evidence, Ted Turner was once again the Mouth of the South, and Turner—knocking heads, spreading charm, and publicly bashing his old enemy, Rupert Murdoch, with all the old fire and glee—had given Time Warner the appearance and perhaps the substance of the sort of dynamic enterprise it had never been. Meanwhile, TCI sat passively on the sidelines. No outsider could say just when Malone had disappeared from the scene—in the tight-knit Denver cable company, almost nobody knew that he was no longer running his company until he announced his return—but something had very definitely changed at TCI.

It was always hard to see inside TCI, but Malone was still present and very much in charge during the late summer of 1995 when he and Murdoch agreed to merge their sports operations. It was almost the last of the old Malone that anyone was to see: the emotionless logician, sitting with preternatural stillness at a marathon negotiating session in his Englewood headquarters, dealing with one of the few men he considered his equal.

There had always been something curiously one-sided about their relationship, almost as if Malone—not without calculation or an eye to his bottom line—was trying to placate the man at the very moments when he could have damaged him the most, and he had never failed to leap to Rupert Murdoch's side in an hour of need. He had given the struggling Fox network a vital boost by agreeing to put Fox on his cable systems when Murdoch and Diller were struggling desperately to find an audience. When Murdoch was nearly driven into bankruptcy in the early 1990s, Malone had lent him money vital to his survival. Now, in August 1995, they met to consult their mutual advantage.

With fifteen regional sports networks, TCI was the largest sports programmer in America. Murdoch owned a satellite whose broadcast footprint extended from Israel to Japan and reached two-thirds of the human race, and American sports were immensely popular in Asia. ESPN saw great possibilities there, and so did Malone and Murdoch. In America, the prospects were interesting; there was still a lot of regional sports programming that ESPN did not control. The minds met and the deal was done. With the merger of the TCI and Fox sports operations and Murdoch's satellite, they would be competitive with the cable channel that had revealed that Malone was no longer in charge of his world. Next, Malone and Murdoch decided to take on CNN.

Murdoch had always wanted CNN, but with the Time Warner–Turner merger CNN was beyond his reach, perhaps permanently. Like Malone, Murdoch was a tenacious man once he got an idea into his head. Unlike Malone, he also believed he had a talent for programming. Trying to establish a twenty-four-hour news service from scratch, he was offering cable operators $10 for every viewer they delivered into his hands. It was an offer of unprecedented generosity, it had driven ABC to scuttle its own planned twenty-four-hour news service, and it had otherwise failed to meet with conspicuous success. Murdoch's notion of a news story was known to be somewhat strange. Except at CNN and ABC, the news business, no matter how well run, was not a profit center; everybody else lost money, lots of it, in television news. And CNN was like IBM in its heyday; any news programmer that tried to go head-to-head with CNN invariably signed its death warrant. A new twenty-four-hour news service—especially a twenty-four-hour news service that paid $10 a head for viewers who probably wouldn't watch it in significant numbers unless the Japanese bombed Pearl Harbor—looked like a terrible idea.

For his part, Malone was already a major stockholder in Time Warner, Time Warner owned CNN, and if Malone got involved with Murdoch's news service, a long-anticipated moment would arrive. Malone would run into himself coming around a corner. He would be competing with himself. In financial parlance, there was a heck of a lot of downside to Murdoch's news service, and there wasn't a heck of a lot of up.

Nonetheless, TCI agreed to step into the vacuum as Murdoch's launch network. In exchange for $120 million and an option on 20 percent of the new channel, TCI agreed to make the programming available to 10 million of its customers, which instantly suggested a couple of things. TCI needed money, perhaps desperately. A company that needed money, perhaps desperately, had lost much of its power to maneuver. TCI was no longer guided by cold logic. The hand on the tiller was enfeebled, and perhaps there was no hand on the tiller at all. For his next move, Murdoch attacked TCI. Malone's string had finally run out.

AS THE DECADE OF THE 1990s PIVOTED AROUND ITS middle years, many things returned to haunt TCI. Next in line was direct satellite broadcasting.

Malone had always said that the initials of direct satellite broadcasting—DBS—stood for Don't Be Stupid. The receiving dish was huge, awkward, and ugly; it had been a seemingly urgent but nonexistent problem with the receiving dishes that had inspired Woo Paik to defy the laws of physics and invent digital television. Satellite signals were easily stolen, and the weather—and sun spots, and the northern lights—interfered with them. The paying audience was small. There was nothing on DBS that wasn't available on cable, and because the cable companies had bought the rights to certain channels, there were more programs on cable than there were on DBS. Rupert Murdoch, of course, was deeply interested in his European and Asian satellites, but in America Murdoch had placed his bets on Fox, his terrestrial network. Then, in the early 1990s, the DirecTV division of Hughes–General Motors used Woo Paik's breakthrough to digitize the satellite signal, and Malone's world changed again.

Once the new digital satellites were launched, vast numbers of potential customers could receive crisp and superior digital television on as many as 200 channels without paying a penny to John Malone—or, for that matter, putting up with Malone's idea of customer service. The "communicopia" had finally arrived, and Malone hadn't done it. The old ten-foot satellite dishes had cost upward of $3,000; the small, chic new dishes—roughly the size of pizza pans—cost as little as $200, and competition was driving the price ever lower. Among competing DBS services, the rivalry was so fierce that Preston Padden, Rupert Murdoch's satellite chief, joked: "Take this free dish and we'll buy you a house to bolt it onto." In 1995 and 1996, nearly 3 million customers signed on. Digital DBS was the most successful new-product rollout in the history of consumer electronics. Sixty percent of the new customers lived in rural areas served by cable. Almost half of Malone's customers lived in rural areas and were not well served by his cable. He had been milking the systems for years, and the economics of the game were no longer in his favor. Digital DBS was a spear aimed directly at the heart of TCI.

The existing rural cable systems—TCI's and others—had cost billions of dollars to build, operators like TCI needed millions of subscribers to pay at least some of their debts, and the cost of wiring each viewer's house was $600. A digital DBS system cost millions of dollars to build and launch and could turn a profit with tens of thousands of viewers. The customers paid for the antenna, and the cost of sending a satellite signal to a viewer's home was $5.00. Malone could no longer lock up his programming and neither could anybody else, because the government had ruled that DBS companies could buy any programming that was available over cable. DBS charged its customers around $25 a month, and nothing seriously bad or annoying ever happened to the crisp, abundant DBS channels unless the satellite burned out or fell down. TCI's service often left something to be desired, and in 1996 the company—freed from regulation by the new Telecommunications Act—abruptly raised its rates by 13 percent, $3.75 per customer.

By the third quarter of the year—ironically, the year interactive cable television was supposed to take the country by storm—TCI had lost at least 70,000 customers. Americans would give up many things before they abandoned their television; more American households owned television sets than owned flush toilets. It was likely that many, if not most, of the lost 70,000 customers had migrated to DBS.

Seventy thousand lost customers were not a lot of lost customers. Compared with TCI's 14 million other customers (and the 3 million customers served by TCI's indirect investments), they were a trickle, not a tide. Malone had always been extremely good at explaining such things, although in recent years Malone's explanations had developed an unhappy tendency to cut in two directions. He had persuaded the financial community that TCI's debt was a powerful asset, not an immense liability, and his message had endured for a decade before the financial community turned on him. He had talked up cable telephones for years; it wasn't until 1996 that it became apparent that he was talking through his hat. He had almost single-handedly stampeded his industry in pursuit of the 500-channel world. But he was equally good at describing the failings and limitations of his competitors, and digital DBS, as it happened, had a few of them.

Two-way communications weren't possible on digital DBS, at

least not yet; it was digital but not interactive, and it couldn't carry telephone signals. A DBS home receiver served only one television set in a house, and many American homes had more than one set. In dense cities like New York and Chicago, there were daunting difficulties in offering DBS to the occupants of high-rise apartment buildings, and for regulatory and practical reasons, DBS didn't offer local programming. For the moment, DBS was a form of television with one bell—a clear picture—and one whistle—lots of channels. It was time for Malone to step confidently forward, clear the air, and calm the latest case of jitters Wall Street had developed over his lost 70,000 customers. Malone did not step forward.

As it happened, and despite Malone's many discouraging words about the satellite business, TCI was not badly equipped in this regard. In 1990, hedging its bets, TCI had joined with six other telecommunications companies to form Primestar, a partnership devoted to DBS. Primestar launched its first bird in 1990 and went digital in 1994. Nor was TCI's share of the partnership, Primestar by TCI, doing badly. In 1995, the service added 450,000 new customers for a total of 552,000—an increase, as TCI never ceased to remind anyone who would listen, of 443 percent. It didn't have 200 channels, but it had 95, and nobody on earth made a habit of watching 95 channels. Ninety-five channels or 200 channels brought back the old spectrum glut problem of the 1960s, before Levin revolutionized the business. Malone didn't explain that, either. Instead, TCI found itself engaged in a fashion sweepstakes, and it was losing a war of perception rather than a war of reality. When it came to new technologies, Wall Street was famous for sinning in haste and repenting at leisure, throwing bushels of money at the next big thing and then watching in horror as the cash was consumed in the ensuing conflagration. For Wall Street, the newest next big thing was a digital DBS with a huge number of channels, and in this regard TCI was sadly lacking.

In its first year of operation, EchoStar, one of the smallest of the DBS start-ups, signed up 430,000 customers for 120 channels, DirecTV offered 175 channels, and they were the latest darlings of

Wall Street. To get back in the game—which had almost nothing to do with viewers, viewing habits, or television—TCI was building a shiny new satellite that would enable it to broadcast between 130 and 140 channels. It was at this point that Rupert Murdoch perceived his opportunity.

THE PRIZE ONCE AGAIN INVOLVED A FORM OF REAL estate—in this case, real estate in outer space. Murdoch, who regarded cable systems as a huge waste of money, was intimately familiar with outer space. He was also remarkably, some said maddeningly, adept at getting governments to do exactly what he wanted. In Britain, the Thatcher government had conceded that his satellite was "technically illegal." Murdoch was allowed to use it anyway, to his considerable enrichment. In America, his Fox network was almost certainly illegal. The FCC gave him a waiver and allowed him to run it anyway. He had done many piratical and perhaps dastardly things in his life and gotten away with them, but he had never attacked John Malone, perhaps because Malone had never gotten his hands on something that Murdoch wanted. Now he had.

When it came to telecommunications, only three orbital pathways covered mainland America—or CONUS, as it was called, for the Continental United States. Satellites in the three paths had to be separated by 9 degrees of distance; any closer, and their signals began to interfere with each other. All three orbits were either fully occupied or fully leased, and Malone had secured one of those leases, or so he believed. Moreover, like many shrewd executives seeking the favor of the Clinton administration, he had attempted to secure his position by obtaining the assistance of an Arkansas businessman. The Clinton administration had demonstrated that it would do many things, some of them strange, if an Arkansas businessman was involved.

The businessman in question was David Garner, a Little Rock entrepreneur who owned a company called Advanced Communications. By a prodigious stroke of good fortune, Advanced Communications held a license to launch a satellite into one of the three coveted orbits, and Garner proved to be a man who was open for business; in 1994, he sold his slot to TCI for $45 million in Malone's favorite currency, TCI stock. There was a problem, but it did not appear to be insurmountable.

Garner had never launched a satellite because he'd never been able to raise enough money to catch up with the rapidly evolving technology, and with no satellite in orbit, his license would expire at the end of 1994. Garner accordingly applied to the FCC for a construction extension that would buy TCI the necessary time to launch its bird, beam down its new channels, and persuade Wall Street that it was still a hot technology company. The FCC had never denied a construction extension, but the FCC, headed by Vice President Gore's lifelong friend, no longer liked John Malone very much. Garner did not receive a construction extension.

On April 27, 1995, Reed Hundt's FCC announced that the license had expired. No orbital slot had ever been auctioned, but auctions were all the rage now, and the FCC proceeded to hold one. The winning bidder—for $682 million—was MCI, the long-distance company, then involved in a close alliance with Murdoch's Newscorp. The two companies planned to have their own satellite up and running by 1997 as the vehicle for Murdoch's own DBS service, the American version of his fabulously successful television venture in Europe. So far, nothing unusual seemed to have happened. Satellites were Murdoch's preferred broadcasting mediums, a telephone company had put up the money, and the national treasury was further and painlessly enriched. Still, there was at least one feature of interest. TCI had recently spent billions to expand its cable network, it had spent more billions to race into the telephone business, and it was pouring billions more into the rewiring of its urban systems. But it hadn't topped MCI's bid. There seemed to be truth in the rumor that TCI, lately the imperial power of the television industry, was out of money.

Briefly, TCI fought back. First, the company tried to join forces with the victorious Murdoch. TCI owned an advanced DBS satellite but had no orbit to put it in, Murdoch had access to an orbit but no satellite, and there was an obvious convergence of interest. The talks went nowhere; there were complications. Murdoch did not actually own the orbital slot and MCI was growing increasingly uneasy with their alliance. Still, the failure to close some kind of a deal was unlike Malone, the daring and resourceful masked rider of the plains. Instead, TCI tried an end run that depended on the goodwill of a hostile government whose regulatory agency would not lose any points by kicking the stuffing out of John Malone.

Canada would be the answer. TCI would sell its satellite to a Canadian company, Telesat. Telesat would then launch the bird into a vacant Canadian orbit, TCI would obtain a license from the Canadian government, and TCI would broadcast its signal into the United States. Murdoch, the owner of an Australian company that controlled an American broadcasting network, lobbied heavily against the deal. Once again, the FCC turned TCI down—pending, it said, the necessary licenses from the Canadian government. Canadian officials said they would grant the necessary licenses. At the end of October 1996, the FCC refused to grant TCI permission to broadcast from Canada. It was a memorable month. In October 1996, it finally became clear that almost everything else at TCI had gone haywire, too.

THE CREDIT RATING WAS SHOT. THE BOSS HAD VANISHED. The alliance with Microsoft was at an end. TCI had spent an estimated $4 billion to lay the optical fiber and install the electronic switches for a telephone venture that had either collapsed or was on indefinite hold, while using the fiber and switches to bring a tenth of its subscribers an abundance of new channels and a modest version of digital interactive television that was far from the bright original promise. TCI's new, vast, empty $100 million National Digital Television Center at the Englewood headquarters could send six compressed signals—six television shows or six movies—over a single old analog channel, bounce them off an older satellite, beam them down to its earth stations, and distribute them to the half of its subscribers that didn't live out in the country. For a fee, other cable systems could pick up the signal, make minor adjustments in their equipment, and provide their customers with cheap digital television. As TCI never ceased to boast, nobody else had anything remotely like the National Digital Television Center. But until somebody figured out how to manufacture millions of digital set-top boxes, the compressed signals could not be decoded in the vast majority of the nation's homes, and Malone might as well have been broadcasting in Serbo-Croatian.

General Instrument may have invented digital television, but it continued to discover that manufacturing set-top boxes wasn't as easy as falling off a log. It wasn't even as easy as manufacturing a carburetor.

In the last months of 1996, General Instrument finally succeeded in shipping TCI 40,000 of the devices. "All has been forgiven now," said a GI spokesman. "Hopefully." All was not forgiven. At current production rates, TCI estimated that only a quarter of its customers would have digital boxes by 1999. And when TCI, having burned haystacks of money, finally became a digital television company in the memorable month of October 1996, there was nothing remarkable about it.

One hundred and forty channels were piped to a handful of viewers in West Hartford, Connecticut. Most of the new channels offered near-video-on-demand—glorified pay-per-view—and the sort of viewing fare, such as spin-offs of HBO, that was available almost everywhere. It was not the television of the future. It was more television. This, in the end, was what it had all been about. And for TCI in October 1996 the end seemed very near.

BESET WITHOUT AND HEMORRHAGING MONEY WITHIN, THE company had returned to its old reliable standby, squeezing cash out of its cable systems. Next, someone at TCI took a close look at the books and discovered an astonishing thing. Some programming services, like Rupert Murdoch's untried news channel, would actually pay good money for one of TCI's channels. Other programming services—ESPN, for example—charged a bundle. The logic of the situation seemed inescapable. TCI would remove the programmers that cost the most money and replace them with the programmers that paid the most. In the Denver metropolitan area, TCI's nerve center, this interesting but not very bright experiment produced something that resembled a middle-class riot. At TCI, the touch of the master was definitely missing.

In Denver, the company removed Viacom's popular MTV and VH1 channels from its system. To the surprise of nobody but TCI, Viacom showed fight and struck back. With the local news media whipping the situation into a froth, it established "MTV Shelters" in local music stores, where the faithful could watch shows beamed down from a satellite, lent its support to an anti-TCI rally, and sent talent to stir up the crowd. Viacom's chairman, Sumner Redstone, having made his point, picked up the phone, and TCI relented. TCI had never been known for the subtlety of its customer relations, but it had never blacked out two must-see channels in a major metropolitan area. In Denver, Malone's leaderless company briefly resembled a man who decided to economize by not eating. Next, it decided to economize by burning down part of its house.

Abruptly, TCI announced that it was suspending orders from its suppliers, including General Instrument. Executive salaries were slashed, some by as much as 20 percent. Twenty-five hundred employees were laid off. The company's airplanes were sold. John Malone announced his return and immediately repudiated everything he had said and done for years.

"It's not true that I have no interest in cable," he said.

———

ONLY A FEW THINGS HAD EVER BEEN KNOWN FOR CERTAIN about John Malone, and the list seemed to grow shorter, not longer, with the passage of time. He was fifty-five years old. In Maine, he owned a new plaything, an eighty-foot yacht, the *Liberty*, made of intricately laid wood and carbon fiber and described by *The Wall Street Journal* as "stunning." He had never made his billion, but he was distinctly comfortable; he paid himself more than $13 million a year, and his holdings in TCI were worth around $550 million. It was not revealed when his sabbatical had begun, where he had spent it, or why. TCI had never been a talkative company.

He still appeared at trade gatherings, speaking as usual without notes, but he no longer appeared at many of them. He had never let an outsider get too close to him, but now his aversion to contact emerged in the most literal possible way; at an industry dinner in New York, his executives hustled him into an elevator before a *Business Week* reporter could get a good look at his face. TCI finally acknowledged that he was ill but did not say with what. Others said he had leukemia.

WHATEVER HAD HAPPENED AND WHEREVER HE HAD BEEN, Malone—looking much like his old self—made his comeback appearance before an audience of analysts in Phoenix in late October 1996. Things, Malone assured his audience, were not as bad as they seemed. TCI's cash flow was up for the quarter. That was true, but the cash flow hadn't risen nearly so much as TCI pretended. The suspension of supplier shipments was of no great moment, Malone said; TCI had plenty of digital set-top boxes. In fact, TCI didn't have enough digital set-top boxes to wire a medium-sized city. Inventory controls would be tightened, Malone continued. He failed to mention the persistent rumors that TCI had somehow managed to misplace $50 million of its inventory. The Hartford test of interactive television, he concluded, was going well.

Three weeks later, on November 17, Bob Magness died. The old rancher was seventy-two, and his personal fortune was estimated in the vicinity of $1 billion; his stake in TCI had been very good to him. It did not appear that it was going to be nearly as good to John Malone.

By all reports, Magness had left 90 percent of his holding to his two sons, Kim and Gary, and the rest to his wife and an unnamed charity. These things could not be known with any certainty. Although a will is a public document, the Magness will could not be read. It had been locked away, placed "under security" by the Denver court, and no explanation was forthcoming for this all but unprecedented event.

Evidently, Magness had created no trusts, the favorite tax shelters of wealthy people who acknowledge their mortality. The second Mrs. Magness would not pay taxes on her inheritance and neither would the unknown charity, but the sons most definitely would, and the Magness sons were destined to receive the largest single block of TCI shares in existence. For John Malone, this was big trouble.

The Internal Revenue Service was not expected to be lenient. To pay the death duties, Kim and Gary Magness would have to sell a large portion of their holding in a stock market that no longer doted on TCI, but the continued financial health of the Magness heirs was the least of Malone's worries. Together, Magness and Malone had controlled TCI and run it like a private business. Now, a good portion of the company was in danger of falling into hands whose owners might have different or unfriendly agendas. Malone could lose control. For a change, however, the latest impending crisis revolved around money and finance, not technology. Malone had always been very good when it came to money and finance.

To the world at large, he presented himself as a man who had undergone a radical change of heart. TCI, he startlingly announced, had been run by a pack of fools, himself included.

For starters in the new gospel according to Malone, debt was a curse. The time had come for TCI to face reality, pay off its creditors, make a profit, and do some hard thinking. Getting into the telephone business might not have been a mistake, exactly, but there had been too much hype and he blamed himself. The same went for digital television and his new Internet service, @Home. No doubt they would pay off someday—and pay off big—but in the meanwhile a chastened and reformed TCI would get back to basics. Getting back to basics consisted of bringing plain old television to the home.

He resigned as president, assumed the chairmanship, and no longer even pretended to manage the company. But he was vastly interested in the old TCI subsidiary, Liberty Media, where the pro-gramming assets were concentrated. Liberty's name, like the name of his new yacht, did not appear to be an accident.

Malone had long been a master of creating complications where none should exist—unless, of course, the complications were deliber-ately intended to cause a certain amount of useful confusion. Ma-lone's plan for Liberty was so complicated—and, on the surface, in-comprehensible—that one professional analyst, a man carefully schooled in such things, had to read the relevant documents three times. He insisted on remaining anonymous. Wall Street analysts are supposed to be sharp as tacks, but Malone had that sort of effect on the best of people.

At the time of the failed Bell Atlantic merger, Liberty had been reabsorbed by TCI. It was on Liberty that Malone now pinned his hopes.

In a blinding series of fast shuffles that revealed the familiar fist of John Malone, Liberty would provide the Magness boys with money to pay their estate taxes in exchange for their holdings in Liberty. Actually, TCI would provide the money, because Liberty was still a part of TCI. (Having paid their estate taxes, the Magness boys would retain their TCI holdings.) Next and once again, Liberty would be-come an independent company, and Malone, having paid neither money nor taxes for the privilege, would become Liberty's controlling stockholder because the Magness boys' shares would now be owned and controlled by Malone. In this scenario, since Malone had been liquidating his holdings in TCI, the Magness boys would control TCI, its mountain of debt, its failed telephone strategy, its dud technology, and the shiny new satellite sitting in the basement. Malone, if all went according to the apparent plan, would squeal off into the night with Liberty and the programming assets—now enhanced to include *The MacNeil-Lehrer NewsHour* and a piece of the Court TV channel—that had recently been TCI's most valuable possessions. The devil, as always, would take the hindmost. Confronted with this scenario, and a dispute with their stepmother, the Magness boys went to court, setting off a two-year battle which ended in late 1997 on more favorable terms for the heirs. Liberty was not spun off.

When the dust settled, Malone controlled TCI, with it Liberty, and was paid $150 million for the privilege.

Malone had often described Bob Magness as his father figure and mentor, but he was not a man to be inhibited by any sentiments for his fallen chief.

"It's fun being Darth Vader again," he announced when he reemerged from seclusion in October. With his customary selective candor, he neglected to add that, unlike Darth Vader, he proposed to make his getaway. If the Liberty maneuver didn't work, he would think of something else.

The Media Lab at Ten

AS BEFITTED A MODERN ROMANCE OF ACADEMIC CAPITAL-
ism, the tenth anniversary of the MIT Media Lab was celebrated
with appropriate symbolism and a certain amount of pomp, although
the architectural omens were not auspicious. At ten minutes after ten
o'clock in the morning on the tenth day of 1995's tenth month, the
festivities began on the stage of MIT's Kresge Auditorium, the sort of
1950s-style, take-me-to-your-leader building that was designed to slip
seamlessly into a future that never happened.

On the stage was Douglas Adams, author of *The Hitchhiker's
Guide to the Galaxy*, a man well trained in after-dinner speaking, a
uniquely British art that makes the listener, should he be so luckless
as to open his mouth in the speaker's presence, feel as though nothing would emerge but snakes and toads. Outside, under a huge

tented marquee, coffee and Danish were available. Guests were given tote bags emblazoned with the numerals 10-10, representing the date, time, and anniversary; the numbers 1 and 0 of the binary digital code were at the heart of everything the Lab did, tried to do, and sometimes actually accomplished. There were other gifts as well: a watch, a specially manufactured mouse pad, and a wearable Lego block that, properly activated, could communicate with another guest's Lego block. A visitor to the Media Lab on its tenth anniversary had not exactly stumbled into the heart of the military-industrial complex.

Later, lunch was served in handsome Japanese-style containers embossed with the ubiquitous numerals, as were the labels on the many circulating bottles of white wine. At one of the tables, executives from Compaq Computer—cool men from a hot company that was one of the Lab's corporate sponsors—turned the food apparatus in their hands and, not for the first time, exchanged a significant glance. In cheeseparing times, when funding for scientific research was shriveling everywhere else for lack of ready cash, the Media Lab had spent its benefactors' money to customize hundreds of lunch buckets. It could afford to.

In 1995, by far the largest part of the Lab's $25 million in annual funding was provided by 105 corporate sponsors, including such technological heavyweights as Compaq, Sony, and IBM, but also counting among their numbers Nike, the sneaker company. The Danish toy manufacturer, Lego, was another longtime donor to the Lab. So was Nintendo, the Japanese toy manufacturer, whose most conspicuous contributions to the advancement of planetary culture were the addictive video games Super Mario Brothers and Robocop. The average corporate donation was $200,000. Most of the rest of the Lab's money came from government grants, but not, perhaps significantly, from the National Science Foundation, and not, perhaps significantly, for lack of trying. According to Nicholas Negroponte, the Lab's co-founder, the NSF had turned down every one of the Lab's requests for the last decade.

Still, the Lab could hardly complain; corporate contributions were growing by 30 percent a year at a time when the rest of MIT, battered by the collapse of the Evil Empire and the newfound parsimony of the private sector, had seen its grants fall by 30 percent. In 1995, MIT posted a deficit of $9.2 million. It could be argued, and was, that this was not necessarily a bad thing, that there was no longer any need, if there ever had been, for the nation to discover bold new cutting-edge ways to blow the planet to smithereens. But it could also be argued, and was, that the Media Lab, despite all its money and because of its loudly proclaimed fascination with gadgets and playthings, was not practicing grown-up science. It could be argued, and was, that the Media Lab was not practicing science at all.

ON THE STAGE OF THE KRESGE, THE PARADE OF SPEAKERS did little to dispel this somewhat sour notion. The Media Lab demonstrated that it had managed to both reinvent and improve Maxwell Smart's shoe phone. Wearing a tiny experimental computer in his footgear (where, in perfected form, it would recharge itself as its owner walked, using the compressive energy now wasted as the owner propels himself to a destination), a Lab member shook hands with a similarly equipped colleague. Their low-powered but electrically charged bodies had been converted into small local-area computer networks. On a screen behind them, they digitally exchanged business cards. In the future, it was suggested, one of them might download a file by throwing his arm around the other's shoulders. Over lunch, the Compaq executives dryly wondered why the demonstration had not been carried to its logical conclusion.

It was clear, however, that the Lab was determined to carry digital interactivity to the most distant boundaries of its founder's dreams. The Lab owned machines for embroidering computer circuitry into shirts and pants, as though ordinary clothing was so much useless shrubbery covering the soon to be tapped, conductive real estate of the human frame. Confronted with computerized shoes and digital pants, the mind's eye of an observer conjured the image of a yellowing publication from the early twentieth century, open to an ad for a dog's treadmill attached to an electric generator, accompanied by the slogan "Make Him Earn His Keep!" By the time of the Lab's tenth anniversary, it was becoming increasingly apparent that the digital faithful were taking an increasingly cavalier attitude toward the temple of the spirit, combined with a notion, breathtaking in its arrogant naïveté, that any digital idea was probably a good idea, no matter how lunatic it might appear in the eyes of the uninitiated. This impression took on the form of prophecy when a famous graduate student, Steve Mann, appeared in the back of the darkened Kresge auditorium.

A pair of antennas sprouted from his beanie. His eyes were covered with enormous black goggles. Around his waist was a wearable computer. Everything Mann saw—although he did not appear to see it very well; the famous graduate student was assisted to his seat by another graduate student—traveled from his goggles to his belt and from his belt to his beanie, where the image was transmitted to his home page on the World Wide Web. A subsequent peep at the Web revealed that Mann had visited the campus lunchroom. He hoped his research would one day help the visually impaired, or so he said. He had, his adviser told the *New York Times*, a long way to go.

Still, Mann's celebrity, such as it was, was of the famous-for-being-mildly-strange sort. Like someone who had discovered a radish in the shape of Indiana, he was good filler on a slow news day, a novelty item for the computer magazines, and a campus character. The same could not be said for the figure who now strode forward into the footlights far below. Seymour Papert was a man of genuine professional accomplishment.

PAPERT WAS A RECOGNIZED EXPERT IN THE CONTRO-versial field of computers and education. He had invented Logo, a digital language comprehensible to children. He had been co-director of MIT's artificial intelligence laboratory. Currently, he was the Lab's Lego Professor of Learning Research; in addition to finding many uses for computers in the classroom, he had found many uses for Lego blocks.

Papert was one of the Media Lab's genuine stars, trotted out on every possible occasion for the benefit of the press and the television cameras. On the occasion of the tenth anniversary, he seemed to have fallen under the Lab's curious spell, sounding for all the world like a pitchman on late-night television—a very dignified pitchman—trying to sell a fabulous vegetable-slicing machine that no one had quite gotten around to inventing. To illustrate, he told an anecdote about accidentally burning some sauce in a pan.

Papert had cried "Stupid!" referring to himself, but one day soon, he said, he would cry "Stupid!" referring to the pan. The saucepan of the future would contain a microchip that would warn its owner of impending mishaps. Similarly, the refrigerator of the future would inform its owner that it was out of milk, and the owner's doorknob would answer the phone. It was all quite sad, a first-class mind awash in the domestic trivia of a cartoonish future. As a teacher, Papert had once been intimately familiar with the untidy, undigital, uncool world beyond the campus, but the Lab had a curious way of clouding the keenest mind. To many observers, the Lab had especially clouded the mind of Papert's colleague Walter Bender, who soon took his place on the Kresge stage. Bender was widely regarded as a man who had devoted his life to solving a problem that did not exist by creating an entirely new problem that should never have existed.

Walter Bender caught more flak than any other member of the Lab, up to and including Nicholas Negroponte. Even the most determined of Negroponte's detractors acknowledged that the arrogant crackpot occasionally had something interesting to say, but Bender's critics regarded him as a seriously deluded man. In the eyes of his most vehement critics, Walter Bender was positively dangerous.

On the Kresge stage that morning, he remarked that he had considered wearing a raincoat during his public appearances, to deflect the soft fruit and other missiles that seemed to come his way every time he opened his mouth in a public forum. Bender directed the News in the Future project, a longtime and favorite undertaking of the Lab. Its oft-stated goal was to create a newspaper called the *Daily Me*, based on two readily observable phenomena: the onward march of digital science and the fact that newspapers and television news operations generate vastly more material than they can possibly use. Bender's *Daily Me*, like Negroponte's ideal digital television, would be a newspaper customized to the interests of its reader.

In its latest incarnation, it would be delivered on a digitally friendly medium that resembled paper. By monitoring its subscriber's preferences in articles, the *Daily Me* would gradually weed out all the tiresome items its subscriber either ignored or skimmed. Instead, it would present a rich banquet of stories tailored to the subscriber's interests. Negroponte, in his 1995 book, *Being Digital*, suggested that the *Daily Me* could be equipped with something called a "slider," enabling the subscriber to adjust the political content of the stories from far right to far left, in a way congenial to the subscriber's out-look. In this, the *Daily Me* would resemble the public spaces of the Internet, just then coming into wild favor as a sort of electronic asylum for refugees from talk radio, religious fanatics, ignoramuses, survivalists, cranks, racists, neo-Nazis, and a monstrous regiment of people with the mental age of a fourteen-year-old equipped with a ski mask and a horse pistol. A number of people who did not wish Walter Bender well noted that an earlier version of his pet project had been called *Newspeek*, a word phonetically identical to the mind-control-ling, monochromatic, totalitarian language created by George Orwell in *1984*.

Other implications of Bender's project were not lost on outsiders. An alert reporter for *Advertising Age* swiftly combined Papert's chat-tering digital appliances with Bender's malleable news sheet and con-jured a future where the family car, sensing that its tires were worn, could flood the morning *Me* with tire ads. The reporter thought this was a hell of an idea. How the larger public good was thus served remained somewhat obscure.

The larger public good, as it happened, was much on Nicholas Negroponte's mind that morning.

The co-founder of the Media Lab did not bound forward on the Kresge stage accompanied by a rock star's acclamation. Very little short of the uncaged arrival of a living velociraptor is capable of bringing a scientific gathering—or the congregation of a decorous church; the two are not dissimilar—to its feet in full-throated cry. Still, Negroponte's arrival was clearly an exceptional moment; it almost seemed as though there was a change in the air pressure and the ambient lighting. Dressed as always in a well-tailored suit and his trademark blue-striped shirt, Negroponte was not only the co-founder of the Lab but its presiding intellect and voice to the world. To the faithful, he was the prophet of the digital revolution.

He traveled hundreds of thousands of miles a year, attending conferences, giving speeches, visiting sponsors and prospective sponsors. A couple of years before, he had promised that he would cut back and spend more time at home—because some people felt that the administrator of a lab should spend some time administering the lab—but he had not. He no longer had an office at the Lab and was pleased by his liberation from furniture and walls; the computer that recorded his e-mail was sufficient, or so he felt. NN or Nicholas, as he was called, spent upward of three hours a day reading and answering his e-mail. On a visit to Bell Labs, he had not won the hearts of his scholarly hosts by producing a laptop computer and reading his e-mail while they were trying to talk to him. He wrote a monthly back-page column in *Wired*, the hot book of computer magazines. He was an opinionated and very confident man.

Today his subject was pornography on the Internet. On the whole, he was in favor of it. He did not, however, mention interactive television, although he had once—and very recently—seen the home television set as the vehicle of choice for the convergence of video, computers, and telephones. The Lab continued to work on it, of course; the Lab kept his fingers in any pie as long as the sponsors continued to pay the bills, but Malone and Levin had disappointed Nicholas Negroponte. The interactive television they were attempting to create bore only a glancing resemblance to the future he had anticipated, and the wonders of the Internet now brightened his eye. Moreover, the inhabitants of the Lab had perceived a stunning new digital future whose implications obliterated everything that had gone before, even if it had never actually happened. For humankind, the digital revolution led directly to a remarkable reward, and it was left to the Lab's other star performer, Marvin Minsky, to reveal what it was.

Minsky was one of the founders of the science of artificial intelligence, a great beached whale of a technology whose goal was to make computers as smart as humans. Things had not gone well for artificial intelligence. In 1992, after a decade of work and $400 million down the drain, the Japanese abandoned their Fifth Generation Project, their full-court press to perfect AI and thus dominate the computer industry. The Fifth Generation Project had failed because it hadn't worked very well, nobody was very interested in it, and the world's computer industry had gone off in an entirely different direction that made Microsoft's Bill Gates into the richest man in the world. The Japanese offered their software, free, to anybody who wanted it.

To a Media Lab obsessed with smart refrigerators, this suggested nothing, nor did Minsky choose to shed light on the subject. Instead, and puzzlingly, he began his remarks by describing how, seated in his Massachusetts office, he had recently moved the arm of a primitive robot in Australia.

"Am I forgetting something, or didn't we go to the moon once?" muttered one of his distant listeners.

"Yeah, a couple of times," said his companion. "We also developed a polio vaccine."

On the stage, Minsky finished with the Australian robot. Warming to a new subject, he informed his listeners that computers would soon grant humankind the gift of eternal life, through a merger of biological and electronic life forms. He was not the first speaker to raise the possibility. Earlier in the day, Pattie Maes, the Sony Career Development Professor of Media Arts and Sciences, had also raised the possibility of an impending merger. It had made Maes distinctly uneasy, but to Minsky it was no mere possibility and for him it held no terrors. Human and electronic life forms would inevitably merge. The resulting supersmart entity would live forever.

THE SEARCH FOR THE PHILOSOPHER'S STONE, THE MAGical, forever undiscovered rock that would transmute base metals into gold, had been a remarkably effective way of persuading the king to pay a medieval alchemist's bills. But in alchemy, the real payoff was the Elixir of Life. At the Media Lab, smart houses and smarter newspapers were the Philosopher's Stone, the ever elusive but plausible-sounding goals that persuaded the likes of Lego, Nintendo, and Sony to endow the professorial chairs and keep the Lab awash in cash. The payoff remained the same.

In this, the Lab was far from alone in its thinking. The great religions of the world had long pondered the liberation of the spirit from the flesh. So, on a secular but equally obsessive level, had modern science fiction. Not since the Middle Ages, however, had humanity been promised immortality as an off-the-shelf consumer product.

TO HIS CREDIT, NICHOLAS NEGROPONTE DID NOT BELIEVE in artificial life. A computer or a television set or a smart building or a robot would do what its programmer told it to do, but Negroponte pointed out that obedience, even obedience to complicated orders that resulted in the imitation of intelligent life, was by no means awareness and a sense of self. It was not even identical—not even similar—to the mindless life of the amoeba and the flatworm. Nor would it ever be. Nicholas Negroponte was one of the many men who went overboard on the subject of the digital revolution, but he never swam or drifted very far from the ship. The digital future, stubbornly exhibiting a mind of its own and repeatedly falling into the hands of pedestrian thinkers like Jerry Levin and John Malone, continued to disappoint him, but there was always some new discovery—or some new use for an old discovery—that would make Negroponte's day and Negroponte's living. Others might find the future frustrating or financially ruinous because it hadn't happened yet and almost never turned out according to plan, but there was always a buck in it for the right sort of man. Nicholas Negroponte was not averse to the trappings and the rewards of wealth.

At the end of the day, when the tenth-anniversary celebration was over and the Kresge emptied out, his guests were served oysters, smoked salmon, and walnuts with their wine. Interactive television had not been discussed. Everyone who tried it lost money and became a laughingstock, and that would never do. Nicholas Negroponte had revised the future accordingly, and the Media Lab had moved on to other things.

LIKE TCI, TIME WARNER—TRUE TO ITS WORD AND ITS captain's vision—also attempted to mine fairy gold in the telephone business. The test bed was Rochester, New York. "It's sort of a step function," Jim Chiddix explained. "You have to buy a beginner-level switch, and then as you gain customers, you expand the system in modular fashion." By the end of 1995, following the expenditure of many advertising dollars and a personal visit by Chairman Levin to rally the troops, Time Warner had signed up just 1 percent of the telephone customers in Rochester, and not much was heard of the experiment thereafter. Time Warner also proposed to enter the telephone business in Ohio, encountered spirited resistance from Ameritech, the regional Bell, and went nowhere. The interactive television experiment in Orlando was suspended in September 1997. Like TCI, Time Warner was now fascinated with the Internet. Like other television companies, including the broadcasters, Time Warner had also become keenly interested in the newly perfected digital form of HDTV developed in America, not because of the picture quality but because digital HDTV made it possible to send as many as six channels of television and services down a single old analog pipe. Thanks largely to Ted Turner, who was widely perceived to be running the company with vigor and skill after a long drought, the price of Time Warner's stock finally began to rise. The company still made no money.

John Malone stepped down as president of TCI in early 1997 and assumed the vacant chairmanship. But Malone, who claimed he was no longer interested in day-to-day operations, was soon back in fighting trim. It was a timely recovery, for the struggle over the Bob Magness estate—the largest in Colorado history—had reached new heights of interfamilial ugliness, with the Magness sons suing their stepmother, the stepmother laying claim to a full half of the inheritance rather than the beggarly $55 million, including the family mansion and Arabian horses, she had been assigned in the will, and huge inheritance taxes looming. (There was no denying that Bob Magness, a man who felt no love for the government or its tax authorities, had left a strangely basic will. In Colorado, a story circulated that a second, far more sophisticated will had been drawn, sheltering many of the Magness assets, but it had been completed just as the old tycoon fell deep into his final illness. Thought was given, the story went, to placing a pen in Magness's near-lifeless hand and guiding his signature on the new document, but someone thought better of it.) To make matters even more interesting, rumors began to circulate that Bill Gates's Microsoft, which had just made a $1 billion investment in Comcast, tried to persuade Comcast to bid for the 20 percent of TCI owned by the Magness estate, a move that would have forever dashed John Malone's hopes of controlling the company he and Magness had built. But Malone, as predicted, thought of something: It was not necessary to activate the Liberty escape vehicle after all. TCI paid the Magness heirs $124 million in exchange for the right to buy the family's shares if the family decided to sell or if their heirs died.

Under a simultaneous and nearly identical agreement, TCI paid Malone $150 million. It will be noted that no shares actually changed hands. Under the terms of the agreement, Malone also received an irrevocable right to vote the Magness estate's shares as he saw fit, making his control of the company secure while promising him a second handsome payday at his shareholders' expense if he ever decided to take a hike. (As a result of the complicated maneuvering over the estate, TCI—and therefore Malone—became the owners of the *Salt Lake Tribune.*) Meanwhile, Malone revealed that all of his old interests, so recently dashed and humbled, had been rekindled. He hadn't really meant that TCI should finally begin making some money, he said. He'd only meant that TCI should find a better way of managing its debt. He announced that TCI would spend $1.9 billion to bring its customers the next generation of digital, interactive television. His announcement was viewed with a certain amount of skepticism—he had, after all, spent somewhere in the vicinity of $4 billion to give a scant 520,000 of his 14 million customers access to digital television the first time he tried it, and the other cable guys had finally awakened to the fact that people weren't very interested in much of anything digital television could do in its current form. But he was once again acknowledged as the leader of his industry when he successfully played off Sun Microsystems against Microsoft in their competition to provide the software for the next generation of set-top boxes, and reminded Silicon Valley (and Bill Gates) who was boss in cable television, even if the boss (as seemed possible) was still wrong about the future. TCI, the most technologically backward of major cable companies, returned to favor on Wall Street; it was a trick Malone had turned before, and now he turned it again. And, thanks to TCI's sports broadcasting alliance with Murdoch's Newscorp, TCI owned rights to half the Los Angeles Dodgers if the National League approved Murdoch's purchase of the team. TCI decided to pass.

Sumner Redstone, having borrowed too much money to purchase Paramount, fired his chief executive officer and took the post himself. Losses continued at Viacom, largely because of an earnings collapse at the Blockbuster Video subsidiary. Although Viacom's Paramount Studios owned a large piece of *Titanic*, the first movie to gross more than a billion dollars, Redstone still had no reason to think kindly of Barry Diller.

Rupert Murdoch parted company with MCI. His publishing house, HarperCollins, canceled its agreement to publish a book by Christopher Patten, the last British governor of Hong Kong. Pandemonium ensued, but the book was certain to outrage the Chinese government. Murdoch still entertained great hopes for his television business in China. With Rupert Murdoch, as with John Malone, the old ways died hard.

As this book went to press, it was announced that AT&T would acquire TCI in a stock and debt-assumption deal valued at $37.3 billion. The media went wild. AT&T's chairman, Michael Armstrong, like Ray Smith before him, could not contain his delight at the prospect of seizing the future boldly by the horns while amassing riches beyond the dreams of avarice. John Malone also expressed his pleasure.

This time, there was no talk of the 500-channel universe. Instead, AT&T would use TCI's cables to invade and dominate the market in the Next Great Thing, the Internet and its sidekick, the World Wide Web. It was unclear if AT&T understood just how, or even approximately, a cable system worked. AT&T also proposed to use TCI's cables to piggyback its telephone service. Just how it planned to do this—especially in view of the fact that everybody else who had tried it had fallen flat on his face—AT&T did not say. There would be home shopping. There would be home banking. There would be games. Perhaps there would even be a Picturephone.

For his part, Malone would at last be free of TCI's staggering debt, its restive and disgruntled customers, and his obsolete cable systems. They would now be AT&T's babies—and according to some estimates, AT&T could also expect to spend at least $10 billion to upgrade TCI's systems. Why AT&T thought this was a good idea, AT&T also did not say.

On paper, Malone would at last become a billionaire—almost twice over. He would become one of the largest, if not the largest, stockholders in AT&T. Although Liberty Media, where Malone had quietly transferred the bulk of his personal fortune, would officially become part of the AT&T family, John Malone would run it as his own company, with all the powers and abilities of an independent executive. It would issue its own stock, independently of AT&T. For all intents and purposes, it would be Malone's private empire, containing all of the programming assets—and the 44 percent of *TV Guide* that it had recently bought—that had once been, and were no longer, the most valuable possessions of TCI. It would also be a very rich private empire; as part of the proposed deal, Liberty, although it had only thirteen employees, would receive $5.5 billion from AT&T, and Malone would know how to put the money to good use.

If the deal went through—if Michael Armstrong, unlike Ray Smith before him, did not surmise his peril—Malone would have triumphed.

NOTES

---

1. A WONDERFUL BUSINESS

p. 9 . . . it was 1948. Interesting material on the dawn of cable can be found, among many other places, in *Broadcasting*, 11/21/88, and *Dun's Business Review*, 11/81.

p. 11 . . . one day in 1952. The passages on Bill Daniels draw heavily on "An Oral History Interview: Bill Daniels, Cable Television Pioneer," National Cable Television Center and Museum, Pennsylvania State University, University Park, Pa.

p. 14 ". . . an engineer living in the house." David E. and Marshall Jon Fisher, *Tube: The Invention of Television* (Washington, D.C.: Counterpoint, 1996), p. 328.

p. 16 . . . the Denver suburb of the cable barons. All Glenn Jones quotes come from author interview, 10/22/96.

p. 17 . . . a minimum of risk. *Dun's Business Review*, 5/65, p. 45.

p. 18 . . . a place called Manhattan Island. *Business Week*, 1/19/66, pp. 100–1.

p. 21 . . . the telephone companies . . . For a quick tutorial on the telephone-cable war, see *Broadcasting*, 10/19/64, pp. 28–30; 10/17/66, pp. 44–48; and 3/4/68, pp. 62–63. Also *Forbes*, 5/11/81, pp. 205–9.

p. 21 . . . no money coming in as a result. See *Broadcasting*, 3/18/68, pp. 53–54.

p. 24 ". . . I need to get out." Anita Sharpe, *The Wall Street Journal*, 11/27/95, p. A10. A detailed study of Turner's mental state (and perhaps the best biography of the man yet written) can be found in Porter Bibb, *It Ain't as Easy as It Looks: Ted Turner's Amazing Story* (New York: Crown Publishers, 1993).

p. 27 . . . in the words of one commentator. Maggie Mahar, *Barron's*, 7/11/88, p. 21.

2. A MIRROR IN THE SKY

p. 29 . . . seven times his purchase price. John Malone gave a number of interviews in the late 1980s. The radio anecdote is found in *Business Week*, 10/6/87, p. 90.

p. 30 ". . . in electrical engineering." Author interview (undated), Fall 1990.

p. 30 ". . . in the business side." Ibid.

p. 31 ". . . in statistics and math." Ibid.

p. 31 The Malones' relationship was extensively discussed by Ken Auletta in *The New Yorker*, 2/7/94, pp. 52–67.

p. 32 ". . . the vehicle for that." Author interview, Fall 1990.

p. 32 ". . . stuck in traffic." Ibid.

p. 33 . . . grown to nearly 37,000. The outlines of the Magness saga can be found in L. J. Davis, *New York Times Business World*, 12/2/90, p. 38.

p. 33 ". . . Bob just bought." Author interview, 10/22/96.

p. 35 ". . . to borrow money." Author interview, Fall 1990.

p. 35 ". . . whaleshit," Malone said. *Business Week*, 10/6/87, p. 91.

p. 36 . . . Malone said dismissively. Ibid.

p. 37 . . . to become a bag carrier. The Levin story has also appeared extensively in print. For concise summaries, see Connie Bruck, *Master of the Game* (New York: Penguin Group, 1994), pp. 247–50; Richard Clurman, *To the End of Time* (New York: Simon & Schuster, 1992), pp. 147–50; and Michael Oneal, *Business Week*, 12/11/95, pp. 87–96.

p. 37 . . . Henry Luce. The Henry Luce story is not exactly obscure. See Robert E. Herzstein, *Henry R. Luce: A Political Portrait of the Man Who Created the American Century* (New York: Charles Scribner's Sons, 1994); and Curtis Prendergast with Geoffrey Colvin, *The World of Time Inc.: The Intimate History of a Changing Enterprise, 1960–1980* (New York: Atheneum, 1986), together with companion volumes.

p. 38 . . . mighty corporate empire. For eyewitness accounts of the early days of cable, the author is indebted to Daniel Burke, past president of Capital Cities/ABC and Les Brown, former *New York Times* television critic and editor of the now vanished *Channels* magazine, where we all had some glorious times.

p. 40 . . . undertake an experiment. Details of the HBO satellite experience can be found in Clurman, pp. 39, 147–50; Bruck, pp. 247–52; *Broadcasting*, 11/21/88, pp. 35–49; and "Cable Milestones" (draft), 10/23/96, National Cable Television Center and Museum, Pennsylvania State University, University Park, Pa.

p. 43 ". . . We passed." Rukeyser in conversation with the author.

3. The Bystander, the Land Rush, and the Wired Nation

p. 45 . . . John Malone's expense. Howard Rudnitsky and Edward F. Cone, *Forbes*, 4/6/87, p. 126.

p. 46 . . . L. J. Davis, *New York Times Business World*, 12/2/90, p. 38. Slightly different versions of the TCI turnaround appeared in *Business Week, Forbes, Fortune*, and *Barron's*.

p. 46 ". . . for us," Malone said. Author interview, Fall 1990.

p. 47 ". . . are ruined professionally." Quoted in Christopher Knowlton, *Fortune*, 7/31/89. For other details, see *Forbes*, 10/6/87; Maggie Mahar, *Barron's*, 8/1/88, p. 9; and Ken Auletta, *The New Yorker*, 2/7/94, p. 58.

p. 47 . . . lost its case. The Boulder story, like the Vail and Jefferson City stories, can be found in most summaries of TCI's early history. For a fairly complete account, see Geraldine Fabrikant, *New York Times*, 10/19/83, p. D1.

p. 48 . . . its prime regulators. Author interview quoted in *New York Times Business World*, 12/2/90, p. 38.

p. 53 . . . rent-a-citizen. A widespread and brazen practice. See *Broadcasting*, 5/21/88, p. 44, and *The Economist*, 6/20/81, p. 29.

p. 53 . . . charged much more. The extra payoffs took a variety of forms. One was bribery. See *The Economist*, 6/20/81, pp. 27–28. The British publication's coverage of the American cable scene has been consistently excellent.

p. 53 . . . thousands of trees. To be precise, 20,000 trees. *Barron's*, 7/4/83, p. 6, and *The Economist*, 6/20/81, p. 27.

p. 53 . . . killing his dog. *The Economist*, 6/20/81, p. 29. Sacramento's trees, Newton's library, the Illinois waterworks, and the bizarre flux of superfluous channels gave the press a brief but heady field day. See *Barron's*, 7/4/83, p. 6.

p. 53 . . . wanted cable television. *Business Week*, 7/22/85, p. 127.

p. 54 . . . the Wired World. And generate a small, largely forgotten literature on the subject. See Ralph Lee Smith, *The Wired Nation* (New York: Harper & Row, 1972); *Business Week*, 8/16/67, p. 65, and 12/8/80, p. 65; *The Economist*, 4/8/72, pp. 65–66, and 10/25/80, p. 97; *Forbes*, 5/11/81, pp. 205–9; and just about any issue of *Broadcasting* in the late 1960s.

p. 55 ". . . Aladdin and his lamp." Quoted in *Forbes*, 3/1/72, p. 33.

p. 55 . . . economics of broadcasting. *Broadcasting*, 7/8/73, p. 78.

p. 56 . . . experiment went nowhere. *Broadcasting*, 7/8/73, p. 21.

p. 56 . . . called light paths. *Communications News*, 9/76, p. 41.

p. 57 ". . . the subscription system." Quoted in *Broadcasting*, 11/15/82, p. 56.

p. 58 ". . . what it is." Ibid., p. 57.

p. 59 . . . of Cary Grant. Much of the following inevitably draws on Connie Bruck's *Master of the Game*, the only (and very fine) biography of Ross yet to appear. Also see Richard Clurman, *To the End of Time*, pp. 54–60.

p. 59 . . . running it to Malone. Bruck, p. 68 and p. 218; author interview, Fall 1990.

p. 61 ". . . blood and vomit." *The Economist*, 7/29/78, p. 62.

p. 61 . . . had been laid. A wonderfully deadpan discussion of pornography, VCRs, and Qube can be found in Tony Schwartz's "The TV Pornography Boom," *New York Times Magazine*, 8/13/81, pp. 44 ff.

p. 62 . . . from the sex channel. Ibid.

p. 63 . . . other than "Lulu Smith." C. Gerald Fraser, *New York Times*, 11/15/80, p. 48.

p. 63 . . . contemplated suicide themselves. Tony Schwartz, *New York Times*, 6/18/80, p. C31.

p. 63 ". . . of her song." *The Economist*, 7/29/78, p. 63.

p. 64 . . . around the floor. Dava Sobel, *New York Times*, 1/27/81, pp. C1–C2.

p. 64 . . . newspaper cost $5. *Broadcasting*, 1/12/81, p. 76.

p. 66 ". . . people around here." Quoted in Margaret Yao, *The Wall Street Journal*, 9/30/81, p. 31.

4. THE TROLL AND THE WIZARD

p. 68 . . . John Malone was. Verne Gay, *Advertising Age*, 11/9/87, p. 40; Maggie Mahar, *Barron's*, 8/1/88, p. 9; author interview, 1985; author interview, Fall 1990.

p. 68 . . . was nearly speechless. Author interview, 1985.

p. 69 . . . exceeded his grasp. Gay, *Advertising Age*, 11/9/87, p. 40; Mahar, *Barron's*, 8/1/88, p. 9.

p. 70 . . . told a visitor. Mahar, *Barron's*, 8/1/88, p. 7.

p. 70 ". . . necessarily a business." Quoted in Burstein and Kline, *Road Warriors: Dreams and Nightmares Along the Information Highway* (New York: Dutton, 1995), p. 36.

p. 70 . . . had always wanted. The details of Malone's life are drawn from a variety of sources, of which the best and most complete is Ken Auletta, *The New Yorker*, 2/7/94, pp. 52–67.

p. 71 ". . . under the bridge," Author interview, Fall 1990.

p. 71 ". . . you get conflicted." Quoted in Mahar, *Barron's*, 7/11/88, p. 7.

p. 72 . . . by a machine. Ibid., p. 8.

p. 72 . . . into the night. Connie Bruck, *Master of the Game*, p. 165.

p. 73 . . . around their necks. Laura Landro and Dennis Kneale, *The Wall Street Journal*, 6/4/84, p. 2.

p. 74 . . . sealed with concrete. Richard Clurman, *To the End of Time*, pp. 114–15.

p. 75 ". . . That was it." Author interview, Fall 1990.

p. 75 . . . television any longer. *Business Week*, 10/6/87, p. 92.

p. 75 . . . of fine Montrachet. Kristin Lentwyler, *Scientific American*, 9/95, p. 87. Because the Media Lab and Negroponte seem to be positively unnerved by the presence of outsiders and the possibility of criticism (see Negroponte's wounded and awkward rebuttal of Professor Joseph Pelton, *Telecommunications*, 1/93, pp. 41–42), much of the material on the following pages is drawn from Negroponte's book *Being Digital* (New York: Alfred A. Knopf, 1995).

p. 76 . . . with many enemies. There are a number of memorable passages on this subject in Joel Brinkley's *Defining Vision: The Battle for the Future of Television* (Orlando: Harcourt, Brace, 1997). For that matter, Brinkley doesn't seem to like Negroponte very much himself. I was a party to many conversations with computer scientists on the vexed problem of Negroponte's personality and truthfulness, but the scientists in question, however eager they were to be quoted on any other subject, any subject at all, prefer to remain anonymous and uncited.

p. 76 . . . the private sector. Quoted in Lentwyler, *Scientific American*, 9/95, pp. 51–52.

p. 78 . . . the tycoon explained. The reporter in question was, of course, yours truly.

pp. 82–83 ". . . and demanding applications." Quoted by Gary McWilliams, *Business Week*, 2/10/92, p. 122.

5. IN THE HALL OF THE MOUNTAIN KING

p. 87 . . . in ESPN's fees. Author interview, Fall 1990. Described in L. J. Davis, *New York Times Business World*, 12/2/90, p. 51.

p. 88 ". . . great big swallows." Author interview, Fall 1990.

p. 88 ". . . interest than taxes." Quoted in Davis, *New York Times Business World*, 12/2/90, p. 38.

p. 88 ". . . of the future." Quoted in *Business Week*, 11/23/81, p. 74.

p. 89 ". . . in the first place." Johnnie L. Roberts and Laura Landro, *The Wall Street Journal*, 9/27/93, p. A16.

p. 90 ". . . water-tight bulkheads." Quoted in Maggie Mahar, *Barron's*, 8/1/88, p. 30.

p. 91 . . . $1.3 billion. *Business Week*, 10/6/87, p. 88.

p. 91 . . . fire-sale prices. Christopher Knowlton, *Fortune*, 7/31/89, p. 100.

p. 91 . . . 91,000 percent. Ibid., p. 97.

p. 91 ". . . squeeze people's tails." Quoted by Andrew Kupfer in *Fortune*, 6/28/93, p. 92.

p. 93 . . . said Malone indulgently. Ibid.

p. 95 . . . of the thought. Mahar, *Barron's*, 7/11/88, p. 21.

p. 95 ". . . or Time Inc.," he said. Ibid.

p. 96 ". . . is . . . John Malone." Ibid., p. 7.

p. 97 . . . was thrown out. This was a vexed and much discussed subject. See Ronald Grover, *Business Week*, 5/27/92, p. 74; Roberts and Landro, *The Wall Street Journal*, 9/27/93, p. A15; and Ken Auletta, *The New Yorker*, 2/7/94, pp. 59–60.

p. 98 . . . of his hand. Mahar, *Barron's*, 8/1/88, p. 9.

p. 101 . . . duty is unknown. Connie Bruck, *Master of the Game*, p. 236.

p. 102 ". . . his entertainment junk." Richard Clurman, *To the End of Time*, pp. 38–39.

pp. 102–3 . . . not his line of work. Ibid.

p. 104 . . . a small matter. Much of the following account, including Levin's role, is drawn from Christopher M. Byron, *The Fanciest Dive* (New York: New American Library, 1986).

p. 106 ". . . on Time's treasury." Quoted in Connie Bruck, *Master of the Game*, p. 253.

p. 108 "Be my guest," said Ross. Bruck, p. 202.

p. 109 ". . . to be small." Ibid., p. 236.

p. 113 ". . . left Cape Canaveral." Ibid., p. 272.

6. John Malone and the Laws of Physics

p. 116 . . . for his company. Geraldine Fabrikant, *New York Times*, 11/16/89, p. D1.

p. 116 ". . . of their ears." Quoted in Maggie Mahar, *Barron's*, 8/1/88, p. 29.

p. 119 . . . terrible, throbbing headache. Author interview.

p. 119 ". . . personal about it." Author interview, Fall 1990. Also Andrew Kupfer, *Fortune*, 6/28/93, p. 98. Malone didn't just say it once. He kept on saying it. This was not a good idea.

p. 126 . . . the American marketplace. By far the best treatment of the HDTV story can be found in Joel Brinkley, *Defining Vision*.

p. 126 ". . . for electronics!" Quoted in ibid., p. 41.

7. The Shark Goes Fishing

p. 136 ". . . and catching porpoises." Author interview, Fall 1990.

p. 139 . . . very large bag. Although the Liberty spin-off—like most of Malone's large and often puzzling maneuvers—attracted a great deal of attention and was much commented upon, a superbly cogent analysis, the best of all, was written by Carol J. Loomis in *Fortune*, 11/15/93, p. 94.

p. 145 . . . it would be. Barry Diller, speech delivered before the American Magazine Conference. Reprinted in *Wired*, 2/95, pp. 82–84.

p. 146 . . . on the ropes. Geraldine Fabrikant, *New York Times*, 4/23/93, p. 49; Andrew Kupfer, *Fortune*, 6/28/93, p. 98; *The Economist*, 7/10/93, p. 59.

p. 147 . . . of tomato soup. For a quick survey of recent Paramount history, see L. J. Davis, *Buzz*, 10/93, pp. 73–77, 114–20.

p. 149 . . . almost everyone else's. Malone's version of his background maneuvers can be found in Ken Auletta, *The New Yorker*, 2/7/94, pp. 64–66.

8. The Bell Atlantic Way

p. 155 . . . He was dyslexic. An excellent short biography of Ray Smith can be found in John J. Keller, *The Wall Street Journal*, 12/10/93, p. A1.

p. 156 ". . . send you packing." Ibid., p. A6.

p. 157 ". . . is not applauding." Ibid.

p. 162 "England," he said. Author interview, 2/23/98.

p. 172 . . . dickered some more. Mark Landler and Bart Ziegler, *Business Week*, 10/25/93, pp. 32–33.

p. 173 ". . . We're techies." Author interview, 2/23/98.

p. 175 ". . . become legendary . . ." Quoted by Allen R. Myerson in the *New York Times*, 10/14/93, p. D11.

9. The Death and Rebirth of an Illusion

p. 177 . . . senior vice president. Leslie Cauley, *The Wall Street Journal*, 3/3/94, p. B12.

p. 178 . . . eighth-largest movie chain. Details of Redstone's life and career have appeared in many places. See Lois Therrien, *Forbes*, 10/20/86, pp. 77 and 80.

p. 178 ". . . go to work." Quoted by David Lieberman and Lois Therrien in *Business Week*, 3/16/87, p. 42.

p. 179 ". . . of the future." Speech before the National Press Club, 10/19/94.

p. 180 ". . . a competitive deal." Quoted by Kenneth N. Gilpin in the *New York Times*, 9/24/93, p. D4.

p. 181 ". . . John C. Malone." Quoted by Johnnie L. Roberts and Laura Landro in *The Wall Street Journal*, 9/27/93, p. A1.

p. 181 ". . . a small investment . . ." Quoted by Bernard Weinraub in the *New York Times*, 10/14/93, p. D10.

p. 182 . . . Nobody believed it. Ronald Grover, *Business Week*, 5/27/92, p. 75.

p. 183 ". . . advantage of it!" Quoted by Mark Robichaux in *The Wall Street Journal*, 11/17/93, p. B12.

p. 183 ". . . memo was regrettable." Ibid.

p. 190 . . . usual grueling pace. Ken Auletta, *The New Yorker*, 2/7/94, p. 61.

p. 191 . . . outside counsel. Dennis Kneale, Johnny L. Roberts, and Leslie Cauley, *The Wall Street Journal*, 2/25/94, p. A1.

p. 191 ". . . the movie *Rashomon*." Interview, *Wired*, 2/95, p. 110.

10. THE COURT OF THE BORGIAS

p. 194 ". . . order of magnitude." *Wired*, 7/97, p. 130.

p. 195 ". . . to John Malone." Dennis McAlpine, quoted by Eben Shapiro and Mark Robichaux in *The Wall Street Journal*, p. A3.

p. 195 ". . . do with Barry." TCI news release.

p. 200 . . . wonderful business again. The best analysis of Malone's reasoning on this subject can be found in Carol J. Loomis and Andrew Kupfer, *Fortune*, 1/13/97, pp. 67–74.

p. 201 . . . Camus's *The Stranger*. *Vanity Fair*, 10/95, p. 273.

p. 205 . . . engineer in 1986. All Chiddix quotes come from author interview, 11/2/95.

p. 212 . . . to do next. Much of the following is drawn from Time Warner technical specifications and personal reporting by the author.

p. 216 . . . them had failed. Andrew Feinberg, *New York Times*, 9/25/88, "Sunday Business," p. 4.

p. 216 . . . sold to QVC. *New York Times*, 3/31/89, p. D5.

p. 216 ". . . for our competitors." Author interview, Fall 1990.

p. 216 . . . stumbled onto something. Peter Carlin, *New York Times Magazine*, 2/28/93, p. 38.

11. THE END OF SOMETHING ELSE

p. 221 ". . . and it's spectacular." Author interview, 8/1/96.

p. 221 . . . O'Neal turned green. Author interviews, Orlando, 10/95.

p. 229 . . . owned its veto. At a time of intense interest in the media moguls, the maneuvers leading up to Levin's purchase of Turner Broadcasting were covered like the Gulf War or the invasion of North Africa. Outstanding reporting can be found in Connie Bruck, *The New Yorker*, 2/19/96, pp. 55–69.

p. 231 . . . did anybody else. Anita Sharpe, *The Wall Street Journal*, 11/27/95, pp. A1 and A10.

p. 231 ". . . just about anything." Ibid.

p. 231 . . . quietly to Atlanta. Bruck, *The New Yorker*, 2/19/96, p. 68. Bruck says "squash." Other versions say "crush."

12. THE END OF THE AFFAIR

p. 234 ". . . as he could." Quoted by Robert Lacey in *Ford: The Men and the Machine* (New York: Little, Brown, 1986), p. 303.

p. 237 . . . Wherever he was. Mark Robichaux, *The Wall Street Journal*, 2/26/96, pp. A1 and A7.

p. 237 . . . to say so. Author interview, 1/95.

p. 245 ". . . bolt it onto." Quoted by Robichaux in *The Wall Street Journal*, 11/7/96, p. A1.

Notes

p. 251 ". . . Hopefully." Conversation with author, 12/96.

p. 252 ". . . cable," he said. Quoted by Geraldine Fabrikant and Mark Landler in the *New York Times*, 12/9/96, p. D1.

p. 253 . . . as "stunning." Robichaux, *The Wall Street Journal*, 2/2/97, p. 3.

p. 253 . . . he had leukemia. Personal reporting by the author.

p. 256 . . . seclusion in October. Quoted by Fabrikant and Landler, *New York Times*, 12/9/96, p. D1.

Afterword: The Media Lab at Ten

p. 257 . . . that never happened. The majority of this chapter is based on personal reporting by the author.

p. 260 . . . way to go. *New York Times*, 1/14/96.

p. 262 . . . the subscriber's outlook. Nicholas Negroponte, *Being Digital*, p. 154.

p. 263 . . . of an idea. Lorene Shenazy, *Advertising Age*, 8/5/86, p. 28.

p. 266 ". . . in modular fashion." Author interview, 11/2/95.

ACKNOWLEDGMENTS

To PARAPHRASE A CONSPICUOUS LATE AMERICAN, I would like to make a couple of things perfectly clear. First, I am not a Luddite; I might have gotten a big kick out of the Pleistocene when I was fourteen or so, but that was long ago. In other words, I like it here. A cozy berth in the world of the present, however, is not necessarily identical (although it sometimes is) with a refusal to perceive that when a new technology is introduced, things become seriously strange.

The invention of digital television will inevitably result in one or many consumer products. Some of them may even be useful and some of them almost certainly will not, and at the moment of this writing it seems likely to the point of certitude that the digital products in question will not be identical to—or even resemble, except remotely—the digital products that have been promised. I speak, of course, of high-definition television, a technology for whose swift and decisive death the nation's broadcasters pray daily and with fervor. But the fate of high-definition television will be decided in the immediate future, and this is a book about the immediate past. Specifically, it is a book about what happened when John Malone and the nation's other cable barons attempted to rewire their systems to bring the public a form of digital, interactive television that would replace the computer, transform the telephone business, and make its owners as rich as Croesus. Digital interactive television was scheduled to arrive in the nation's homes as early as 1996. Despite the expenditure of billions, it didn't. This book tells why.

Second, in the writing of this book, I was forced to fall back heavily on the rough first draft of history in the form of newspaper and magazine reporting, some of it acute, some of it bedazzled by the wonders of the digital realm, and quite a lot of it insightful and deluded at the same time. Alas, although many books have been written about computers, the Internet, and Bill Gates, there exists no single volume on the cable industry and the fata morgana of interactive television that I could pinch, rewrite in my own pellucid prose, and pass off as my own. Instead, it became necessary to buckle down to work, prowl the files—the splendid people in Brooklyn's Cadman Plaza Business Library deserve a special vote of thanks—and do the job myself.

Then there was the human factor. Without the unique knowledge and sound advice of Bob Woletz, my old colleague on the *New York Times's Business World*, it would have been extremely hard to figure out what the book was supposed to be about and even harder to write it. Moreover, it is unlikely that any book of any sort would have been possible if Marylin Bender and Bob Stock, the supreme beings at *Business World*, hadn't turned Mr. Woletz and Mr. Davis loose on TCI in the first place. Those were great days.

Singled out, too, are Les Brown, Merrill Brown, and Steve Behrens of the late, lamented magazine *Channels*, who did their level best to take a business reporter who knew nothing useful about television and turn him into a television reporter who knew a thing or two about business; if the result turned out half-baked, it is not their fault, nor is it the fault of the magazine's owner, Norman Lear, who made certain that the generous paychecks did not bounce. Last, there was the invaluable contribution of Judith Rascoe, an indefatigable reader who scrutinized every page of the manuscript, sometimes several times, and devised the remarkably effective Judy Test. It worked like this: if I wrote something I thought I understood and she definitely knew she didn't, I was set the task of rewriting it until she did.

I was unable to speak with John Malone during the course of this project, although not for lack of trying. Instead, I was given two tours of TCI's vast, empty, $100 million National Digital Television Center, where nothing much was going on in 1995 and even less in 1996. Mr. Malone does not talk to the press unless it serves his purposes (the current book definitely does not), and he had vanished from his usual haunts. Back in 1990, however, when I wore a different hat and John Malone was eager to contemplate his visage in America's newspaper of record, he gave me an extensive and remarkably informative interview, on which I have drawn—and I was also able to secure the cooperation, grudging though it seemed, of David Beddow, senior vice president, TCI Technology Ventures, and of Brian Hayashi. At Time Warner, chairman Gerald Levin did discuss his goals and ambitions, although it is unlikely that he will be pleased with the result. Also at Time Warner, valuable help was given by Mike Luftman, Ed Adler, John Dunn, Daniel Levy, and James P. Ludington.

Raymond Smith, the engaging and fluent chairman of Bell Atlantic—and a man with an amateur thespian's eye for the telling detail—walked me carefully through his negotiations with John Malone; if we differ on a few points it is because Mr. Smith understandably has his perspective, and I have mine. This is part of the game. At Lucent Technologies–Bell Labs, the charming George Moffatt served an excellent lunch, while John Mailhot and Ed Szurkowski offered their perspectives on HDTV, digital television, and the pitfalls of interactivity. Nicholas Negroponte of the Media Lab did not make himself available, despite repeated requests through a number of intermediaries.

I would also like to thank, in no particular order, Marlowe Froke of the National Cable Television Center and Museum; Glenn Jones of Jones Intercable; Mr. and Mrs. George Durfey of Portola Valley, California; Vinnie Grosso and Rosemary Lomazzo of AT&T; Saul Schapiro of the FCC; Bud Rukeyser of NBC; Michael Fitzpatrick, Roland Wolfram, and Craig Watts of Pacific Bell that was; Henry Breitrose of Stanford University; Virginia Henderson of Silicon Graphics; Casey Sheldon, Krishna Natarajan, and Jeff Holove of Hewlett-Packard; and Dan Burke, Steve Silverman, and Veronica Pollard of ABC. Greg Critser, formerly of *Buzz* magazine and later of *Worth*, did yeoman service as sounding board and friend, a role shared with Chris Orr of *Mother Jones*. Thanks, guys.

It was Margarett Loke, then of the *New York Times Magazine*, who proposed an article on Sony and Hollywood that contained an intriguing germ of an idea, from which the current book has grown. My inestimable agent, Gordon Kato, was the first to perceive its possibilities—Lord knows, I didn't see them. At Doubleday, Bill Thomas, a young man with all the near-vanished virtues of an old-school editor, saw the project through three broken deadlines and four drafts, making pertinent suggestions, nudging Homer when he nodded, and calmly guiding the work to its conclusion. At times, slogging on, I was reminded of Abraham Lincoln's man who was ridden out of town on a rail: if it hadn't been for the honor, I'd rather have walked, but Gordon and Bill never doubted that the journey was worthy of the road.

If there are any mistakes in the pages that follow, my friends, colleagues, and the many helpful strangers who sped the work are absolved from blame; the fault is mine alone, and I will take the rap. It isn't often that a writer is given an opportunity to tell a story that has never been told, and I am a lucky man.

L. J. DAVIS

Brooklyn and San Francisco, 1995–97

INDEX